# Praise for *The Quaking of America*

"Resmaa Menakem's *The Quaking of America*
is a brilliant and effective guide to embodied
social change. All of us need to read this
book—and then act on it."

**Angela Rye,** NPR political analyst
and former CNN commentator

"Wow. Just wow. Prepare to *see what is coming*. Prepare
to *feel the urgency*. Prepare to *be changed*. This is a book
that will wake you up, excite, and terrify you. But
Resmaa won't leave you there; all along the way he
gives you the practices to do the work of healing into
action. And he delivers all of this in riveting prose.
Resmaa Menakem is a visionary, and his work is
absolutely essential for antiracist practice. We need
this book in as many hands as possible."

**Robin DiAngelo, PhD,** *New York Times* bestselling
author of *White Fragility* and *Nice Racism*

"Resmaa Menakem is one of our country's most gifted
racial healers. His brilliant new book could not be more
timely—a volume our country, our bodies, and our
humanity desperately need. *The Quaking of America* offers
wisdom and liberation, not only for Black, Brown, or
Indigenous folk, but for all Americans."

**Michael Eric Dyson,** bestselling author of
*Entertaining Race* and *Long Time Coming*

"As author Resmaa Menakem makes plain, there's nothing in our society that makes expanding progress and social inclusion inevitable. These things happen because wise, brave, and committed people make them happen. But they also happen because spiritually well people make them happen—people who understand the importance of self-care for the struggles ahead. *The Quaking of America* is more than an insightful book about the challenged state of American multiracial democracy. It is a user's guide, an instruction manual on how to transform your body, yourself, and this country into their highest and noblest aspirations."

**Keith Ellison**, Attorney General of Minnesota

"A storm is coming. But this is not a scare-mongering book intended to threaten your nervous system. It's just the opposite. This book is not just for Black, Indigenous, and white Jewish or Muslim 'bodies of culture' who might be deemed the enemy in such a culture war. Regardless of the pigment of your skin, if you want to prepare your body to take ethical, spiritual action should you be forced to risk your life in order to choose sides, this is your book. Filled with somatic trauma-healing practices intended to build bodily resilience so your actions can live up to your antiracist intentions, this book could save your life, help you save other lives, or even prepare you to prevent a civil war or survive one. If you're an American and you believe in democracy and equal human rights for all beings, I'm not exaggerating when I say this might be the most important book you read this century."

**Lissa Rankin, MD,** *New York Times* bestselling author of *Mind Over Medicine* and *Sacred Medicine*

"Resmaa teaches us a new understanding and vantage point of our physical and personal relationship with people different from ourselves. He brings revolutionary insights to the value of connecting with depths of information our bodies hold onto, acquired through life's experiences. He leads us to crucial and deeper connections with our inner truths and provides us with a pathway to building more meaningful relationships and empathy for all people."

**Pete Carroll**, Head Coach and Executive
Vice President of the NFL's Seattle Seahawks

"*The Quaking of America* is a profoundly needed bridge over today's troubled waters. Resmaa teaches us how to be present and embodied, even in conflict. This book should be in all our hands. For all our sakes, please read this book and share it with a friend."

**Peter A. Levine, PhD**, author of *Waking the Tiger*,
*Healing Trauma*, and *In an Unspoken Voice*

"One . . . two . . . three . . . BOOM! Precisely how I've experienced Resmaa's work in my life, our company, and in the world. He is a critical voice in reclaiming our bodies and thus our freedom."

**Audrey Cavenecia**, Chief Content Officer and award-winning producer at Amplify Voices (a Pete Carroll Company)

"There really are no words that can adequately describe the pouring of incisive foresight and actionable content into a book as Resmaa Menakem has done. We would be remiss not to grasp *The Quaking of America* as a critical operations manual for the salvaging of this utterly imperfect democracy."

**Rev. angel Kyodo williams**, coauthor,
*Radical Dharma: Talking Race, Love and Liberation*

Thank You

# THE
# QUAKING
## OF
# AMERICA

## AN EMBODIED GUIDE TO
## NAVIGATING OUR NATION'S UPHEAVAL
## AND RACIAL RECKONING

## RESMAA MENAKEM

CENTRAL RECOVERY PRESS
LAS VEGAS, NV

**Central Recovery Press** (CRP) is committed to publishing exceptional materials addressing addiction treatment, recovery, and behavioral healthcare topics. For more information, visit www.centralrecoverypress.com.

27 26 25 24 23 22    1 2 3 4 5

*Library of Congress Cataloging-in-Publication Data*

Names: Menakem, Resmaa, author.
Title: The quaking of America : an embodied guide to navigating our
   nation's upheaval and racial reckoning / Resmaa Menakem, MSW, LICSW,
   SEP.
Description: Las Vegas, Nevada : Central Recovery Press, [2021] | Summary:
   "The New York Times bestselling author of My Grandmother's Hands surveys
   the deteriorating political climate and presents an urgent call for
   action to save ourselves and our country"-- Provided by publisher.
Identifiers: LCCN 2021052546 (print) | LCCN 2021052547 (ebook) | ISBN
   9781949481662 (hardback) | ISBN 9781949481747 (paperback) | ISBN
   9781949481679 (ebook)
Subjects: LCSH: United States--Social conditions--2020- | Political
   participation--United States--History--21st century.
Classification: LCC HN59.3 .M46 2021  (print) | LCC HN59.3  (ebook) | DDC
   306.0973--dc23/eng/20211223
LC record available at https://lccn.loc.gov/2021052546
LC ebook record available at https://lccn.loc.gov/2021052547

Photo of Resmaa Menakem courtesy of Bruce Silcox Photography.

**Publisher's Note:**
This book contains general information about trauma, racialized trauma, somatic healing methods, and related matters. This information is not medical advice. This book is not an alternative to medical advice from your doctor or other professional healthcare provider.

Our books represent the experiences and opinions of their authors only. Every effort has been made to ensure that events, institutions, and statistics presented in our books as facts are accurate and up-to-date. To protect their privacy, the names of some of the people, places, and institutions in this book may have been changed.

**Author's Note:**
This book is for informational purposes only. It is not intended as psychotherapy from a qualified counselor or a replacement for it. If you feel you can benefit from therapy, please contact a trained mental health professional.

*Cover design by The Book Designers and interior design by Sara Streifel, Think Creative Design.*

*This book is dedicated to the memory of*

**Lucille Walls** and **Addie Coleman**
my grandmothers and ancestors

**Tabi Deba Orang**
Thank you, my ancestor, for always guiding my
thoughts, words, and deeds.

**Dr. David Schnarch** and **Dr. James Maddock**
Thank you for being my mentors.

**Jodi Nowak**
Thank you for being my friend.

**Amelia Brown, Vesta Mason, Braxton Taylor,
Dale Smith,** and **Mac Walton**
Thank you for being my inspirations—
and now my ancestors.


To all those who have gone before me,
I am humbled by your love and dedication.

Thank you.

# CONTENTS

**The past and present rules of white-body supremacy (or WBS):**

- The white body deems itself the supreme standard against which the humanity of all other bodies is measured and judged, both structurally and philosophically.

- Only the white body is fully human. All other bodies, or **bodies of culture**, are lesser primates—deviants from the human standard.

- The white body—and only the white body—is inherently pure and virtuous.

- The many different types of bodies of culture can be ranked on a vertical continuum. At the bottom are Black and Indigenous bodies.

- Only white bodies get to define who is fully human and who is not.

- White bodies get to change this definition whenever they please—which they do constantly.

- WBS is a pigmentocracy. Body pigmentation is primary—not identity.

**Somatic Abolitionism is:**

- a living, embodied practice and culture of antiracism

- a return to the age-old wisdom of human bodies respecting, honoring, and resonating with other human bodies

- the resourcing of energies that are always present in your body, in the collective body, and in creation

- an emergent process

- a way of being in creation

- a form of growing up

- an embodied response to the problems of white-body supremacy

The practice of Somatic Abolitionism requires endurance, stamina, ongoing adjustment, emergent discipline, and discernment. These can be built, day by day, through reps.

*So we're just sick of it, you know, and we're not gonna take it anymore. I see a civil war coming. I do.*

Attendee at Donald Trump's October 9, 2021
rally in Des Moines, Iowa

*It is little wonder that about two-fifths of Republicans (in a poll this year) expressed an openness to political violence under certain circumstances. People in this group are not being stigmatized. They have the effective endorsement of a former president and likely GOP presidential nominee in 2024.*

Michael Gerson in the *Washington Post*,
September 27, 2021

*Be ready to fight. Congress needs to hear glass breaking, doors being kicked in, and blood from their BLM and Pantifa slave soldiers being spilled. Get violent. Stop calling this a march, or rally, or a protest. Go there ready for war. We get our President or we die. NOTHING else will achieve this goal.*

from an FBI report dated January 5, 2021,
quoting a recent online thread

*Civil war is coming, people, get your guns.*

Jason Lefkowitz at an August 29,
2021 rally in Santa Monica, California

*When do we get to use the guns? . . . How many elections are they going to steal before we kill these people?*

Audience member at a 2021 pro-Trump event

*We're going to be in a civil war because the militia will be taking over.*

"Ron," a Trump supporter speaking to CNN journalist
Donie O'Sullivan on June 26, 2021

**To all Americans who hope
to incite a civil war:**

We see you.

We know your plans.

We will be ready to defend ourselves and
what this country could be against you.


**To all bodies of culture:**

You are not defective, or deviant,
or inadequate. You are human.

You are not crazy.
What you see happening is real.

The GOP and its complicitors seek
to end democracy and establish a
dictatorship of white-body supremacy.

You will need to defend yourself and
your ancestors' dream for America.

Find and stand with each other.

If you can, find and stand with courageous,
committed white bodies who support
liberation, justice, and unfettered democracy.


**To all white liberals and progressives:**

This is not a performance.

This is not a venue for the display of your
good intentions, kindness, and wokeness.

This is our country's most dangerous
internal conflict in over 150 years.

Justice is imperiled. So are you.

You will need to defend
yourself and your country.

Put your body on the street.

Develop a living, embodied antiracist
culture among white bodies.

Find and stand with other bodies who care about
liberation, justice, and an emancipated democracy.


**To all Democrats:**

This moment demands great strength.
Exert it. Keep exerting it.

This moment demands bold unity. Establish and
maintain it. Debate the particulars later.

This moment demands justice. Insist on it.

Stop your feckless handwringing. End your calls
for cordiality and bipartisanship.They are
no substitute for justice and liberation.

If you compromise at the expense of bodies
of culture, particularly Black and Indigenous
bodies, as you have so many times before,
you will accelerate our country's destruction.

**To every American who cares about
liberation and justice:**

The GOP and its complicitors have dedicated
themselves to autocracy, white-body supremacy,
and the destruction of American democracy.

They have been emboldened and
enabled by the complicity of many players—
including the Democratic Party.

To repel this assault, we must organize,
based on our personal and communal interests,
vote in every general election and every primary,
and hold those in elected office accountable.
But we must also do much more.

We must all stand together, arm in arm,
body by body, in the streets of America.

We can argue policy later.

Today we must begin creating a living,
breathing antiracist culture.

# 1

# WHAT IS THIS BOOK?

*For the first time since 1860, a major American political party doesn't believe America is a democracy. No Republican will win a contested primary in 2022 or 2024 who will assert that Biden is a legal president. The effect of this is profound and difficult to predict. But millions of Americans believe the American experiment is ending.*

Stuart Stevens

*The GOP has radicalized. . . . One, they have doubled down on the idea that if democracy doesn't serve their ascendance to power, then it's OK to do away with democracy. Two, they've doubled down on the idea that violence is a perfectly acceptable means to take power. Three, they've decided that the next election will be one where democracy itself is something to attack and beat.*

Umair Haque

*What the United States did not have before 2020 was a large national movement willing to justify mob violence to claim political power. Now it does.*

David Frum

*American democracy relies on the losers of elections respecting
the results and participating in a peaceful transition of power.
If, instead, the losing party tries to override the will of the voters,
that would be the death knell for our system of government.*

from the 2021 report "A Democracy Crisis in the Making"

*It's only by thinking about what was once unfathomable
that we can see the country as it really is.*

Jennifer Szalai

*Pause.*

The quotations at the beginning of each chapter are not window dressing or simple distillations of key points. Each quotation offers its own unique experience and resonances.

After you read each quote, pause briefly. Take note of what emerges in your body.

Later, you may find yourself revisiting some of these quotations. As you do, pause again and notice how your body is responding. As you will discover, while your mind contemplates the wisdom in the words, your body is metabolizing it.

If you like, go to the top of the previous page and begin this chapter again.

*The Quaking of America* is a book of practical, embodied psychology that will help you be ready for what is to come.

No one can perfectly foretell the future. But many signs point to an imminent attempt to overthrow American democracy and incite widespread violence, especially against Black bodies and other bodies of culture.[1] This civil war will likely be incited by the

---

1    I use the term *bodies of culture* instead of *people of color* for three reasons. First, as primatologist Frans de Waal notes, we human beings are "bodies born of other bodies. . . . Bodies matter, which is why anything related to them arouses emotions." Second, the term *people of color* continues to otherize nonwhite bodies by holding them up against the implied norm of white people. In contrast, the term *bodies of culture* deliberately steers clear of any mention of color. Third, many people immediately resonate with the term in positive ways. The term *bodies of culture* is not intended to suggest that white bodies do not have culture (of course they do), any more than a bumper sticker that says, "I love my beagle" suggests that the car's driver hates other dog breeds. What white Americans do *not* have is a living, embodied, antiracist culture. Building such a culture is one of the core focuses of this book.

Republican Party and its many complicitors sometime between the summer of 2022 and early 2025.

At the same time, America is roiling and reverberating with a long-overdue racial reckoning. This reckoning began soon after the murder of George Floyd in May 2020, and it continues to unfold.

This reckoning and our potential civil war are intimately intertwined, in a social and political double helix. As you will see, this book is structured as a similar helix, sometimes moving back and forth between these two strands, sometimes focusing on their intertwining.

This book is not about political strategy, or organizing rallies, or boosting voter turnout, or civil disobedience—though all of these are essential. It's about preparing your body and community for a civil war—and, if possible, preventing it. It's also about leaning into our racial reckoning and beginning to create a living, embodied antiracist culture.

You will not just read this book. You will *do* this book. You will experience it with your body. Often, you will *pause* to process and metabolize your experience.

You will experience this book partly on your own, partly with other people—as a pair, as a triad, and as a community that you help to cultivate.

My intent is that, in your body, you will experience this book as awareness, growth, and healing. Then, over time, as you repeat the body practices in this book, you will bring these benefits into your family, your community, and the world.

If millions of us do this, the shifts in our bodies can shift our culture, our country, and the trajectory of history.

This book is not meant to be read once and then set aside. It is meant to be contemplated, digested, mulled on, argued with, cried over, and perhaps cursed at. You may find yourself dog-earing particular pages, or writing notes in the margins, or returning to certain passages again and again. This is a book to have a relationship with—perhaps a transformative one.

That said, this is a book of healing, not a book of therapy. Both healing and therapy are important—and, for many people, both are necessary. Good therapy often leads to healing. Nevertheless, there is a fundamental difference between the two.

All of us are born into a set of structures, circumstances, and contexts. These may nurture and support us in some ways, and ravage and weather us in others. Effective therapy helps us to address our ravaging and weathering.

Therapy is also personal. It involves individuals, couples, or family groups. In therapy, we draw a circle, repair the broken pieces within it, and fill in the missing ones.

In contrast, healing is both individual and communal. It involves far more than mere repair. In healing, we connect to energies that are always with us, in us, and around us—energies that always have been here and always will be. While healing is often experienced personally, it is built into the very structures of our bodies, our planet, and the cosmos.

Healing naturally resonates and radiates outward. It can begin with an individual and cascade into a family, group, or community. It can also move in the other direction, beginning with a community, group, or family and cascading through individual bodies.

Healing is a reminder of what we already are and what we have always been part of.

I originally envisioned that in 2021 I would write a sequel to *My Grandmother's Hands*. But in the first two months of that year, events in the US unfolded in unprecedented, perilous, and sometimes deadly ways. It soon became clear that we Americans need a very different book in order to move through both the racial reckoning and the crisis of democracy we will almost certainly face in 2022 through 2025. *The Quaking of America* is that book.

By the time you read this in 2022 or later, the interwoven racial reckoning, national upheaval, widespread mayhem, and (perhaps) civil war may all be current events—or highlights of American history. Or maybe they have somehow been pushed further into your near future. So let me set the context of this book by listing just six of the headlines that appeared on the *Washington Post*'s home page on the day I'm writing this paragraph, November 18, 2021:

- Paul Gosar killed his colleague in a cartoon. Kevin McCarthy is killing democracy in real life.
- Matt Gaetz says he might offer Kyle Rittenhouse a job as a congressional intern as jury debates the teen's case.
- The Republican effort to govern by threat.
- Insurrectionists are finally receiving justice. But the GOP is more unhinged than ever.
- Trust is a key ingredient in "functional institutions"—and Congress is fresh out of it.
- Man who raped four teenagers gets no jail time; judge says "Incarceration isn't appropriate."

At the end of each chapter of this volume, you'll be invited to explore your body and its experience in one or more new dimensions—starting now.

In these initial chapters, you'll experience your body in some very simple, elemental ways—the same ways that many living creatures do. Then, in later chapters, using other practices, you'll begin tempering and conditioning your body and your mind. As you work through this book, new body practices will build on—and sometimes combine with—earlier ones.

These practices will help you move into settledness and steadiness when you are under stress. When you find yourself in the midst of conflict, they will also help you act from your integrity and the best parts of yourself.

The body practices in this book won't involve strenuous physical exercise. Instead, you'll focus on building your body's discernment and resilience, especially in the face of stress or conflict.[2] As you'll see, building these involves exploration, curiosity, and repetition.

While I don't expect every reader to do every body practice in this book, these practices are not optional add-ons. Unless you involve your body—practice after practice, time after time, rep

---

2    I do also recommend regular physical exercise, such as walking, jogging, swimming, cycling, or working out. Any exercise should of course be appropriate for your ability and physical condition. Consult with a qualified health care professional before beginning any new, strenuous, or unusual exercise regimen.

after rep—you will bypass the main purpose and value of this book.

Test out each body practice at least a few times. Then review the effects that each one has had on your body. Which ones helped it to cultivate settledness? Which ones helped you stay present and fully engaged? Which ones helped you tolerate discomfort? Which ones most helped you build discernment? Which most encouraged you to act from the best parts of yourself? Which practices were especially pleasurable or meaningful?

Thereafter, continue to practice any or all of the activities that you find helpful.

Every human body is unique. Please honor your own body's abilities, limitations, and warning signals. Adapt (or, if necessary, skip) any body practice in this book as your body directs you to.

Don't just do each practice once; return to some of them over and over, whenever you sense that one of them can be helpful. Some practices are designed to be integrated into your daily life. Others are meant to be revisited periodically. (With each revisiting, compare your body's current response with its earlier responses.) A few practices are designed to be repeated for the rest of your life.

These body practices aren't a self-help program or a lockstep process. They're a form of emergent conditioning. A practice that resonates deeply with you today may not seem as meaningful a week, month, or year from now—or one that seems less meaningful today may have more resonance in the future.

If your body becomes so uncomfortable with a particular practice that you can't get through it, no worries. Move on to a different practice. Weeks or months from now, you can circle back to that uncomfortable activity—at which point you may discover that your body responds very differently.

In Chapter 6, I'll give you guidance for writing about your experience with the body practices in that chapter and beyond. You're of course welcome to write about earlier body practices as well.

As you move through the first half of this book, you'll do the body practices on your own. Beginning with Chapter 25, though, I'll ask you to do them both on your own and with others, so you can experience the benefits of both individual and collective practice.

Please begin with the body practice below, which will remind your body of its elemental nature.

BODY PRACTICE
## CURLING AND UNCURLING

This is the most basic movement of human bodies—and of the bodies of many other living creatures. It is also something you began doing when you were still in your mother's womb.

Lie on your side on a bed, a yoga mat, or some other comfortable surface. Take a few slow, deep breaths. Then slowly curl yourself up into the shape of a fetus. Take three more slow breaths. Then slowly uncurl again until your spine and legs fully straighten out. Curl and uncurl three times—or more, if your body wants to.

As you curl and uncurl, as well as immediately afterward, notice what you experience in your body. Pay close attention to:

- physical sensations
- urges and impulses
- images
- movements or actions
- judgments
- meanings or explanations

*[Handwritten annotations: "Contraction expansion" — "noticed in fetal position tightness - closed in + closed off - trapped - not spacious" — "one ↓ Free/ elongated/ steady + centered in a feeling of being free"]*

# 2

# WHY A WAR IS
# BEING PLANNED

*The happenings in the world are begging us to wake up.*
*Listen and give attention to what really matters.*

Catrice M. Jackson

*The Republican Party today is not a movement dedicated to ideas*
*but a tribe devoted to self-preservation, defined by anger and*
*emotions, and organized around a clannish loyalty to its leader.*

Fareed Zakaria

*The Republican Party is an existential threat to the constitutional*
*order and viability of the United States, dedicated to an*
*authoritarian vision and the obliteration of a pluralistic*
*society. . . . The GOP has become a neofascist cult of personality,*
*dedicated to the accumulation of raw power for its own sake by*
*dividing Americans using lies, fear, and hatred.*

Alexander Ziperovich

*There seems to be no answer to the question of what the*
*modern Republican Party wouldn't do to maintain its grasp*
*on power. The fact that this question is unanswerable means*
*that we are in dangerous and uncharted territory.*

Lawson Miller

*The rich ruling class has used tribalism, a primitive caveman*
*instinct, to their advantage since the beginning of time. They use*
*it to divide and conquer us. . . . You can observe the same old trick*
*everywhere in America today. . . . That doesn't just happen all by*
*itself. There are always voices instigating these fights.*

Oliver Markus Malloy

In November 2020, after losing in the most transparent and secure election in American history, Donald Trump refused to concede. Instead, he insisted, without evidence, that he had actually won in a landslide, and that his victory had been stolen from him by a widespread conspiracy of liberals, government officials (the "Deep State"), and voting machine manufacturers.

Most Republicans in both Congressional chambers fell in line behind him, echoing the same claims and refusing to acknowledge Biden's win. Right-wing television, radio, and social media broadcast these lies relentlessly, until 75 percent of Republicans—over fifty million Americans—believed them.

On January 6, 2021, at the urging of Trump, his surrogates and champions, and organizers on social media, about eight hundred people stormed the US Capitol, attacked police, and broke into offices and the Senate chamber. Five people died in the riot, and one hundred forty police officers were injured. As of January 2022, seven hundred twenty-five of the rioters were arrested and charged with crimes; one hundred sixty-five pleaded guilty. (The US Department of Justice estimates that as many as 2500 may eventually be charged.) On the same day, violent clashes also broke out in Los Angeles and the state capitols of Washington, Oregon, and California.

In the months afterward, this event was widely viewed as a violent attempt to overturn the legitimate results of the recent election. Only later would most of the country and world begin to see January 6 as the rioters themselves did: as the first significant battle in a new civil war.[3]

---

3   General Mark Milley, who was chairman of the Joint Chiefs of Staff in 2021, described the January 6 storming of the Capitol as "a precursor to something worse down the road." Milley also said that he feared Trump was searching for a "Reichstag moment."

Based on extensive online chatter calling for a second attack on January 20—on both the US Capitol and statehouses across the country—security at all of these buildings was greatly increased. Presumably because of this enhanced protection, none of the anticipated attacks occurred.

Following the attempted coup, Trump consolidated his near-total control of the Republican Party. Since then, he, the party, and right-wing media have continued to spread the same Big Lie: that Trump was the actual winner of the 2020 presidential election and that Biden's victory—and his presidency—are fraudulent and illegitimate. By mid-2021, over seven hundred Republicans running for public office had made this Big Lie one of the defining issues of their campaigns.

Thus, by mid-2021, the Trump-controlled Republican Party stood for four things: (1) Donald Trump, (2) the Big Lie, (3) the suppression or death of American democracy, and (4) white-body supremacy. The party took a firm, clear stand *against* the right to vote, the validity of election results, the peaceful and orderly transfer of power, racial justice and equity, the accountability of its leaders, the very process of governance, and truth itself. Since then, its actions and its messaging have clearly demonstrated that it is not interested in governance, or in the rights of all Americans, but in dominance.[4] As Ed Pilkington observed, "Increasingly the institutional machinery of the Republican Party is organized around fealty to the big lie and the willingness to steal the next election."

Meanwhile, to rally and organize its followers, and to recruit new ones, the Republican Party has been using techniques perfected by the Ku Klux Klan and, later, the German and American Nazi Parties and the South African apartheid government.

In 2021, in a widespread attempt to suppress Democratic turnout in the 2022 and 2024 elections, especially among bodies of culture, the Republican Party proposed at least 440 voter-restriction laws in forty-nine states. (In just five of those states—Texas, Georgia, Pennsylvania, Michigan, and Arizona—187 such

---

4    This is not a uniquely American phenomenon. Since I wrote *My Grandmother's Hands*, leaders of many of the world's most populous nations—most notably Vladimir Putin in Russia, Xi Jinping in China, Recep Tayyip Erdogan in Turkey, Narendra Modi in India, and Jair Bolsonaro in Brazil—have also become the centers of autocratic personality cults. Some of these openly oppress racial, ethnic, or religious minorities (Uighurs and Tibetans in China, Muslims and Christians in India, Indigenous people in Brazil).

new laws were proposed, including 59 in Texas alone.) The largest concentration of these bills has been in the states that were most closely contested in the 2020 presidential election. Many of these bills proposed limiting or eliminating mail-in ballots, drive-up voting, 24/7 voting, and/or early voting. Others established tougher voter ID requirements. Still others authorized the widespread purging of voter rolls for no legitimate reason. Some proposed laws politicized the oversight of elections by giving state legislatures, secretaries of state, or election boards the ability to arbitrarily overturn legitimate election results. Many of these laws passed in states where the Republican Party controlled both the legislature and the governorship. By the end of 2021, at least nineteen states passed legislation that made it harder to vote.

In another, parallel GOP initiative, beginning in the summer of 2021—in thousands of towns, cities, counties, and states— huge numbers of pro-authoritarian, pro-Trump, anti-democracy GOP supporters signed up to become election monitors, precinct officers, and poll workers. Many hundreds of others became candidates for election boards and other election-related positions—including many state-level secretaries of state. (In the 2022 election, ten out of fifteen declared Republican candidates for secretary of state in the swing states of Arizona, Georgia, Michigan, Nevada, and Wisconsin either declared that the 2020 presidential election was stolen or called for their state's election results to be invalidated or further investigated.) The former chair of the Michigan Republican Party, Jeff Timmer, summed up the situation this way: "This is a great big flashing red warning sign. The officials who fulfilled their legal duty after the last election are now being replaced by people who are pledging to throw a wrench in the gears of the next election. It tells you that they are planning nothing but chaos and that they have a strategy to disrupt the certification of the next election." Joanna Lydgate, the CEO of the nonpartisan States United Democracy Center, sounded an even louder alarm: "Having election deniers run elections is like having arsonists take over the fire department."

Much of the inspiration for this groundswell of faux volunteerism and interest in holding public office came from former Trump strategist and advisor Steve Bannon, who repeatedly encouraged the above strategies in his podcast.[5] (He summed up the strategy this way: "We're taking over school boards, we're taking over the Republican Party through the precinct committee strategy. We're taking over all the elections. Suck on this!")

In Republican-dominated states where officials are appointed to key positions, some pro-authoritarian Republicans were simply handed the keys to an entire elections apparatus. In Texas, for example, Republican governor Greg Abbott appointed as secretary of state John Scott, one of the lawyers who represented Donald Trump in his lawsuit challenging Pennsylvania's election results. In an attempted parallel move, Arizona state representative Shawnna Bolick proposed a law that would empower the Arizona legislature (currently controlled by the GOP) to overrule the certification of popular vote results by the state's own secretary of state. The state of Georgia has done something similar, enacting a new voting law that strips power from state and local elections officials and gives it to the state legislature (which is currently Republican). As the *New York Times* noted in a January 1, 2022 editorial, "Jan. 6 is not in the past; it is every day. . . . the Capitol riot continues in statehouses across the country, in a bloodless, legalized form that no police officer can arrest and that no prosecutor can try in court."

Meanwhile, in 2022 primaries for city, county, state, and national elected officials throughout the country, the GOP has thrown its weight behind pro-Trump, ultra-ultra-right candidates. These candidates are not mere clones of Paul Gosar and Madison Cawthorn. As conservative talk-show host and former Republican congressman Joe Walsh noted, "I talked to these folks every day, and for people who think Matt Gaetz and Marjorie Taylor Greene and Lauren Boebert are nuts, they ain't seen nothing yet. The Republicans at the state and local level are way, way more gone than the Republicans in Washington. . . . So you're going to get a far larger number of wackadoodle Republicans elected to Congress in 2022 because they will reflect the craziness that's going on state and locally right now." As Alicia Andrews, chair of the Oklahoma

---

5    Simultaneously, the Republican Party also advanced a variety of non–election-related efforts to marginalize certain groups, take away people's rights, and otherwise make Americans' lives smaller, more painful, more dangerous, and more restrictive.

Democratic Party, explained, "Their stated strategy is start at the municipal level, take over the state, take over the nation. So while everybody's talking about the infrastructure plan and the Build Back Better plan, they're rubbing their hands together and making differences in states." Greg Sargent put it more simply and succinctly: "Republicans are increasingly running for office on an open vow to subvert future election losses."

At the same time, some Republicans and their media surrogates have encouraged physical threats—or made such threats themselves—against current elections officials. In 2021, the Brennan Center for Justice reported that a third of all US election officials felt unsafe in their jobs—and that one in six had received threats. One goal of such threats is to bend these officials to the will of MAGA supporters. Another is to get them to resign in fear, frustration, or exhaustion. They can then be replaced with MAGA minions who may be willing to challenge or overturn legitimate vote counts—or declare free and fair elections to be rife with imaginary fraud.

These efforts have eight goals:

1. To suppress voting among Democrats in general, and bodies of culture in particular, using all possible methods. These also include nonstop legal challenges; the challenging and rejection of legitimate ballots; the denial or limiting of voting opportunities, especially for bodies of culture; and the direct intimidation of voters.

2. To put anti-democracy activists in positions of authority. In any election resulting in a GOP loss, these authorities can invoke their official roles and present bogus challenges and claims of having witnessed fraud. ("I saw a UPS truck pull up and drop off five thousand ballots, all marked for the Democratic candidate. Everyone else ignored the truck because they're socialist traitors working for the Deep State.")

3. To overturn legitimate GOP losses wherever and whenever possible, in defiance of the will of voters. ("The voting machine tallies are incorrect. They show the Democratic candidate winning by over 56,000 votes. As the duly appointed official overseeing this election,

13

I hereby certify that the Republican candidate actually won by 670,000 votes.")

4. To sow widespread doubt about the fairness and accuracy of many specific contests—and to encourage distrust in all elections officials, as well as our entire elections system.

5. To create a tsunami of challenges of every type, at every level, to thousands of specific electoral contests.

6. To attempt to grind to a halt our entire elections apparatus—and, in the process, jam up our court dockets as well.

7. To stoke ever more fury, fear, and mistrust among voters—and to encourage people to turn on each other.

8. To destroy any shared sense of public good, truth, facts, or reality, both in relation to American elections and in general.

Republicans in every state, at every level, will insist that all of this is necessary to ensure "election integrity" and to "restore voter confidence" that every electoral contest is "free and fair." In fact, of course, it will be an Orwellian and Hitlerian Big Lie. Everything the GOP will do—and, as I write this, is currently doing—in the name of "election integrity" is clearly intended to *undermine* election integrity and voter confidence.

Throughout much of 2021 and early 2022, the most pro-authoritarian elements of the GOP also conducted "forensic audits" in Arizona, Michigan, Pennsylvania, Texas, and Wisconsin. (As I write this paragraph near the end of 2021, only the Arizona audit is complete, and GOP operatives are demanding many more such audits elsewhere.) These events were pure theater—absurd sham "investigations" intended to stoke ever-greater fury and distrust in elections among people who were gullible enough to take them seriously. Regardless of what these faux audits ostensibly show, the GOP will declare that their candidate actually won. (The day after Arizona's fake audit concluded that Biden won the state by *more* votes than elections officials and prior investigations had determined, Trump announced at a rally, "We won at the Arizona forensic audit yesterday at a level that you wouldn't believe." A day earlier, he proclaimed that the sham audit "conclusively shows there were enough fraudulent votes, mystery votes, and fake votes to change the outcome of the election 4 or 5 times over.") In any case, the results of any such audit are irrelevant. The mere *existence* of each such audit will be used to undermine faith in our elections. As former US secretary of labor Robert Reich observed, "It's a vicious cycle. As Trump continues to stoke his base with his Big Lie that the election was stolen, Republican lawmakers—out to advance their careers and entrench the GOP—are adding fuel to the fire, pushing more Americans into Trump's paranoid nightmare."

The GOP tested out the use of a parallel Big Lie in the vote to recall California governor Gavin Newsom in September 2021. A week before the vote, Fox network host Tomi Lahren declared, "The only thing that will save Gavin Newsom is voter fraud. Pay attention to the voter fraud going on in California because it's going to have big consequences not only for that state but for upcoming elections." The campaign of Larry Elder, the leading Republican gubernatorial candidate, claimed on its website *before Election Day* that it had detected fraud that would change the outcome of the vote. It explained: "Instances of undocumented ballots have been discovered. . . . When . . . officials, either through laziness or incompetence, allow thieves to steal amidst the dead of night and cheat our ballot box, we can no longer rely on its contents. . . . They say that in America, there are four boxes of liberty. The soapbox, the ballot box, the jury box, and the ammo box. Will we now have to fight the California jury box, in the hope that the final box— the one most akin to Pandora's—remains closed?" In short, the unspecified (and unsubstantiated) fraud that somehow occurred before Election Day might force Californians to take up arms and revolt. In person, Elder also declared, "They're going to cheat, we know that." Donald Trump called the vote "totally rigged."

For the 2021 Republican Party, this comment was not anomalous. A few days earlier, in a speech to the Macon County, Georgia Republican Party, North Carolina congressman Madison Cawthorn advised the crowd to begin stockpiling ammunition for what he said was likely American-versus-American violence in the wake of future elections. Widespread election fraud, Cawthorn said, would "lead to one place, and that's bloodshed."

15

After the California vote, however, which Newsom won handily with 62 percent of voter support, Elder swiftly conceded, urging his supporters to be "gracious in defeat."

Looking ahead to both 2022 and 2024, Donald Trump announced with great conviction, "There is no way they will win elections without cheating. There's no way." Steve Bannon echoed the sentiment on his podcast, "They're Democrats. They're going to try to steal it. They can't win elections they don't steal, right?" In short, no future win by any Democrat could, by definition, ever be legitimate.

*Washington Post* columnist Dana Milbank put it this way:

> Reckless, irresponsible GOP leaders and candidates have convinced their voters that there are only two possible outcomes in any election:
>
> A.   The Republican wins.
> B.   The Democrat stole the election.

By early 2022, the Republican Party found itself in an unprecedented position. Its most vocal and steadfast supporters—the people who reliably vote in primaries—overwhelmingly and unrepentantly supported Trump's Big Lie; complete, unquestioned loyalty to him; his restoration to power; the creation of one-party autocratic rule; and, to a somewhat lesser degree, the transformation of the United States into a white-body supremacist and/or evangelical Christian nation. GOP voters made it equally clear that they adored Trump and had no serious interest in anyone else as their 2024 presidential candidate.

Trump himself all but formally announced that he planned to run for reelection in 2024. From his followers' donations, he built a huge campaign war chest. He spent much of 2021 and early 2022 making it clear to all Republican candidates, and the world, that he demanded absolute, complete, unquestioned fealty from every Republican who wanted to hold public office. He loudly and endlessly repeated this message: *The Republican Party is the Trump Party. Every Republican candidate for any office must get 100 percent on the MAGA train. If you run for office and are not entirely subservient to me, I will throw my support behind a competing candidate—if necessary, even a Democrat.*

As a result, in the 2022 GOP primary elections across the country, many candidates for governorships, US Senate, US House, state attorneys general, and state secretaries of state ran on some variation of this platform: *Donald Trump is our authentically elected president. The 2020 elections were rigged by Democrats and other villains, who stole the election from him. Any future election in which a Democrat receives more votes will also be rigged. Once I am in office, I will have four key priorities. The first is to restore Trump to the presidency. The second is to ensure that, after any election in my state or district, the Republican candidate will take office, regardless of the vote count. The third is to do everything I can to ensure that no Democrat-supported idea or initiative ever gets passed. The fourth is to return America to its rightful owners.[6] As a patriot, I will use every tool—legal or illegal, ethical or unethical, peaceful or violent—to achieve these goals.* Some candidates spoke this full message out loud, but most only hinted at parts of it or used coded language.

I'm writing this paragraph in late December 2021, just before this book goes to press. I can see that the elections of 2022 and 2024 will be utterly unlike any pre-2020 election in our nation's history. Each one will be—in the words of former Republican strategist Rick Wilson—"a chain fight in a biker bar in Frogsass, Alabama."

As of the end of 2021, here is how the election of 2022—and/or the election of 2024—appears likely to play out:

The winners of many GOP primaries will run in the November general election on platforms calling for an end to American democracy and the establishment of one-party autocratic rule. Regardless of how Americans actually vote, however, in many locations the Republican Party will repeat the Trump and GOP playbook from 2020, attempting to take power through any means possible, both legal and illegal. These will involve thousands of court challenges; threats of violence against election officials, secretaries of state, and their families; Republican-led secretaries of state, state legislatures, and election boards refusing

---

6    Many GOP voters will hear *rightful owners* as *white Christians born in the United States.* In March 2021, Glenn Ellmers published an essay in *American Mind,* a publication of the conservative Claremont Institute, in which he wrote that "most people who live in the United States today—certainly more than half—are not Americans in any meaningful sense of the term." It does not require careful literary analysis to understand that, for Ellmers, *American Mind,* and the Claremont Institute, *an American in any meaningful sense* is a dog-whistle term for *a white Christian born in the United States.*

to certify, or attempting to overturn, legitimate voting results; widespread demands for thousands of recounts; and a massive nationwide disinformation campaign. Many of these efforts will be partly planned, implemented, aided, and/or abetted by sitting Republican members of the US House and Senate.[7]

As part of this strategy, Republicans will point relentlessly to the "results" of earlier fraudulent "audits," sometimes lying about the audits' own results. Many more such audits will be demanded—and, to the degree possible, undertaken—by GOP officials and voters in as many locations as possible, throwing our entire elections system into chaos.

If, through any means, the GOP manages to take back the US House of Representative in the 2022 election, here are its likely plans, all of which it has discussed very publicly:

1. Block any and every piece of legislation proposed by the Democratic Party. Make Congress unable to accomplish *anything*. Perhaps make it impossible to keep the government running, or pay its bills, or fund Social Security payments. Create as much of a deliberate meltdown as possible. Then loudly, widely, and relentlessly blame Democrats for everything.

2. Immediately begin impeachment proceedings again President Biden for bogus crimes against humanity, the state, and the Constitution. Make this into a never-ending media circus, in which Republican operatives announce, 24/7, that Biden is the biggest traitor and worst criminal in American history. Draw out the impeachment process for as long as possible, so that the media are forced to cover it, week after week, month after month. If and when the process ends—in inevitable failure—perhaps impeach Biden again, for different imaginary crimes. Perhaps force his resignation "for the good of the country." If this occurs, the day after President Harris takes office, perhaps initiate impeachment proceedings against her, and begin the process anew.

---

7    We now know that the January 6 demonstration that turned into a sacking of the US Capitol was planned with the active assistance of GOP House members Marjorie Taylor Greene, Paul Gosar, Lauren Boebert, Mo Brooks, Andy Biggs, Madison Cawthorn, and Louie Gohmert, and/or some of their top staffers, as well as with the active participation of Trump's chief of staff, Mark Meadows.

3.  In parallel fashion, announce faux House-led "investigations" of Biden's cabinet members, key advisors, and chief of staff, as well as other powerful Democrats. Haul them in front of House committees for Joe McCarthy-style "questioning" (e.g., "When did you first decide you wanted to destroy the Constitution and make Communism the law of our land?"). Strip some or all Democratic House members of their committee assignments. Charge a raft of powerful Democrats with contempt of Congress.[8]

4.  Elect anti-democracy Trump ally Kevin McCarthy—or an even more abject Trump sycophant such as Jim Jordan or Elise Stefanik—as the Speaker of the House. Perhaps elect Trump himself. Although this is entirely without precedent, it is also entirely legal. The Speaker of the House does not need to hold any elected office. As of this writing in late 2021, Trump has not dismissed the idea. On a talk show, he said of the proposition, "You know, it's very interesting. That's so interesting."

If Democrats maintain control of the House but Republicans gain control of the Senate, the GOP will be unable to follow the second and fourth parts of the above strategy—but they will almost certainly follow the first, as well as a senatorial version of the third.

Whatever scenario plays out, the GOP hopes to provoke white-hot rage, profound disgust, deep suspicion, and swirling confusion in hundreds of millions of American bodies—bodies of all colors and political persuasions. On a larger scale, it hopes to generate social and political chaos—and, perhaps, mayhem.

---

8    On November 17, 2021, on the House floor, then-House Minority Leader Kevin McCarthy pledged to investigate a range of powerful Democrats if Republicans take control of the House in early 2023. A few months earlier, Republican House member Jim Banks vowed that if the GOP wins control of the House, every Democrat and every Republican who served on the committee investigating the January 6, 2021 Capitol riot would be removed from *every* House committee. GOP House member Lauren Boebert announced her hope and plan to charge unnamed Democrats with contempt of Congress. In September 2021, Saule Omarova, President Joe Biden's nominee for the job of comptroller of the currency, appeared before the US Senate Banking Committee as part of her confirmation process. Omarova was born in Kazakhstan and emigrated to the United States in 1991. At the hearing, Republican Senator John Kennedy said to her, "I don't know whether to call you professor or comrade."

If Donald Trump runs for president in 2024, which appears highly likely, he will focus his campaign on this message: *I won the 2020 presidential election, which was stolen from me by the Democrats in the greatest crime in American history. Now, I promise you, they're going to do it again. I'm going to win in a landslide, and the Democrats, Antifa, and the Deep State are going to rig things so that I seem to lose. But we're not going to let them get away with it, are we? We're going to take America back—by any means necessary!* In addition to "Make America Great Again," his likely campaign slogan will be "Stop Another Steal."

Trump's game plan is already obvious: If he wins enough electoral votes to secure the presidency, he and his followers will insist that the election was flawless. If he doesn't, he and the GOP will declare that the entire election was rigged and fraudulent. They will use every method, and every opportunity—legal or illegal, peaceful or violent—to upend the election, destroy American democracy, and install him as this country's chief executive (and absolute ruler).

If you are reading this between 2022 and 2025, it will likely already be clear to you that Trump is never going away—and will never stop wreaking widespread havoc—until he is dead or in prison. If he is not in the news for more than a few days, it is because he is either reloading, with the help of his many minions and complicitors, or physically ill.

You may recall from one of your history classes that, in 1923, Adolf Hitler attempted to overthrow the German government, in what has become known as the Beer Hall Putsch. For this crime, Hitler was arrested, tried, and sentenced to five years in prison, but released after only nine months, in December 1924.[9] After his release, he regrouped and—having learned from his first coup attempt—steadily consolidated power and led a second, successful coup. By 1934, he was the absolute dictator of a country of over sixty-five million people.

By design, the overall effect of all of these efforts will be to infuriate nearly all American voters—and to sow deep, widespread distrust in our entire elections system.

---

9    Historians will likely note that December 2024, the period immediately after the 2024 presidential election, marks exactly one hundred years after Hitler left prison and resumed his rise to absolute power.

Among many GOP voters, especially those who support a white supremacist and/or Christian autocracy, this fury will be channeled toward fomenting widespread mayhem and bloodshed.

However, a repeat of the January 6 mob violence at the US Capitol, and similar attacks on state capitols, looks very unlikely. Having learned from that attack, state and federal officials will ensure that before, during, and immediately after the 2022 and 2024 elections, the US Capitol and all fifty state capitols will be well protected. Ballot processing centers, courtrooms, and other potential targets will also receive robust security. Thus, new riots by groups of hundreds or thousands of people will fail. Many Republican leaders, and many potential perpetrators of GOP-inspired gang violence, will recognize this.

Thus, in 2022 and 2024, and perhaps beyond, a central Republican Party strategy for maintaining and growing its power in Washington may be *to incite violence by millions of its followers throughout as much of the country as possible.*[10]

Because the most obvious targets will be well protected, this war will likely be fought in the streets—in ordinary neighborhoods, in downtowns, and in gathering places such as town squares, parks, fairgrounds, and shopping malls. Right-wing thugs may swiftly attack one of these soft targets, create carnage and mayhem, then just as swiftly withdraw and move on to another, knowing that it's impossible to protect every public space in the country.

This will likely be guerilla warfare, focused simultaneously (or perhaps sequentially) on many thousands of different soft targets across the United States. Some may be hit from multiple directions at once, over and over. More often, though, the war may resemble a deadly game of whack-a-mole. A shopping mall may be attacked, and security guards, police, and perhaps National Guard troops will rush to protect it. But by the time they arrive, the attackers will have disappeared. Then, a few minutes later, the

---

10    This strategy is not new, novel, or particularly American. Stalin used it. Hitler used it. Throughout history, many other dictators and wannabe dictators have used it. As I write this footnote near the end of 2021, far-right French presidential candidate Eric Zemmour is trying to use it. He is currently on trial for hate speech. Earlier, Zemmour warned of a coming civil war in France between "those who do not wish to abandon the identity of France, which is to say its Christian, and White, identity" and people who accept "the Islamization of France." Zemmour has proposed, among other things, to halt all legal migration to France and to ban all foreign-sounding first names. He also pointed a rifle at journalists and told them, "The fun's over."

amusement park across town (or a hundred miles away) may be attacked by a different band of murderous "patriots."

Currently, most pro-democracy American bodies are utterly unprepared for such widespread violence and brutality. This book will help prepare them.

This book will help prepare *you.*

*Pause.*

Before you read further, check in with your body.

How is it responding to the possibility of widespread brutality and chaos—and to the prospect of armed rioters in your own town or neighborhood?

Where does your body constrict or recoil?

What emotions are you experiencing—and where in your body do you experience them?

What urges do you experience?

What images and meanings are emerging?

*Pause again.* Take a few slow, deep breaths.

You've just begun your journey into Somatic Abolitionism. Welcome.

## BODY PRACTICE
## MINDFUL STRETCHING

Stretch often and regularly—multiple times a day.

Whenever you have the urge, stretch all or part of your body in whatever ways it wants to stretch (unless you're in a situation where stretching might be seen as disrespectful). When you wake up in the morning, deliberately stretch as you lie in bed. Stretch again when you first stand up. Keep doing these daily stretches until they become a habit.

Pay close attention to your body as you stretch.

These should be natural stretches, not gymnastics. Just notice the pull and expansion of your muscles. Notice where there is constriction or release, pleasure or pain—and breathe.

You are not stretching just to experience release or relief. You are beginning a practice of noticing what emerges in your body, as it moves from one state or position to another.

*[handwritten margin note: Adrenaline shakiness—it occurs in the solar plexus. tensing]*

# 3

# WHAT THE WAR PLAN LOOKS LIKE

*About 31 million American adults* . . . *sympathize with the statement that "because things have gotten so far off track, true American patriots may have to resort to violence in order to save our country."*

Aaron Blake

*Seeing the people—ordinary citizens—take up arms at the call of a demagogue is what gives authoritarians confidence. . . . Because they don't need the military on their side. They need your local real estate agent. What you're left with then is a society that faces its greatest threat from within.*

Sikandar Hayat Khan

*The coup on Jan. 6 was a turning point—at least that's how history will remember it. . . . Violence was normalized. The Big Lies were acted upon. Brutality was normalized. . . . Nazism is what happens when a fascist movement unites, hardens, and develops.*

Umair Haque

> *The true goal of totalitarian propaganda is not persuasion, but organization. . . . What convinces masses are not facts, and not even invented facts, but only the consistency of the system of which they are presumably part.*
>
> Hannah Arendt

> *We are already in a constitutional crisis. The destruction of democracy might not come until November 2024, but critical steps in that direction are happening now.*
>
> Robert Kagan

In order to win this civil war, the Republican Party will need to activate millions—if not tens of millions—of people. Many will be armed.

The playbook for much of this war has already been written. Parts of it have been field-tested—first, briefly, in the run-up to the 2016 election, then in the aftermath of the elections of 2020 and 2021. Here is the most likely scenario:

Beginning immediately after the 2022 and / or 2024 primaries, Republican candidates will baselessly claim that plans are already underway to steal the election from them—just as it was ostensibly stolen from Donald Trump in 2020. Different candidates will pin the blame on different thieves (liberals, Democrats, Black Lives Matter, the Deep State, Antifa, Nancy Pelosi, George Soros,[11] the Biden administration, etc.), but the central message will always be the same: *America's enemies plan to steal the election from American patriots.*

For months, this message will be spread 24/7 by national right-wing television and radio networks, by right-wing pundits and personalities, by elected Republican leaders, by millions of Russian bots, on thousands of websites, and throughout social media. The primary audience for this message will be the tens

---

11    Soros, a wealthy Jewish philanthropist who has given over $15 billion to a variety of pro-democracy, pro-education causes, is widely imagined by the political right to be the head of a nonexistent international Jewish conspiracy. His name has become one of the most common anti-Semitic dog whistles. Just as *critical race theory* is a substitute for the N word, *George Soros* is a substitute for the K word.

of millions of Americans who already believe that in 2020 the presidency was stolen from Donald Trump.

Immediately after the 2022 and/or 2024 elections, unless the Republican Party wins control of both houses of Congress (and, in 2024, the presidency as well), the message will shift to this: *Every Republican win was the result of a free, fair election. Every Republican loss was the result of widespread fraud committed by a conspiracy of traitors. Once again, your candidates' legitimate victories have been stolen.* These messages will be repeated relentlessly by all of the party's loyal outlets of misinformation and disinformation.

As the weeks pass—probably in January, after the holidays are no longer a distraction—the central message will likely shift to *Because of widespread election fraud, your beloved country and way of life are being stolen from you. They will both soon be gone—forever.*

Soon a call to action will be added: *Patriots! Our elections have been hijacked by our enemies. There is only one way to stop them from stealing America and turning it into a socialist hell. You need to take your country back! You know what to do.*

Unlike in January 2021, when Donald Trump used similar words to whip a crowd of several thousand into a frenzy, this call for mob violence will go out to tens of millions of self-identified "patriots" throughout the country.

Meanwhile, throughout 2022, 2023, 2024, and perhaps 2025, many GOP senators and House members will do everything they can to make the federal government as dysfunctional and impotent as possible—and, if they can, to grind it to a complete stop. This became a Republican strategy in the 1990s, under the leadership of then-Speaker of the House Newt Gingrich. The GOP deployed it repeatedly in the decades that followed.

Until the war is well underway, many Republican lawmakers and leaders will carefully avoid explicit calls for violence, while calling for it implicitly—loudly, clearly, all the time, in all parts of the country, and through all available methods of communication. Just as Trump and his surrogates did after January 6, 2021, they will insist that their calls are for peaceful protest, political organizing, and changing the minds of voters in the next election cycle. Nearly everyone will recognize these statements as lies.

I've just described the most likely scenario, but the Republican Party and its media surrogates may deploy one (or more) of these variations instead:

- Followers may be incited to "take back your country" on Election Day. Under this plan, groups of armed rioters would storm polling places, especially in left-leaning precincts. Even if this mob violence fails, it could render many elections (or the results in many precincts) void, creating extensive chaos. In some locales, the election may then need to be rescheduled and rerun. During this new election, the same maneuver can simply be repeated—if necessary, over and over. The prospect of further violence on any subsequent Election Day may depress voter turnout, especially in Democratic-leaning areas.

- As above, but the call to "take back your country" may come earlier, shortly after the primaries, once all Republican nominees have been identified.

- GOP operatives at the local and state level may overturn or challenge legitimate election results; make up false voting tallies and/or "find" nonexistent votes; attempt to manipulate voting machines or discard ballots; harass, threaten, sue, defame, or physically harm honest elections officials who try to do their jobs honorably; after the 2024 election, appoint and certify slates of electors to the Electoral College that do not reflect the election laws of their state and/or the will of its voters; file thousands of frivolous lawsuits; or simply scream "FRAUD!" endlessly at the tops of their lungs. Their primary goal may be to install Republican candidates everywhere they can, regardless of any actual vote totals. Their secondary goal may be to create so much pandemonium, disaster, and fury that few people will trust any election results from that (or any) locale. If this occurs in thousands of locations, many Americans will no longer trust the results of the entire election—or our voting system as a whole. All of this may be followed by the call to "take back your country."

- In January of 2025, GOP Congressional legislators may use procedural tactics involving the counting of electoral votes to overturn the will of American voters. This might involve objecting to legitimate electoral votes and/or electors, attempting to accept some illegitimate votes and/or electors, or voiding the entire electoral process and throwing the election to the House of Representatives. In this last scenario, House members would simply vote for whatever presidential and vice presidential candidates they wished, with each state (not each House member) having one vote. This would almost certainly result in the Republican nominee—presumably Donald Trump— being "elected" president. This might be followed by GOP leaders urging followers throughout the US to "take back your country."[12]

What I've described here and in the previous chapter is a prediction, not the result of insider knowledge, psychic powers, or divine revelation. It is simply a description of what, to me and many others, seems likely to unfold. It is not our country's unavoidable destiny.[13]

That said, Republican lawmakers and officials will likely vehemently deny that any of the above scripts is (or ever was) their plan, even as they execute it faithfully. They will still more vehemently deny that they seek to incite a largely racialized war. Then they may insist that *I* am the one trying to provoke such a

---

12    I hope that the Democrats are not so foolish and gutless that they allow things to get to this point. If they do, I hope they are not so foolish and gutless that they follow Al Gore's lead from 2000 and permit Trump to take office, ostensibly for the stability of the nation, or to "heal divisions," or to "put aside partisan rancor" in "a spirit of reconciliation." I hope that they are not so foolish and gutless that they call for calm and tell their fellow Dems to respond to violence and thuggery with peacefulness. If the Democratic Party does any of these things, the GOP will likely see it as extreme weakness and a form of surrender. They may then swiftly and violently attempt to take full authoritarian control of our national government.

13    One other scenario that may lead to a civil war—but that would not be explicitly planned by the GOP—seems possible. If, in 2024, Donald Trump legitimately wins the majority of electoral votes in a free and fair election—especially if he loses the popular vote for the second time—many Americans, sensing that the end of democracy is at hand, may spontaneously rise up against the impending autocracy that would almost certainly emerge under a second Trump presidency. But this uprising would also be *against* the legitimate results of our country's election laws. These laws are deeply flawed and have needed to be changed for well over a century. Nevertheless, because such an uprising would refuse to accept the legitimacy of those laws, it is difficult to see how, should this scenario play out, a democratic United States would survive.

war, perhaps in concert with Black Lives Matter, Antifa, George Soros, proponents of critical race theory, Chuck Schumer, the Biden administration, et al. This too may be a piece of their plan.

As part of this propaganda effort, some Republican leaders may baselessly claim that Black Lives Matter is planning its own violent revolt. Of course, no such revolt is being planned or contemplated.

But don't take my word for this; take the word of the FBI, the Department of Homeland Security, and every other domestic intelligence-gathering agency. These are people who have never been great friends to bodies of culture, especially Black and Indigenous bodies—or to our quest for justice and liberation. Yet they will confirm what I have just told you. They will also tell you that the single greatest, most persistent, and most lethal domestic threat to the United States is violent insurgency by white nationalists.

*Pause.*

What are you experiencing in your body right now?

## BODY PRACTICE
## **WIGGLING**

For twenty seconds, wiggle any set of joints that wants to loosen or move, one set at a time. This might include:

- Wiggling your ankles from side to side, or up and down, or in circles.
- Wiggling your knees from side to side, or back and forth, or up and down.
- Wiggling your hips and the base of your spine from side to side, or forward and backward, or in circles.
- Wiggling your shoulders forward and backward, or from side to side, or up and down, or in circles.
- Wiggling your elbows back and forth, or in circles.
- Wiggling your wrists from side to side, or up and down, or in circles.
- Wiggling your fingers in any directions.
- Wiggling your head from side to side, or in circles.

It's fine to wiggle while standing up, while seated or kneeling, or while lying down.

If you like, try wiggling when you first awaken in the morning, before you get out of bed. When you're done wiggling, *pause* for a few breaths.

BODY PRACTICE
## GROUNDING AND ORIENTING

Find a safe and fairly quiet location. Sit or stand comfortably. Keep your eyes open, but keep your gaze soft and let it drop. Take three slow, deep breaths.

Notice the outline of your skin and the slight pressure of the air around it. Experience the firmer pressure of the floor or earth beneath your feet. If you're seated, experience the pressure of the seat beneath you.

Notice your breath as it enters and leaves your nose, your windpipe, your lungs, and your belly. (Although air doesn't literally fill our bellies, that is the sensation that many of us experience.) For a few breaths, simply follow the air as it flows into and out of your body.

Notice any other sensations in your body: the bend in your knees; your spine, straight or curved; a breeze in your hair; your belly and any tension you hold there; and your chest, expanding and releasing with each breath.

Start at the bottom of your body. Notice the very slight pressure of your socks or shoes or sandals against your feet. Notice any warmth or coolness, any tightness or relaxation, and any pleasurable or painful sensation.

Then slowly move your awareness up your body, first through your calves and shins, then to your knees, then up through the rest of your legs. Notice any change in temperature, any constriction or release, and any pleasure or pain. Pay attention to where your body touches your underwear, your socks or stockings, your shirt or blouse, your pants or skirt or dress.

Continue this process all the way up your body, until you reach the top of your head.

Then turn your head and slowly look around in all directions, including behind you. (You will need to rotate your entire upper body to do this.) Then look up, then down at your feet.

As you look around, orient yourself in the surrounding space. If you're indoors, notice the height of the ceiling, the height and color of each wall, any doors or windows, and any other details that stand out. If you're outside, take note of any boundaries, such as a fence, a footpath, a road, the edge of a clearing, or the shore of a pond. Notice any plant or animal life nearby. Note any sounds you hear, any smells that fill the air, any warmth or coolness, or any colors that stand out. Also notice any sensations you experience in your head, neck, and shoulders as they move.

One full cycle of this practice should take you about a minute. One cycle is enough, but do two or more if you like.

Please do this grounding and orienting practice at least once a day, every day. You'll find it especially useful during times of high stress or conflict.

But don't wait until you're in a high-stress situation to do this practice. Repeating these body practices when your body is settled will help you temper and condition it. This will help it be better prepared for when high-stress situations emerge.

Many people find it helpful to ground and orient themselves each morning, when they first get out of bed and stand up.

# 4

# BODIES AND LOGIC

*A lie once told remains a lie, but a lie told
a thousand times becomes the truth.*

attributed to Joseph Goebbels

*Many consequential Republicans decided their best bet is to keep
their contracting coalition in a state of constant agitation and fear,
combatants in a never-ending culture war, "embattled warriors
making a last stand against the demise of everything." And that,
in turn, requires them to feed the base ever greater falsehoods.*

Peter Wehner

*False stories have an intrinsic advantage over the truth when it comes
to uniting people. If you want to gauge group loyalty, requiring people
to believe an absurdity is a far better test than asking them to believe
the truth. . . . If all your neighbors believe the same outrageous tale,
you can count on them to stand together in times of crisis.*

Yuval Noah Harari

*Pause.*

What do you experience in your body right now?

The Republican Party's relentless accusations of fraud, theft, and conspiracy won't just be false. They'll also be illogical and contradictory—just as many of the Republican Party's messages were in 2020 and 2021. For example, how is it possible that when Donald Trump and Marjorie Taylor Greene appeared on the same ballot in Georgia, Greene was elected fairly, while Trump won the state in a landslide but somehow had his victory stolen from him? How can the January 6 carnage and chaos be simultaneously a minor incident overblown by the media; a legitimate and victorious fight for freedom and American values; a murderous, despicable plot by Black Lives Matter and Antifa designed to discredit American patriots; a faked "false flag" incident meant to hoodwink the American public; a top-secret FBI operation; and a normal, peaceful visit by a batch of tourists?

Yes, these outcomes are contradictory, mutually exclusive, and impossible. But impossibility doesn't matter, because *none of the Republican Party's core messages is cognitive. Each is designed to speak directly to our bodies, not our cognitive brains.*

Unlike our cerebral cortex, the rest of the human body is not designed to understand logic or context. It doesn't give a damn whether something makes sense. *All it wants is to be safe*—and it is designed to create, maintain, or reclaim that safety at all costs. (We'll dive deeper into this in later chapters.)[14]

The Republican Party's central messages all share the same purposes: to make the bodies of their followers sense that they are unsafe and under attack; to activate the past trauma (especially racialized trauma) stuck in those bodies; to activate intense terror and fury in response to that trauma; and to incite a huge buildup of energy that needs to be either metabolized or expressed.

In short, the Republican Party hopes to incite a civil war by evoking a collective trauma response in tens of millions of American bodies.

Which is why, in order to prevent this war—or, if war is unavoidable, to successfully resist and prevail—we need to begin not with strategy or politics, but with tempering and conditioning our bodies.

---

14    Also, as David Frum has noted, for Trump partisans, "Their argument doesn't have to make sense, because their constituency doesn't care about it making sense. Their constituency cares about being given permission to disregard and despise the legal rules that once bound U.S. society. That's the game, and that's how Bannon & Co. will play the game."

BODY PRACTICE
# PAUSING AND NOTICING

Most of us imagine that our body is a machine operated by a mini-me inside our head. But that's an illusion. We're not backhoes or bulldozers.

We are bodies. The mini-me that you imagine inside your head is not the dictator of your body but one of its thousands of interacting energy flows.

The practice below can help you regularly experience and re-member your bodyness. It can be done almost anytime and almost anywhere.

*Pause.* Just *pause.* Stop moving. Stop worrying and speculating and hoping. Just notice what your body is experiencing right now.

Don't try to figure anything out. Don't try to understand. Don't try to come up with an explanation or an answer. Don't check to see if you're doing this practice right. *Just pause.* Just notice. Just experience your body.

Then go back to whatever you were doing.

Do this practice over and over—at least several times a day, until it becomes a habit.

Over time, you will be able to pause and notice whenever you want. You will also be able to pause and notice whenever you sense that something seems off, or someone or something—especially your body—needs your attention.


BODY PRACTICE
# ENTERING AND LEAVING

This practice combines elements from Grounding and Orienting (Chapter 3) and Pausing and Noticing (immediately above).

When you first enter or leave a room—or walk through a doorway into a theater or train or airplane or gym—simply *pause* and stand still for three breaths. Look around you 360 degrees. Orient yourself in the space. Notice what changes you experience in your body. Then resume whatever you were doing.

You can also do this when you get into or out of a car, on or off a bicycle, or into or out of an elevator.

Don't do this practice when other bodies are nearby and your pausing might block their movement. Also (of course) don't do this with a moving vehicle or while you're driving.

# 5

# YOUR BODY IS THE KEY

*When everything around you is crazy,*
*it is ingenious to stay calm.*

Mehmet Murat ildan

*When someone upends your world, and the rest of the*
*world feels utterly upside down: be calm. Some people*
*need you to be their safe haven.*

Kirsten Robinson

*Pause.*

Once the war is underway, no one knows how it will play out in your state, town, or neighborhood. You can't know how you will be involved, either. Will you march in the streets in support of unfettered democracy, justice, and liberation, in concert with thousands of other American bodies? Will you stand arm-in-arm in a long line of bodies, helping to protect a government building from attack by a mob? Or will none of this turn out to be necessary? No one can say in advance.

What *can* be said is that strong, collective, nonviolent resistance is the most effective way to prevent a coup. Much more on this in Chapters 32 and 33.

Here's what else can be said: if you are a nice and respectful human being, your niceness and respect will not protect you. Good intentions will not protect you. If you are a liberal or progressive, your politics will not protect you. The Democratic Party and its legislators will not protect you. They will have good ideas, strong words, solid arguments, and the best intentions. The other side will have rifles, machine guns, handguns, bayonets, bombs, knives, and plans to murder people. Some will also be certain that God commends their cause—and their violence.

As events play out, what additional measures will you need to take to protect yourself, your family, and any communities that you have cultivated? Do you put your loaded rifle by your bed before you go to sleep, in case you need to defend yourself inside your own home? Do you carry a legal handgun for self-protection as you go about your daily business? If so, have you been properly trained in gun use and safety? Do you learn a martial art or hand-to-hand self-defense? Will you meet with your neighbors to discuss how to protect and defend your block? You will need to discern and decide as events emerge. (I'll say much more about these questions in Chapter 36.)

Once (and if) the war unfolds, however, its events will surely activate the trauma in your body—especially your racialized trauma. This will likely happen many times, during multiple situations and encounters.

Each time, when you sense the beginnings of this activation, your task will be the same: slow down; *pause* (when possible); settle and pay attention to your body; notice what is unfolding around you; stay with whatever emotions you experience without squelching them, fleeing from them, or blowing them into another person; then act from the best parts of yourself.

Whatever strategies, alliances, or activities you become involved with, they will require the same things from you: presence, discernment, and a settled, well-resourced[15] body.

As I wrote in *My Grandmother's Hands*,

> Few skills are more essential than the ability to settle your body. If you can settle your body, you are more likely to be calm, alert, and fully present, no matter what is going on around you. A settled body enables you to harmonize and connect with other bodies around you, while encouraging those bodies to settle as well. Gather

---

15   We'll look at what it means to have a well-resourced body in Chapter 29.

together a large group of unsettled bodies—or assemble a group of bodies and then unsettle them—and you get a mob or a riot. But bring a large group of settled bodies together and you have a potential movement—and a potential force for tremendous good in the world. A calm, settled body is the foundation for health, for healing, for helping others, and for changing the world.

As you practice the body activities in this book, and complete rep after rep, you will steadily build your own presence and discernment. You will also become more adept at helping your body settle, no matter what is going on around you.

You don't need to have read *My Grandmother's Hands* to use this book and get great value from it. But your experience with that book will help you get the most from this one. So, if you can, please do read (or reread) *My Grandmother's Hands* alongside *The Quaking of America*. That book focuses primarily on the healing of trauma, especially racialized trauma. You will find Chapters 32 – 47 of *The Quaking of America* particularly useful as the civil war unfolds.

## BODY PRACTICE
## MINDFUL MOVING

Our bodies are designed to move, not stay in one place and one position for hours at a time.

Move yours for at least forty-five minutes every day—or, if that is too much, for as long as your body is able. This can be all at once or in multiple, briefer periods—for instance, stopping to do a few squats or push-ups several times a day.

You don't need to go to the gym for this. Walking, jogging, swimming, cycling, and skating all work.

If you don't like those options, you can play touch football, or tennis, or golf, or basketball, or even ping pong. If you use a wheelchair, play wheelchair basketball, or go wheelchair bowling.

If you're by yourself, shoot baskets, or play outside with your dog, or put on some music and dance. Do tai chi or qigong. Practice a martial art. Turn cartwheels or do somersaults. Shovel snow, mow the lawn, or rake leaves.

Whatever activity you choose, pay attention to what your body experiences.

All of these activities can help your body become more nimble and responsive. They can help you to develop grit and discernment. They can also help you become more aware of your body's energy flows and signals.

# 6

# YOUR BODY'S
# SIX INTELLIGENCES

*Human beings are not static objects animated by spirit,*
*but expressions of a living and sacred process.*

Liz Koch

*I learn how to listen to my body. I must listen or I will die. . . .*
*I must learn the difference between fear and danger.*

Sonya Renee Taylor

*If you're not physically and mentally prepared for what life*
*is going to throw at you, then you're just going to crumble.*
*And then, you're no good to anybody.*

David Goggins

We normally think of *intelligence* as a set of cognitive activities:
thinking, reasoning, deliberating, solving problems, and so on.
But that definition sells us all short. Human intelligence is far
more insightful—and far more varied—than just what we think.

Our bodies constantly flow with multiple forms of intelligence,
which can be divided into these six categories[16]:

---

16    When I teach workshops and classes, I'm a bit more nuanced and detailed about some of these
categories. For the purposes of this book, however, the ones expressed here strike the best balance of
clarity, simplicity, and usefulness. My six categories are based on the work of therapist Peter Levine, a key
figure in embodied therapy and the healing of trauma. Dr. Levine created a somewhat similar process
called SIBAM or SIMBA, which I learned from his organization, Somatic Experiencing International. You
can find out more about Dr. Levine and his work at www.traumahealing.com.

- Vibrations (the charge or energetic quality that your body picks up from a person or situation)

- Images and thoughts (memories, ideas, visions, fantasies, etc.)

- Meanings (explanations, stories, comparisons, connections, cognitive judgments, etc.)

- Behaviors, impulses, and urges (what your body does, plus what it wants to do that you don't act on)

- Affect and emotions (fear, joy, disgust, delight, anxiety, pride, grief, longing, etc.)

- Sensations (pressure, tightness, release, heat, cold, numbness, etc.)

Notice that these categories honor more than just your cognitive brain—and that they don't separate it from your body's other intelligences. Notice, too, how they provide far more information than purely cognitive experience.

These multiple intelligences tend to work together. For example, when you experience a sensation—say, your cat's tongue licking the back of your hand—you might also experience an image (a visual memory of when your cat did the same thing a few days ago); a behavior (moving your hand and scratching the cat behind its ear) or urge (an impulse to scratch the cat that you might not act on); an affect (amusement at what the cat is doing); a meaning (the thought, *Cats are the clowns of the pet world*); a vibration (you sense that your cat wants you to pay attention to her); and so on.

You may not always experience all six intelligences at once, but, as you'll discover, two or more of them will often speak to you simultaneously.

As shorthand, I sometimes refer to these six intelligences as the VIMBAS. If you look at the above list, you'll see that VIMBAS is an acronym made up of the first letter of each intelligence.

As you'll discover, each intelligence has its own range of intertwined textures, speed, rhythms, directions, weights, pressures, and charges. As you pause and take time to fully experience what emerges in your body, you will become more familiar with all of these. You will also learn how they connect and interact with each other.

In the first five chapters of this book, you explored your body in some very simple, focused, and deliberate ways. Those practices helped you develop a habit of paying attention to one or more of these intelligences.

Beginning with this chapter, you'll intentionally explore and cultivate all six of your body's intelligences. This exploration involves multiple ways of slowing down, staying present, and focusing on your body's experience and energies. This exploration is essential for conditioning and tempering your body, for healing trauma, and for staying safe and sane in any high-pressure situation.

As you'll also discover, although each of us experiences the VIMBAS personally, as an individual body, the VIMBAS are also elemental, here-and-now expressions of creation itself.

Sometimes, too, what seems like our individual experience turns out to also be institutional, cultural, intergenerational, or historical. In Chapter 11, I'll explain how this works.

As you do many of the body practices in this book, you'll notice and write down what emerges in you through each form of intelligence. You can always do this on a blank page of a journal or notebook.

On the following page, you'll find a list of the six intelligences, plus a description (or set of examples) for each. If you like, you can make photocopies of this page. Then, as (or after) you do a body practice, you can fill in the blank area after each intelligence with a description of what you experience.

It's quite common for people to approach the body practices in my books and blogs with this plan: *I'm going to use these skills, tools, and techniques to improve my situation and transform myself.* It's a natural and understandable attitude.

But that attitude actually holds people back. If you look at it carefully, you'll see that it's a cousin to the idea that only our cognitive experience qualifies as intelligence.

Notice how your body responds when you read the words *skills* and *tools*.

# VIMBAS: Your Body's Six Intelligences

## Vibrations
*The charge or energetic quality that your body picks up*

## Images and Thoughts
*Memories, ideas, visions, fantasies, etc.*

## Meanings
*Explanations, stories, comparisons, connections, cognitive judgments, etc.*

## Behaviors, Impulses, and Urges
*What your body does, plus what it wants to do that you don't act on*

## Affect and Emotions
*Fear, joy, disgust, delight, anxiety, ride, grief, longing, etc.*

## Sensations
*Pressure, tightness, release, heat, cold, numbness, etc.*

*Pause* right now. Pay attention to your body and its VIMBAS. What are you experiencing in response to those words?

Words such as *skills, tools, techniques,* and *strategies* are associated with analyzing situations, completing tasks, achieving outcomes, and fixing things that are broken.

The body practices I offer are not tools, strategies, techniques, or skills. They give birth to experiences that are far more than just cognitive. They are designed to engage all of your body's intelligences.

With that in mind, imagine your body not as a toolbox but as a *toy box.* Think of each new body practice as a new toy—something to explore, investigate, play with, be curious about, and perhaps share with others.[17]

You can also imagine your body as a living, breathing goodie bag—a container filled with multiple ways to access supportive, healing energies. I call these energies *resource.* We'll look at accessing resource in detail in Chapter 29, and I'll also touch on them briefly elsewhere.

Notice how your body responds when you read the words *toy box* and *goodie bag.*

*Pause* again. Pay attention to your body and its VIMBAS. What are you experiencing in response to those words?

The words *toy box* and *goodie bag* suggest discovery and play. They point to approaches that are open-ended, unbounded, and emergent. They hint at the juiciness and joy of being a human body.

When you envision your body as a toy box and a goodie bag, you can be deeply curious about it. You can slow down, pause, and explore it in detail. You can lean into and appreciate the process of discovery. And you can often take pleasure—and sometimes joy—in what you find.

Beginning with this chapter, many of the body practices in this book include what I call *soul scribing.* This simply means pausing, paying close attention to the VIMBAS your body experiences in that moment, and then noting those experiences *in writing.* Soul scribing helps you access information from all of your body's intelligences.

---

17    My thanks to Dr. Leticia Nieto, who is the source of this important distinction.

You don't need any special talent, experience, or writing ability to soul scribe. You don't even have to write in sentences or paragraphs. You can soul scribe using brief notes, lists, or your own personal shorthand. This might include abbreviations, emojis, pictures, or whatever else you like. (If you want to be more detailed—for example, if you want to keep an embodied journal or diary—that's fine, too.)

For some body practices, you'll soul scribe while you move *through* an experience. More often, though, you'll soul scribe as soon as possible *after the experience is complete.* Occasionally you'll do both.

Some body practices in this book *require* soul scribing; others do not. However, you are always welcome to soul scribe after doing any body practice—or whenever the spirit moves you.

Below are three typical (and excellent) examples of soul scribing. They show how three very different people might soul scribe as part of the body practice at the end of this chapter, "Your Body in the Mirror."

### Dewey

- Kept focusing on my love handles—new, within past year. Wanted to turn away but didn't.

- Experienced some brief disgust. Then kept flashing on Ralph Fiennes in *A Bigger Splash.* Compared my body to his. Told myself that was silly. Then flashed on Jack Black in *Margot at the Wedding.* Compared my package to his. Mine much bigger. That seemed sillier. Instructions said not to critique or evaluate, but that's what came up.

- For several seconds focused on hernia scar. Ran hand over it. Thought it would be sensitive, but isn't. Wondered if it's a turnoff for Lee.

- Pondered how strange human bodies look. Chimp bodies look stranger still. Baboon bodies look much less weird. Wondered why that is.

- My upper arms seem a little bigger. Working out makes a difference.

- Slight tension in belly and upper chest the whole time. Not sure why. Not uncomfortable, just noticeable.

## Marta

- Adjusted mirror so face was cut off, so could focus more on body.
- Surprised, didn't recognize as my body at first.
- Noticed weight loss; surge of approval and pride, then a little spike of shame, in center of chest.
- Memory of mom helping me adjust wedding gown in mirror.
- Noticed I lean to left; brief shock in belly and lower chest; face tightened in worry for few secs.; see osteopath?
- Three thoughts in quick succession: 1) Have hips gotten wider? 2) Hope not. 3) Actually, who cares?
- Whole body liked being unclothed. Be nude more often when home alone!
- One minute seemed more like five; mostly zoned out for last 15-20 seconds.

## Eloise

- I was shocked at how old and worn out my body has gotten. After a few seconds, my chest and gut began to tighten. A thought arose: *El, give yourself a goddamn break. You're almost 80.* Still, after 40 seconds, I had to turn away.
- After a few deep breaths, I was able to turn back and look for another 20 seconds. Suddenly I remembered a time when I was 18. I had taken off all my clothes in a department store dressing room and looked at my body for a long time, evaluating it and giving it a B+. A little shock of loss and grief ran through my chest. Then, unexpectedly, I laughed at myself. But it was a gentle laugh.

As you can see, there's no one right way to soul scribe. That said, here are some useful guidelines:

- Soul scribing is more than just acknowledging or reviewing your body's experience. It also requires the *physical* experience of writing down the VIMBAS. Moving your hand and arm helps you access your body's intelligences. So when you soul scribe, use a pen, pencil, or marker, not a keyboard.

- If using a pen, pencil, or marker isn't possible, speak into your phone or a voice recorder, and later write down (or have someone else write down) your words. If that also isn't possible, then using a keyboard is okay.

- Get yourself a separate book just for soul scribing. This can be a spiral notebook, a bound blank book, a journal with lined pages, a binder with removable pages, etc. Get something that's a pleasure to look at and write in, and that's portable. Experiment until you discover what works best for you.

- Set aside a separate section or set of pages for each body practice. This way, as you repeat the practice over weeks, months, or years, you can easily review how your body's responses to each practice have changed over time.

- Carry your soul-scribing book and pen with you, so you can write whenever something unexpected shows up in your body—or whenever you get the urge.

- If, as you soul scribe, you become temporarily overwhelmed by one or more of the VIMBAS, don't try to force your way through it. Put down your pen and stop writing; if necessary, end the body practice as well. Take a few deep breaths, or a short walk, or both. If necessary, get up and go to another location where your body can experience safety or less activation. Later, when you sense that you're ready, you can try the body practice again.

- If possible, soul scribe at least once a week. Two or three times a week is better; daily is better still.

- Once every three months, set aside an hour or two to go back and review all of your soul scribing during those months—or, if you wish, during the past year, or even longer. As you read your recent comments and compare them to your older ones, notice what is different. If you like, write down the changes that you notice, any new understandings that you have, and/or the VIMBAS you experience in that moment. This regular review will help you recognize the tempering and conditioning that your body has experienced.

As you'll discover, paying close attention to your body at any time, with or without a guided practice, is an important aspect of tempering and conditioning it.

BODY PRACTICE
## YOUR BODY IN THE MIRROR

Pick up your watch, your phone, or a timer. Bring it into your bathroom, or some other private indoor space with a large mirror, and shut the door behind you.

Take off all your clothes, including your underwear and your socks or stockings. Step in front of the mirror.

Look at yourself in the mirror for exactly one minute.

Don't critique or evaluate what you see. Just look.

Notice what you experience in your body. What quakes? What opens? What constricts? What settles? What moves—and where and how? What vibrations and urges does your body experience?

Thoughts, images, and judgments may arise, but don't follow them. Keep returning your attention to your body.

If you have to look away before sixty seconds pass, that's okay. Just notice this. If you can, look back in the mirror before the minute ends.

After one minute, put on your clothes. Say aloud, "My body is an expression of creation itself." (Or, if you prefer, "My body is an expression of the cosmos.") Then leave the room, and soul scribe about your body's experience.

Repeat this activity regularly.

Remember, this body practice is about playing. It's not about endurance, or barreling through, or forcing yourself to override your own urges and impulses. If this practice becomes too much, stop. But come back to it later—a few days, weeks, or months from now—perhaps after you've journeyed deeper into this book.

This practice is about noticing and staying with something meaningful. Be compassionate with yourself. The point of this practice is for you to move through temporary discomfort into a sense of resonance and resource. If you force yourself through, into a hollow sense of accomplishment—as if you've vanquished an internal obstacle—you're pushing yourself too hard.

# 7

# THE FIVE TARGETS
# OF BLAME

*Republicans are playing the long game. . . . They're pumping
their base full of anger toward scientists, healthcare workers,
and teachers. They're stripping everyone of their rights, and
reinstating the old story of great white America, with slave
owners and billionaires as heroes. That's how you control a
population. You create a privileged ethnic class out of the poorly
educated, and you convince them that everyone else is an enemy
who wants what they have. You tell them anything that benefits
someone else is an assault on their personal liberty.*

Jessica Wildfire

*The further a society drifts from the truth,
the more it will hate those who speak it.*

George Orwell

*To err is human. To blame someone else is politics.*

Hubert Humphrey

*The Democrats' naïve belief that policies alone can win the
day is misplaced when opponents will stop at nothing—
not voter suppression, not remorseless disinformation and
not race-baiting—to secure power.*

Jennifer Rubin

In 2022 and / or 2024, as Election Day approaches, five groups will likely be singled out as targets:

1. Bodies of culture[18] of every identity, especially Black and Indigenous bodies

2. Immigrants (and people who look or sound as if they might be immigrants)

3. Pro-justice and pro-liberation activists and politicians

4. Conservatives who are not completely subservient to Donald Trump and the Big Lie

5. Democrats with political power—especially those who align themselves with justice and liberation

In order to better target and dehumanize each member of each group—and to stoke fury against them—all of these groups will be repeatedly described as traitorous, socialist (or Communist), and anti-American.

Here is how each of these specific groups will also be identified, portrayed, and belittled:

| Who someone is | What they will be called | How they will be portrayed |
| --- | --- | --- |
| Anyone with a Black body | Black Lives Matter | Subhuman, violent terrorist seeking to destroy America |
| Anyone with an Indigenous body | Big loser | Savage and worthless |
| Anyone else with a body of culture | Illegal immigrant | Subhuman criminal, job thief, deadbeat, terrorist |

---

18   This group includes Muslim, Jewish, and Latinx people with white-skinned bodies.

| Who someone is | What they will be called | How they will be portrayed |
|---|---|---|
| Anyone speaking Spanish* in public | Illegal immigrant | Subhuman criminal, job thief, deadbeat, terrorist |
| A pro-democracy political activist | Antifa | Violent terrorist seeking to destroy America |
| A pro-democracy conservative | RINO or Super RINO (Republican in Name Only) | The worst and most despicable of all traitors |
| A Democrat with political power | Liberal, elite, socialist | Traitor whose political power is illegitimate |

\* and / or, in some locales, any non-European language

Once the war is well underway, anyone who does not expressly identify with the Republican cause[19] will be placed in one or more of these categories and declared an enemy of America.

As the war proceeds, some Republicans may make Christianity (that is, evangelical, Protestant, pro-Trump Christianity) an additional rallying cry. At first, all Muslim, Jewish, Sikh, Buddhist, and other non-Christian people will be defamed as non- or anti-American Christ haters who seek to destroy not only America but the Christian faith and the worship of God. Over time, this group of enemies may be expanded to also include all Christians who are not explicitly pro-Trump and pro-Republican. It may also be expanded to include all nonwhite bodies, including those who are devout, lifelong Christians.

In his book *How Fascism Works*, Jason Stanley explains this strategy succinctly: "A distinguishing mark of fascist politics is the

---

19  If, as appears very likely, Donald Trump runs for president in 2024, *the Republican cause* will mean *absolute, unwavering, and unquestioning subservience to Donald Trump.*

targeting of ideological enemies and the freeing of all restraints in combating them."

*Pause.*

What are you experiencing in your body right now?

BODY PRACTICE
## METABOLIZING THE RECKONING

In *My Grandmother's Hands*, I described America's racial reckoning this way:

> While we see anger and violence in the streets of our country, the real battlefield is inside our bodies. If we are to survive as a country, it is inside our bodies where this conflict will need to be resolved.

> The conflict has been festering for centuries. Now it must be faced. For America, it is an unavoidable time of reckoning. Our character is being challenged, and the content of that character is being revealed. . . .

> Americans have reached a point of peril and possibility. We will either grow up or grow smaller. This trauma will either burst forth in an explosion of dirty pain,[20] or provide the necessary energy and heat for white Americans to move through clean pain and heal. Only this second outcome will provide us with genuine safety.

When I wrote those words in 2017, I envisioned an either/or choice that we Americans would soon make. But that's not what happened. *We Americans chose to go down both paths at once.*

This both-at-once choice has greatly increased our peril—but it has also greatly increased our opportunities for healing. It may be that a huge, nationwide explosion of dirty pain will be followed by a period of intense growth and renewal.

You and I can't know how all of this will play out. But the reckoning is upon us—and you are part of it.

Find a quiet, safe spot where you can be alone for a few minutes. Sit quietly and comfortably for half a minute. Take a few deep breaths.

Then read the words below aloud. Repeat each sentence three times:

The Reckoning is here.

---

20    *Dirty pain* is the pain of avoidance and denial. We create dirty pain when we act from the smallest and most wounded parts of ourselves. I'll discuss *dirty pain* and *clean pain* in detail in Chapter 9.

I live in a time of great peril and great possibility.

I do not and cannot know what will emerge.

As the future unfolds, I will act from the best parts of myself.

As you read these words, notice what you experience in your body. Take note of any:

- vibrations
- images and thoughts
- meanings, judgments, stories, and explanations
- behaviors, movements, actions, impulses, and urges
- affect and emotions
- sensations

Pay special attention to any urges, any constriction, and any sensation near the bottom of your belly. Notice any pressure, textures, speed, rhythms, direction, weight, or charge that emerges.

You may experience clean pain, such as dread or fear. You may experience a pleasurable sensation, such as relief or release. You might experience both pain and pleasure together.

Take a few more deep, slow breaths.

Then scan your body and notice any places that want to be touched. For the next minute or two, using one or both hands, touch each of these spots in whatever way it wants to be touched—for example:

- lightly pressing
- gently squeezing or gripping
- rubbing
- holding or supporting

You may also want to simply let the palm of your open hand hover above the spot, an inch or two away, for a few breaths. (I'll describe this practice in more detail at the end of Chapter 11.)

Invite this body practice into your life as often as you like. As our racial reckoning unfolds, make a point of doing it whenever you sense peril and possibilities growing. If you like, soul scribe about it.

# 8

# ACTIVE, PASSIVE, AND UNWITTING COMPLICITORS

*Democrats, never tell me again "We got this." Because you don't have this. Stay locked in your bubble that the modern GOP won't have a mob of Bannon's terrorists burn you to the ground and piss on the ashes. An unpunished coup is a training exercise.*

Tweet from Rick Wilson, former Republican strategist,
on October 8, 2021

*Democracy really is at stake, and Democratic lawmakers need to start acting like it. . . . If right wing authoritarianism and fascism take hold in the next few years, and there is an excellent chance that it will, then historians will have no choice but to acknowledge the fact that Democrats handed it right over.*

Lauren Elizabeth

*One party is trying to secure fair and free elections. . . the other party is committed to nothing less than the destruction of American democracy.*

Paul Waldman

*While Democrats squabble over relatively minor differences in how much to spend over how long a time, Republicans have again gone demagogic, raising phony threats about socialism, trillions of dollars of additional debt and a Gestapo-like IRS. . . . As they waver, the voters are turning against them, and the authoritarians are waiting in the wings. . . . Congress will end up back in Republicans' hands, positioning them to be able to overturn the will of the people in 2024.*

Dana Milbank

*Too many in my own party are embracing the former president, are looking the other way. . . . That's how democracies die and we simply cannot let that happen.*

US Representative Liz Cheney

Imagine that I'm planning to carry out a scheme—particularly an illegal or unethical one. Any person, group, or organization that assists me could be called my *complicitor.*

A complicitor can also be any person, group, or organization that sees what I'm doing (or about to do), recognizes that it's illegal or unethical, but doesn't try to stop me.

A complicitor can also be an aider, an abettor, an enabler, a co-conspirator, or sometimes all four.

*Complicitor* is an actual English word. It's not widely used, though it's appeared in media such as the *Washington Post* and the *Arizona Mirror.* It's most often used in law, particularly (for some unknown reason) in the states of Colorado, Kentucky, and Ohio.

The Republican Party could not be what it is today, or enjoy the power and success that it does, without an entire ecosystem of complicitors.

Some GOP complicitors are *active* and *overt*:

- media networks such as Fox News, Newsmax, and One America News

- right-wing, anti-democracy social media sites such as Parler, Gab, 8kun, and The Daily Stormer

- Facebook (which, as whistleblower Frances Haugen revealed, has attempted to polarize people on both the right and the left)
- key media figures and public speakers such as Laura Ingraham, Ben Shapiro, Dinesh D'Souza, and Steve Bannon
- thousands of right-wing groups and organizations, from FreedomWorks (one of the many Koch Brothers organizations) to the Claremont Institute to the Proud Boys
- hundreds of PACs and super PACs
- many foreign organizations, governments, leaders, and operatives, who hope to foment civil war, implode democracy, and encourage autocratic rule in America
- bots from Russia and other countries with anti-American governments, which spread misinformation and disinformation 24/7
- many evangelical Christian ministers, leaders, followers, congregations, and organizations
- many thousands of QAnon adherents and other conspiracy theorists
- tens of millions of individual Americans who embrace the *vehement* or *devout* forms of white-body supremacy[21]

Almost daily, the headlines recount new misdeeds by some or all of these players.

The GOP's efforts to sabotage America's government and people are also supported by a much larger ecosystem of *passive* complicitors. These include:

- most major newspapers, TV and radio networks, and news websites, which treat GOP lies as political messaging and its attempts to destroy American democracy as political strategy[22]

---

21   I'll describe and discuss these and other forms of WBS in Chapter 16.

22   Imagine that you and I live on the same block. Because you disagree with my views, you express your displeasure by burning down my house. That is not neighborhood activism or political expression. It is criminal activity.

- social media platforms such as Twitter, which enable the spread of disinformation and the stoking of rage and cruelty

- hundreds of thousands of businesses, groups, and other organizations that express political "neutrality"—which the Republican Party correctly reads as apathy and indifference to justice, liberation, and small-d democratic governance

- tens of millions of people who either don't recognize, don't understand, or don't care about the growing GOP threat. (Most of these folks suffer from the *complicit, collective* variant of white-body supremacy, which I'll discuss in detail in Chapter 16.)

The Republican Party also has an often *unwitting*—and, for the GOP, hugely beneficial—group of complicitors: the Democratic Party. For decades, the Dems have been feckless and ineffectual in countering the GOP's plan to tear apart America.

In early 2022, the Dems effectively control both houses of Congress and the presidency. Yet every day, 24/7, across America, the Republican Party systematically attacks the foundations of democracy and justice. It does this *in full view of the entire world.* Meanwhile, the Dems dither, squabble among themselves, debate policy, and fail to significantly challenge most of the status quo. As humanity watches in horror, the GOP douses one pillar of American life after another with gasoline and adds to its ever-growing stockpile of torches. In response, the Dems debate the proper diameter of the firehose they hope to use someday.

As Democratic US Representative Sean Maloney put it, "The other side is for insurrection while we're trying to do infrastructure." Rick Wilson, formerly one of the GOP's chief strategists, was less pithy but more eloquent: "Democrats too often want a focus-grouped, pablum policy answer when the world is burning down around them. Republicans . . . know the Democrats will play by the rules, while they play by none at all. . . . Democrats are too politically blind to see the words 'Fuck You' scribbled on the page in Trumpian Sharpie. . . . It's a choice between an aggressive, hard-edged defense of democracy, or accepting the end of our nation as we know it. The people who executed the plan to overthrow America's democracy aren't done fighting to destroy this country . . . not by a long shot."

I'm writing this chapter on October 13, 2021. In the top right of today's washingtonpost.com home page is this headline: "As Democrats dither, Biden bleeds out." Here is another line from the same page: "Less than two weeks after House Democrats missed a deadline . . . the party is staring down another one." And another: "Democrats spar on broader spending bill." These—as well as Representative Sean Maloney's quote in the previous paragraph—are all from the articles on a single page of a single newspaper on a single day.

Not that this is the Democratic Party's only (or worst, or most deep-seated) problem. On that same day, *The Nation* published a piece entitled "Democrats Are Ready to Abandon Black Voters, Again" by Elie Mystal. Here is how Mystal's article begins:

> We have come to a familiar crossroads of American politics. . . a chorus of powerful Democrats has risen up inside the Beltway to tell Democrats that abandoning Black people—the very people who put them in power in the first place—and making performative efforts to win the support of racists, is the only way to stay in power. And Democrats are, predictably, listening. Black people, our concerns, and our agenda, are always the first ones to be thrown overboard, even when we're rowing the damn boat. . . . Black people are always told that progress toward a fair and just country must be deferred for fear of losing white voters.

This is not a matter of the Dems having one very bad day. Eight days earlier, the *Washington Post* published this information in a column by Paul Waldman: "The Bush administration set up a program to torture prisoners, and many of the people who designed and executed it got promoted. Right now the Biden administration is fighting in court to keep the torture program secret. . . . In America, accountability is for the lowly."

A few paragraphs earlier, I described the Democratic Party as the GOP's often-unwitting complicitors. While the Dems' complicity is indeed often unwitting, and sometimes passive, sometimes it is active and overt. Very overt.[23]

The Democratic Party also has a long history of trying to appease, comfort, and pander to centrist and center-left white voters. These are the ostensible swing voters that many Democratic candidates spend much of their time and energy trying to woo. It's also the group that pundits and analysts often focus on. Yes, Democratic candidates want their votes. But they also use this small slice of the electorate as an excuse to not be bold, to not stand up for justice, and to not push hard for a muscular, emancipated democracy.

As Democratic candidates work desperately to attract these voters, they often ignore everyone else, especially many bodies of culture. Steve Phillips explained it this way: "There's been this hierarchy of what battles to fight and which ones to avoid, and this is guided by White appeasement—what policy will not offend White swing voters. It very much dominates policy and political strategy among Democrats." Perry Bacon Jr. put it more succinctly: "The Democrats' White appeasement is their countermove to the Republicans' White grievance." Of course, if you're not white, then neither grievance nor appeasement does you any good.

*Pause.*

Stay with that pause for at least thirty seconds.

What are you experiencing in your body right now? What is emerging in terms of:

- vibrations

- images and thoughts

- meanings, judgments, stories, and explanations

- behaviors, movements, actions, impulses, and urges

- affect and emotions

- sensations

If you like, soul scribe about your experience.

---

23  In fact, white-body supremacy is baked into the Democratic Party just as much as it is into the GOP. In the nineteenth century, the Democrats were vehemently pro-slavery. Until the 1960s and 1970s, many Southern Democrats devoutly opposed civil rights for bodies of culture. Today, the Dems have a mixed record of supporting and encouraging justice, liberation, and an emancipated democracy. That record often looks better than it is because it gets juxtaposed against the Republican Party's goals, plans, rhetoric, and votes in Congress.

If you did not fully understand our situation before, you do now.

If you realize that—wittingly or unwittingly—you have been a part of the Republican Party's complicit ecosystem, now is the time to stop.

If you're thinking, *Hey, democracy is messy,* that's true. But the GOP is actively planning to murder it. Murder is messy, too. So is fascism—though it always wraps itself in a flag of purity.

If you're thinking, *Holy shit, we're in trouble. What can I do?,* take heart. As you will learn, there is a lot you can do. Read on.

## BODY PRACTICE
## STANDING IN YOUR INTEGRITY

Think back to an incident from your past in which you stood firmly in your integrity. For instance:

- As a child, you stood up to a bully.
- Someone asked or invited you to act unethically, and you refused.
- While you were part of a group, you encountered someone who needed assistance, so you stopped to help—even though everyone else in your group ignored them.
- In front of people whom you knew you would offend, you spoke up on behalf of a person or cause you knew was just.
- You physically protected someone who was being threatened.
- You publicly challenged someone or something you knew was immoral.
- You put a close relationship with someone at risk by confronting them about actions they took or words they said.

What did you experience in your body when you first sensed that you needed to take a stand? What did you experience as you acted from your integrity? As events unfolded thereafter? Take note of any:

- vibrations
- images and thoughts
- meanings, judgments, stories, and explanations
- behaviors, movements, actions, impulses, and urges
- affect and emotions
- sensations

Now think back to an incident when you could have stood firmly in your integrity, but didn't—and instead allowed one or more people to be harmed.

What did you experience in your body as you made the decision to not act? As events unfolded afterward? Note any:

- vibrations
- images and thoughts
- meanings, judgments, stories, and explanations
- behaviors, movements, actions, impulses, and urges
- affect and emotions
- sensations

What are you experiencing in your body right now? What, if anything, has shifted, or activated, or settled?

Soul scribe about your body's experience.

# 9

# CLEAN PAIN
# AND DIRTY PAIN

*Sometimes it is necessary to know pain,*
*to be intimate with it, to help others to heal.*

Rev. angel Kyodo williams

*The attempt to escape from pain*
*is what creates more pain.*

Gabor Maté

*Pain is the little voice in your head that tries to hold you*
*back because it knows if you continue you will change.*

Kobe Bryant

*Denial is the ultimate comfort zone.*

David Goggins

Healing and growth always involve discomfort. But so does refusing to heal or grow. Paradoxically, this refusal always creates more pain—both for the person who refuses to grow *and* for the people around them.

Here's another paradox of emotional pain: the only way to ease it is to accept it, work with it, and use it as fuel for growth.

Only by leaning *into* your pain can you move through it and out of it, and metabolize it.

When you accept this pain, and use it to stand in your integrity and activate the best parts of yourself, this is *clean pain*.[24] Clean pain can help you metabolize trauma, resolve conflicts, transform, and grow up.

Nonviolent resistance to oppression, terrorism, and inequality is a form of clean pain. So is Somatic Abolitionism.

Your other option is dirty pain, in which you respond from your most wounded and unexamined parts. You become cruel, or hollow, or conniving, or violent—or you physically or emotionally run away. This only prolongs your pain and deepens whatever conflict activated your initial discomfort.

Dirty pain is the pain of avoidance and denial. When we refuse to accept and metabolize clean pain, or try to blow that pain into other bodies, we create new conflict and difficulty. Meanwhile, our own pain remains unmetabolized.

Dirty pain can manifest as urgency, avoidance, blaming, accusations, hypervigilance, panic, hyperanxiety, hard-and-fast demands, gaslighting, extreme manipulation, desperate attempts to control other people, or violence. Sometimes it shows up as self-harm: drinking, drugging, other addictive behavior, or self-inflicted violence. All of these only make the existing conflict more difficult, more complicated, and more painful.

In short, clean pain is about going *through* something. Dirty pain is about trying to get *around* something.

Being willing to go through something helps you grow up. Trying to get around something makes you more hard-hearted, less mature, and temporarily less able to access your humanity. Also, it never works in the long run—nor, often, in the short run.

Most people choose dirty pain much of the time. They imagine that avoidance, defensiveness, or cruelty will hurt them less than growing and healing. But they always end up hurting others more, and experiencing more pain themselves.

In *My Grandmother's Hands*, I defined clean pain and dirty pain this way:

---

24    The terms *clean pain* and *dirty pain* were popularized by one of my mentors, Dr. David Schnarch, and by Dr. Steven Hayer. Dr. Hayer defines and uses the terms somewhat differently, however.

*Clean pain* is pain that mends and can build your capacity for growth. It's the pain you experience when you know exactly what you need to say or do; when you really, really don't want to say or do it; and when you do it anyway. It's also the pain you experience when you have no idea what to do; when you're scared or worried about what might happen; and when you step forward into the unknown anyway, with honesty and vulnerability.

Experiencing clean pain enables us to engage our integrity and tap into our body's inherent resilience and coherence, in a way that dirty pain does not. Paradoxically, only by walking into our pain or discomfort—experiencing it, moving through it, and metabolizing it—can we grow. It's how the human body works.

Clean pain hurts like hell. But it enables our bodies to grow through our difficulties, develop nuanced skills, and mend our trauma. In this process, the body metabolizes clean pain. The body can then settle; more room for growth is created in its nervous system; and the self becomes freer and more capable, because it now has access to energy that was previously protected, bound, and constricted. When this happens, people's lives often improve in other ways as well. . . .

*Dirty pain* is the pain of avoidance, blame, and denial. When people respond from their most wounded parts, become cruel or violent, or physically or emotionally run away, they experience dirty pain. They also create more of it for themselves and others.

White-body supremacy is a centuries-old form of dirty pain. Attacks on justice, democracy, and equality are also forms of dirty pain.[25] Mob violence against one's fellow citizens is deeply dirty pain.

---

25    I'm not suggesting that our government, laws, and political system, as currently configured, provide us with full democracy, or genuine justice, or anything close to liberation. We often fall short. Indeed, we need to continue to use all legal and ethical means to push all of these closer to their realization.

One key factor in the perpetuation of white-body supremacy is many white bodies' refusal to experience clean pain around race. Instead, usually out of fear and perceived self-interest, they choose the dirty pain of silence or avoidance. This prolongs and spreads the racialized pain. These folks also undermine their own self-interest in the name of attempting to preserve it.

The incipient civil war will require you to choose between clean pain and dirty pain time after time. As you will see, it will also mean deciding whether to let yourself get swept up in the currents of white-body supremacy—or to help build a living, embodied antiracist culture.

In 2021, tennis star Naomi Osaka offered the world a shining example of choosing clean pain over dirty pain.

Osaka, who was ranked the number one player by the Women's Tennis Association, was—like all well-known professional athletes—required to regularly speak to the media. After winning her first match in the 2021 French Open, Osaka announced that she would skip her media obligations because they were harming her mental health. Officials of the French Open responded with a classic dirty-pain move by fining her $15,000, thus trying to force her to choose the dirty pain of subservience over her own mental health. This was a textbook case of powerful bodies demanding full deference from, and full control over, a body of culture[26]—and punishing her for not granting that control.

Osaka responded by choosing clean pain: she withdrew from the event. She explained, "I thought it was better to exercise self-care and skip the press conferences."

Other tennis players supported Osaka's decision. Martina Navratilova tweeted, "This is about more than doing or not doing a press conference. Good luck Naomi—we are all pulling for you!"

Life regularly presents each of us with choices that force us up against ourselves and require us to choose either the clean pain of growth or the dirty pain of harm. In each of these situations, not hurting isn't an option. We don't get to choose between pain and comfort. In fact, when we try to choose comfort, we are actually choosing dirty pain.

---

26  Osaka's mother is Japanese; her father is Haitian.

In every conflict and difficulty that you face, your central question ultimately becomes: are you going to choose clean pain or dirty pain?

BODY PRACTICE
## TEMPERING, CONDITIONING, AND DISCERNING

Think of something that makes you uncomfortable whenever you encounter it. It can be anything—heights, bees, pit bulls, people living on the street, or the way your partner looks at you when they're disappointed with you.

Close your eyes. Imagine that your source of discomfort is in front of your face, just a foot away. Imagine that you're looking right at it.

For three slow, steady breaths, stay with that image. Don't try to run from it, or turn away, or brush it aside. Don't try to do anything about it at all. For three long breaths, simply be with it.

As you do, notice:

- where your body constricts or relaxes
- any other sensations in your body
- any impulse to move or act
- any images or emotions that arise
- any thoughts or stories that pop into your head

Do this once a day. Over time, notice if your body becomes less (or perhaps more) uncomfortable with the thing you imagine. If you wish, soul scribe about this practice.

Then select something else that makes you uncomfortable and begin working with that.

Continue with this process—and one source of discomfort after another— for the rest of your life.

Remember, this practice is part of an emergent process of conditioning and tempering. It is not about shaming or blaming yourself over the particular causes of your discomfort.

## BODY PRACTICE
# OFFERING AND RECEIVING

Stand comfortably with your hands at your sides. Take two or three deep, slow breaths.

Raise and open your hands so that they are directly in front of your belly. Put your open palms together, cupping them slightly.

Then slowly move your hands forward, as if you are offering something to another person—or preparing to receive something from them.

Continue slowly moving your hands forward until you feel a stretch and a natural stopping point in your back muscles. (If you feel any pain, you've stretched your hands too far.)

*Pause* for two or three breaths. Be curious about this spot. Note any:

- vibrations
- images and thoughts
- meanings, judgments, stories, and explanations
- behaviors, movements, actions, impulses, and urges
- affect and emotions
- sensations

Now slowly return your hands to their original position, palms up, directly in front of you.

*Pause* again for two or three breaths. Note any:

- vibrations
- images and thoughts
- meanings, judgments, stories, and explanations
- behaviors, movements, actions, impulses, and urges
- affect and emotions
- sensations

Repeat this practice three times.

# 10

# WHY THE COMING WAR
# WILL BE RACIALIZED

*We're not generating enough angry white guys
to stay in business for the long term.*

Lindsey Graham

*The Republican Party's dalliance with
authoritarianism can be explained in one word: race.*

Dana Milbank

*The Republican Party has become very comfortable with the
formalization of becoming an official White grievance party.*

Stuart Stevens

*The country has long been divided over race, but rarely has there
been such a partisan gap in how Americans use these issues.*

Dan Balz

*Perhaps no issue is more divisive than racial injustice in the US.*

from a 2021 Pew Research Center report

*But the hard truth is that we'll need to brace for something
far worse than the Tea Party, because armed white
supremacists have been further emboldened and organized
under Trumpism and have vowed to be ungovernable.*

from *Indivisible: A Practical Guide for Fixing Our Democracy*

No Republican leader will publicly proclaim the new civil war to involve race. However, the racial divide will be obvious to everyone. At least 95 percent of the people who fight on the Republican side of the war will be white Christians who were born in the United States. (We saw a similar percentage in the people who attacked the US Capitol on January 6, 2021, and in the attendees of the 2021 Conservative Political Action Conference.) On the other side will be Americans of all body pigmentations, religions, and backgrounds.

As part of their strategy, Republican leaders will publicly, repeatedly, and vehemently demonize bodies of culture, especially Black and Indigenous bodies. Mostly they will do it through inference, implication, dog whistles, and other proxy language. However, as I noted earlier, they will often overtly name and blame Black Lives Matter, George Soros, and a handful of other nonwhite and/or non-Christian targets.[27]

By the spring or summer of 2022, white-body supremacy is likely to be an overt (if not central) part of the GOP's standard messaging. In September 2021, Fox host Tucker Carlson and Congressman Matt Gaetz clearly and publicly announced that the United States is undergoing a Great Replacement. This is a neo-Nazi conspiracy theory claiming that an international cabal—made up of Democrats, socialists, Jews, and of course George Soros—is working to flood America with nonwhite immigrants in order to replace the only authentic Americans: white Christians. Gaetz went further, declaring that the Anti-Defamation League (whose mission begins, "To stop the defamation of the Jewish people, and to secure justice and fair treatment to all," and which has been around since 1913), "is a racist organization."

Race will be central to this war for six other reasons:

- **To defeat your enemies, you need to be able to easily spot them.** In most situations, it's not easy to identify a liberal, a Democratic official, or a pro-democracy conservative at a glance. However, you can often quickly tell if someone

---

27  One such example among a great many: in September 2021, on the show *Fox & Friends,* host Brian Kilmeade called out African Americans for not getting Covid vaccinations and thereby spreading the virus. At the time, 43 percent of Black Americans had been vaccinated, but the vaccination rate among white Republicans was far lower. In a study published two months earlier, the people who said they would definitely not get vaccinated were 69 percent white and 58 percent Republican.

does not have white skin. You can just as quickly tell when they are speaking Spanish (or, for that matter, any language other than English), or if they're wearing a headscarf, a hijab, a skullcap, or Hasidic garb.

- **Some Republican followers—that is, members of white nationalist and white-body supremacist groups, as well as some white evangelical ministers—already desire a racialized civil war.** Some have publicly and repeatedly called for such a war, and the number of these calls has been rapidly rising. These folks will be among the war's most vocal and enthusiastic fighters.

- **Most Americans—Americans of all skin pigmentations—have racialized trauma stuck in their bodies.** White-body supremacy is embedded in our institutions, our laws, our language, our religious organizations, and our codes of behavior. It is equally ingrained in our habits, norms, assumptions, vibes, and expectations. Recent discoveries in epigenetics have revealed that it is literally in the cells of our bodies. (Much more about this in Chapter 16.) As a result, racialized trauma has become a common, chronic, unexamined, and unhealed condition of most American bodies.

- **GOP strategists discovered, through careful focus-group testing, that opposition to critical race theory is a powerfully energizing and mobilizing message for right-leaning voters.** The very words *critical race theory* infuriate many members of the Republican base in the same way that *Antifa, the Deep State,* and *socialist* do. Because the three words so reliably activate the racialized trauma stuck in many white Americans' bodies, the phrase *critical race theory* will be repeated relentlessly, as a mantra, by right-wing media. The phrase will be routinely and deliberately misapplied to all race-related news items. In 2021, GOP strategist Christopher Rufo publicly and explicitly explained that this was the Republican plan.[28]

---

28  By the time you read this chapter, the GOP may have wrung every bit of outrage it can from the term. At that point, it will suddenly stop invoking the term and will convene focus groups to test a variety of alternative terms, in the hope of finding one that will activate an equal amount of racialized

In 2021, the most common—and most successful—deployment of this strategy involved public schools. The GOP generated huge successes—and an unprecedented amount of parental outrage—by blaming Democrats for the widespread teaching of critical race theory in public schools.

In fact, critical race theory—like heart transplant surgical techniques and tort law—has never been taught in any American public elementary, middle, junior high, or high school. However, some new GOP-enacted laws slap the name *critical race theory* on something else, then ban that something else. For example, North Dakota recently passed a law banning what it calls "critical race theory," which it redefines it as simply "the theory that racism is not merely the product of learned individual bias or prejudice, but that racism is systematically embedded in American society." This is the rough equivalent of redefining the surgical techniques for *laparotomy via midline transverse incision* as "cut the woman open and pull the baby out of her belly." The GOP now also talks of banning critical race theory—perhaps similarly redefined or dumbed down—at public colleges and universities. Perhaps at some point it will seek to ban this very book. (In 2021, eight states banned the teaching of real and/or faux critical race theory; as I write this paragraph, proposed bans are moving through the legislatures of sixteen other states.)

Remember: the point of the GOP strategy is not to be remotely logical, truthful, or sensible, but to provoke a supercharged racialized trauma response in millions of bodies.

- **Race is the defining issue of American history.** Race has played a central role on the North American continent

---

trauma and provoke a similar degree of outrage. The actual meaning of the words it ultimately selects will be irrelevant; the point is simply to find utterances that infuriate and mobilize its base. Decades ago, simply repeating the N word was sufficient. But as Republican strategist Lee Atwater noted in 1981, the precise meaning of the N word now needs to be invoked via dog-whistle terms, such as, in Atwater's own words, "forced busing, states' rights, and all that stuff." As used by the GOP, *critical race theory* has always been primarily a contemporary, seven-syllable utterance of the N word. As Umair Haque has pointed out, connecting the term to the education of people's children also delivers this false message: *Liberals, Communists, Antifa activists, and minions of George Soros want to brainwash your kids and make them hate America—and you. THEY'RE COMING FOR YOUR CHILDREN!*

since Europeans first began to conquer and colonize it. Throughout US history, there has scarcely been a widespread movement, issue, conflict, trend, or debate that does not have race wrapped inside it.[29] This war will be no exception.

- **Race has long driven issues involving election legitimacy and voting rights.** Do bodies of culture have the right to vote? Legally, this question was answered in 1870, when the Fifteenth Amendment was ratified by Congress. In practice, America has never stopped fighting with itself over this question. For ninety-five years after the Fifteenth Amendment became law, white bodies in (especially) the South used Jim Crow laws and other methods to ensure that bodies of culture could not vote. The hundreds of voter suppression bills introduced in state legislatures by the GOP beginning in 2021, which focus largely on limiting voting opportunities for bodies of culture, reminds us that, today, the answer to this question in many Republicans' (especially white Republicans') minds is still an emphatic *no*.

---

29    This is not a history book, so I won't go into detail on this point. But here is one of many, many examples: in 1787, in order to get Southern states to sign on to the new US Constitution, Northern delegates at the Constitutional Convention agreed to count each enslaved African or African American as three-fifths of a human being—not a full member of the human species. In a later effort to hold the country together, as part of the Compromise of 1850, the US Congress passed the Fugitive Slave Act. The act required that any enslaved person who had made their way to a Northern free state not only could be returned to their owner but legally *had* to be. The act also made the federal government responsible for finding, returning, and trying these enslaved people. In addition, under this law fugitives could not testify on their own behalf, nor were they permitted a trial by jury. A generation later, after the intensely disputed 1876 presidential election, which threatened to tear the US apart, Congress held the country together through the Compromise of 1877, which pulled federal troops out of the South. This resulted in the end of Reconstruction, the beginning of mandatory segregation in the South, and the widespread disenfranchisement of African American voters. In 1938, in order to pass the Fair Labor Standards Act, which was part of the New Deal, President Franklin Roosevelt agreed to specifically exclude protections for professions with large numbers of bodies of culture. In each of these cases—which span over 150 years—the only way that white leaders with differing views were able to forge a compromise was by writing into law a new, additional aspect of white-body supremacy. In late December 2021, the Dems in Congress (with zero Republican support) were on the verge of agreeing on a potentially transformative Build Back Better plan. This would invest $1.8 trillion in America's future safety and prosperity and would substantially address our worldwide climate crisis. In order to pass this initiative, the Dems needed the votes of all their 50 US Senators. Senator Joe Manchin agreed to the great majority of the Dems' agenda items, but insisted that there be no funding for racial equity initiatives. As I write these words on January 9, 2022, the Dems are yet again facing this choice: 1) forge a compromise that hurls bodies of culture under a deadly bus, 2) pitch the entire agenda under that bus, or 3) create a bold and original way forward that throws the first two unacceptable outcomes under that bus.

Donald Trump's rhetoric since the 2020 election has had clear racial undertones. Over and over, he has insisted, with zero evidence, that the election was stolen from him. He has also pointed specifically to (nonexistent) fraud committed in Philadelphia, Detroit, Milwaukee, and other cities and counties with large numbers of bodies of culture.

As historian Timothy Snyder succinctly explains, "Trump's focus on alleged 'irregularities' and 'contested states' comes down to cities where Black people live and vote. At bottom, the fantasy of fraud is that of a crime committed by Black people against white people."[30]

Ted Cruz and ten other Republican senators affirmed their own preference for the disenfranchisement of bodies of culture when, in a January 2021 letter, they encouraged their GOP colleagues to follow the precedent of the Compromise of 1877. (You'll find details on that compromise in the footnote on the previous page.)

All of this is why surviving—or preventing—this civil war depends on more than just organizing and preparation. It also requires laying the foundation for creating a living, embodied antiracist culture.

As you will see, this is the work of Somatic Abolitionism.

## BODY PRACTICE
## ORIENTING FOR SAFETY

Your body is always interacting with the space and energies surrounding it. Orienting your body to these can help you build its capacity for resource and discernment. Regularly orienting your body can also help keep it safe.

Go to a safe and fairly busy public place, such as a train station, airport, park, office building lobby, or shopping mall. Find a spot where you can stand or sit quietly for a few minutes without being in anyone's way.

Begin by taking a few long, slow breaths. Then, breathing normally, slowly turn your head and notice your surroundings. Look first to one side, then the other. Then swivel your shoulders and your head to each side, so that you can look behind you in each direction. Then look up, then down.

---

30 Snyder described the events of January 6, 2021 as "part of a long American argument about who deserves representation."

As you observe your surroundings, answer these questions:

- Where are all the exits or paths leading away?
- What structures or objects will you need to move around in order to leave?
- Where are all the spots through which people can approach you?
- In the event of danger, what spots nearby may provide your body with protection?

Now turn your attention back to your body—but also remain aware of your location. Ask yourself these questions:

- In the event of any danger, what parts of your body will be most vulnerable?
- What can you do to quickly protect those parts of your body? (This might involve crouching, lying prone, or moving behind a structure or corner.)
- Do a very quick body scan. What parts of your body are reacting most strongly? Where do you experience constriction, or fear, or dread, or stuckness, or heat, or any other strong response?

If you like, soul scribe in response to this practice.

## BODY PRACTICE
## ORIENTING WHEN ENTERING OR LEAVING

This practice combines Grounding and Orienting (from Chapter 3), Entering and Leaving (from Chapter 4), and Orienting for Safety (immediately above).

From now on, when you enter or leave a public space, pause (if your situation allows you to). Stand still for three breaths. As you do:

- Ground and orient your body.
- Check your surroundings for exit and entrance routes.
- Do a brief safety check (as in the previous body practice).

Let your body settle into the awareness that you have given it some preparation, readiness, and experience. As a result, should a threat suddenly appear, your body will be far less likely to reflexively slip into a trauma response.

# 11

# WHAT TRAUMA IS AND ISN'T

*Trauma is not what happens to you; trauma is what happens
inside you as a result of what happens to you.*
Gabor Maté

*Although humans rarely die from trauma, if we do not resolve it,
our lives can be severely diminished by its effects.*
Peter A. Levine

Trauma happens mostly in the body, *not* primarily in our emotions
or cognitive brains.

Trauma is the body's response to anything that it perceives as
*too much*, or as happening *too soon* or *too fast*, or as lasting *too long*—
and without receiving sufficient support, resource, or repair.

A trauma response is sudden and reflexive—a way for the
body to survive during what it perceives to be a perilous moment
or event.

One of your body's main concerns is staying safe. So in order
to stay safe during what it experiences as a crisis, your body may
hold onto some of the energy it associates with the event. Later,
at a safer time, you can re-access this energy—this trauma—and
then metabolize it, so that the energy in your nervous system can
flow freely once again.

But until you revisit and process that trauma, it can stay stuck
in your nervous system. This stuckness can diminish your health,

your happiness, your creativity, the quality of your relationships, and your full experience of life.

Unfortunately, much of the time, this revisiting never takes place—and the trauma remains stuck in the body. This is particularly common when an event that inspired a trauma response involves the energies of race.

Trauma is never a defect, a dysfunction, or a personal failure. It is always a protective response—one tied closely to the possibility of repair and to the body's eventual re-establishment of balance and emergence.

Still, with rare exceptions, trauma is not one of the human body's primary experiences. Joy is primary. Love is primary. Healing is primary—and tied to creation. Resource is primary—and always available.

Trauma is the temporary thwarting of joy energy—not its destruction. Trauma is thus an important aspect of our humanity, but it is still secondary.

Trauma is not an event. It's the body's response to an event. But the precipitating event may or may not actually be dangerous.

Because the human body is fast but not logical, it may decide that something is dangerous even when it isn't. Your body may make no distinction between a gunshot and a firecracker, or between falling from a skyscraper and falling off a four-foot wall—especially if it experienced an earlier fall as perilous. Your body may also make no distinction between dangerous closeness (e.g., someone carrying a rifle who stands directly in front of you, shouting insults) and unexpected but safe closeness (e.g., while you're filling out a form online, your partner sneaks up behind you and whispers in your ear).

Different bodies can respond very differently to the same event. Imagine this scenario:

As Martha and Omar are having supper, a mild earthquake shakes their home for twenty seconds, and an empty coffee mug falls off the table and breaks. Martha's body doesn't get overly activated, so she stands up, gets the broom from the kitchen, and sweeps up the pieces. But Omar's body develops a trauma response—an urgent stuckness. Right after the mug shatters, he hurries out the back door, shouting, "Martha, get outside! *Now!*"

Martha dumps the pieces of the broken cup into the trash, then stares out the window at her partner until the quaking stops a few seconds later.

Both Martha's and Omar's cognitive brains forget about the incident within hours. But Omar's body remembers.

Two years later, while they are on vacation, Omar and Martha walk across a floating bridge on a pond. The movements of the bridge remind Omar's body of the long-forgotten earthquake, so it immediately generates a protective response. Omar experiences a twinge of terror, urgency, anger, and agitation. He breaks into a run and hurries to the other side of the pond. Even as he runs, a voice in his head says, *Why the hell am I running?*

Two minutes later, when Martha catches up to him, Omar is wide-eyed and breathing heavily. "What happened?" she asks.

"I don't know," Omar says, speaking from his cognitive brain. But his body knows exactly what happened: its trauma from the earthquake was activated. The trauma energy that was stuck in his body ordered Omar to flee to safety. While this response was unnecessary, it was protective—not defective.

Trauma does not burrow its way into our bodies. The body *develops* trauma and then holds it tightly inside its tissues. This is why trauma always involves a sense of stuckness. In order to heal trauma, the body needs to metabolize that stuck, urgent energy.

Because trauma is developed by the body, it needs to be healed and metabolized within the body. Cognitive practices alone, such as talk therapy, can be helpful, but they usually aren't sufficient.

The key to healing trauma is to recognize and acknowledge its energy, accept and fully experience the fear and clean pain attached to it, and then move through the fear and pain. This often involves completing the action that was thwarted when the body first developed its trauma energy.

Let's return to Omar and Martha. Omar doesn't cognitively understand why he was so terrified as he crossed the bridge, but he recognizes the importance of facing that fear. So he takes Martha's hand and says, "Would you walk with me across the bridge and back?"

Martha giggles. "Sure, babe."

Together, slowly, they cross the bridge once again. As they do, Omar experiences a flash of terror and the urge to drop Martha's hand and rush to the other side. But he simply keeps walking, stopping occasionally and taking a few slow, deep breaths.

Midway across the bridge, he has a powerful urge to leap into the water. But he doesn't. He stops, takes a few deep breaths, squeezes Martha's hand, and then resumes walking at a steady pace.

When they reach the other side, Omar is still anxious and jittery but no longer terrified. "Okay," he says. "Let's cross back."

By the time they have crossed the bridge the third time, Omar is breathing normally. He experiences more room, resonance, and resource in his body.

Neither Omar nor Martha cognitively connects this experience with the earthquake two years earlier. But they don't need to. Omar's body simply needed to complete the action that had been thwarted and to metabolize the urgent trauma energy stuck within it.

This is an organic and emergent process. It's not magical—though it may feel magical at times.

Not everyone will be as quick as Omar to recognize what they need to do to complete their own uncompleted action. They might need to experience several situations that activate the urgent, stuck energy in their body before they recognize what to do. And when they do recognize it, that recognition might or might not be cognitive. A person might think, *I know! I can complete the thwarted action by safely crossing at the same intersection where the bicycle struck me.* But they might not think about the intersection at all. Their body might simply feel drawn to that intersection. Once they cross it without incident two or three times, the energy can begin to be metabolized. Their trauma might become healed without their ever cognitively understanding what happened.

No one, including you, can predict how your body will respond to any particular event. One person can go through war or disaster or abuse and come out the other side without getting overwhelmed or stuck.[31] Someone else can fall off a bicycle and get stuck in a trauma response for decades. A third person can be frightened by something as simple as a loud, unexpected

---

31   Usually this is because they have been able to access some healing resource.

noise. They immediately look around, orient themselves, see that there's no danger, and forget about it. A fourth person can hear the same noise and also briefly become frightened—but instead of forgetting about it, their body may remember it for years.

Your body's reflexive responses can't be reasoned with. Even though your cognitive brain tells you, *It's okay; I only fell four feet, and I landed on grass,* if your body responded to the fall by creating a trauma response, that trauma can stay stuck in your body until you find a way to complete the action and metabolize the energy associated with it.

The longer that trauma goes unacknowledged and its energies go unmetabolized, the more likely it is for its origins to be forgotten. Over months, years, or generations, trauma tends to become decontextualized from its precipitating event or events. In an individual, decontextualized trauma can start to look like personality; in a family, like family traits; and in a people, like culture.

Unmetabolized trauma in an individual often shows up as an ongoing sense of urgency. In daily life, this typically translates into being focused, assiduous, and hard-working. The person may also have a strong urge to address needs or problems right away. To others, this seems like personality. But it may actually be unhealed trauma, which keeps the person's body on high alert.

Not all trauma is associated with a single clear, identifiable event. A sequence of small, recurring, painful events can also engender trauma. (Therapist Nancy Van Dyken calls this *hazy trauma.*)

If you're very thin, and a small child seated next to you in a theater says, "Lady, why are you so skinny?" you'll probably laugh, say "Because it's the way God made me, honey," and forget about it by the following morning. But if your friend tells you at least once a week that you really should put on weight—even though you've explicitly told him several times to stop—then what started as a source of irritation can, over time, turn into trauma and stuckness.

Some trauma isn't personal at all. Trauma may also be *historical, intergenerational,* or *persistent and institutional.*

Imagine that you're walking through a public park and see a noose hanging from a tree. If you have a white body, you may be shocked and disgusted. But if you have a Black body, you may experience a trauma response—a sudden urge to run, or scream, or climb the tree, cut down the noose, and chop it into tiny pieces. That's classic *historical trauma*. Even though you've never had your own life threatened by a lynch mob, your body may hold the historical memory of the lynchings of thousands of Black bodies. This collective anguish from the past—perhaps intertwined with collective racialized anguish from the present—may activate a trauma response in your body.

*Intergenerational trauma* is trauma that gets passed down from caregivers to children—and, often, to grandchildren, great-grandchildren, and beyond. This transmission occurs partly through what people teach their kids and how they raise them, and partly through a parent's gene expression.

If your mother was in two serious auto accidents a few months before you were born, you might inherit a decontextualized lifelong uneasiness about riding in a car—an uneasiness that can't be explained by the events of your own life. While your cognitive mind might not make a connection between cars and danger, the DNA expression in your cells may.

*Persistent and institutional trauma* is trauma resulting from the repeated actions (or inaction) of a socially sanctioned institution—or, in some cases, by a culture.

Imagine that you're a Rohingya whose hometown has been repeatedly raided by the Myanmar military. These raids were conducted impersonally, on your entire village—but of course you and all of your neighbors experienced the trauma very personally, in hundreds of individual human bodies.

It will not surprise you to hear that white-body supremacy can engender any or all of these types of trauma.

White-body supremacy—WBS—also routinely shows up as *vicarious trauma*. This is the trauma of watching someone else be traumatized or of bearing witness to them as they share their story of experiencing trauma.

Many of the people who watched Derek Chauvin murder George Floyd experienced vicarious trauma. You may have experienced it yourself if you watched a video of the murder.

A more specific form of vicarious trauma is *secondary trauma*—the trauma of giving (or trying or wanting to give) aid to someone who is being traumatized or terrorized.

As Donald Williams watched Derek Chauvin murder George Floyd, Williams pleaded repeatedly with Chauvin and his fellow officers to spare Floyd's life. Because the four officers ignored Williams's pleas and would not allow him to assist, Williams may have suffered secondary trauma during the event.

In cases involving a perpetrator and a victim, it's easy to see how the victim might experience trauma. But in many cases, the perpetrator does, too.[32] When someone does something harmful (whether willingly, unwillingly, or accidentally) that may contradict their own sense of morality, this may create trauma in their own body. This form of trauma is often called a *moral injury.*

A moral injury can also occur when someone has the opportunity to prevent harm but fails to; when they attempt to help but are prevented from doing so; when they do help, but their assistance proves useless or makes the situation worse; or when they merely witness an extremely immoral act (such as the deliberate murder of a child).

Because WBS is baked into American culture, most of us have experienced vicarious trauma—and perhaps moral injury as well—many times over. This is one of the fundamental ways in which WBS harms people of all skin tones. Even white bodies that try to stay in a cocoon of white advantage can't completely avoid witnessing, and having their bodies respond to, the subjugation of other human beings.

Trauma is a part of life—and of having a body. Almost every human being has some trauma stuck inside their body.[33]

Yet trauma is not destiny. It can sometimes look like destiny when someone chooses to blow their trauma through others. But you don't have to do that. You can choose to stay with clean pain, move through it, and metabolize it.

---

32   However, I see no evidence to suggest that this was the case for Derek Chauvin.

33   Some people get angry when they learn this, and say to me, "Let me get this straight. You think everyone's traumatized. We're all victims—defective, dysfunctional human wrecks." My answer to that is, *Sure, almost all of us have trauma. We also all have shit and piss inside our bodies. None of this means we're defective, or dysfunctional, or victims. It means we're human.*

When you do this, you protect others from your trauma, much as wearing a mask protects others from being infected by an airborne virus. You offer other human beings safety and the opportunity to build their capacity for resource—both of which can then be passed down through the generations.

This means that when we heal our own trauma, individually and collectively, we don't just heal our own bodies; we help heal the world.

And when, over time, enough bodies heal from historical, intergenerational, and personal trauma and learn to harmonize, that harmony can turn into a culture of resilience, resource, and flow.

## BODY PRACTICE
## **WHAT YOUR BODY WANTS**

This body practice expands on Pausing and Noticing from Chapter 4.

*Pause.* Just *pause.* Stop moving. Just notice what your body is experiencing right now. If you like, quickly scan your body from the bottom of your feet to the top of your head, as you did in Grounding and Orienting (in Chapter 3).

As you pause, ask yourself these questions:

- What wants to move?
- What wants to stretch?
- What wants to be touched, and in what way? What wants gentle or firm pressure? What wants to be rubbed? What wants to be squeezed?
- What wants heat or coolness? What wants moisture or dryness?
- What wants to be left alone?

Spend the next few minutes moving, stretching, rubbing, or otherwise giving your body some of what it wants.

Do this regularly. Although it seems very simple, it is a foundational practice for conditioning and tempering your body, so that it is better able to contend with trauma.

## BODY PRACTICE
# HOVERING

Your body is made up of many interacting energy flows. In earlier practices, you began to explore some of the most familiar flows. In this practice, you'll explore a less familiar one.

Stand or sit comfortably, with your hands at your sides. *Pause.* Pay attention to what your body is experiencing right now. If you like, do a quick body scan, from the bottoms of your feet up through the top of your head.

Notice:

- What parts of your body are stiff or constricted.
- What parts are uncomfortable or in pain.
- What parts are too warm or too cold.

Next, open one of your hands—it doesn't matter which one—so that your palm and fingers form a flat surface.

Move your open hand to a part of your body that is constricted or uncomfortable. Gently hold your open hand an inch or two above that spot, with your palm facing it.

Let your open hand hover above that spot for ten to twenty breaths. Don't move anything. Don't visualize anything. Don't try to imagine or experience a beam of energy flowing out of your palm. Don't do anything except breathe and notice.

Next, move the hand—or your other hand—to another part of your body that is uncomfortable or constricted. Gently hold your palm above that spot for ten to twenty breaths.

Do this for each part of your body that is constricted or uncomfortable.

Afterward, soul scribe if you wish.

# 12

# THE FIVE TRAUMA RESPONSES

*I believe not only that trauma is curable, but that
the healing process can be a catalyst for profound
awakening—a portal opening to emotional and
genuine spiritual transformation.*

Peter A. Levine

*My story may be rooted in trauma,
but it is not my only story.*

Elaine Alec

As we've seen, trauma responses are not cognitive. They are protective emergency responses initiated by the back part of our brain. We humans share this part of our brain with a wide range of other creatures, including lizards, armadillos, mice, dolphins, and gorillas.

In response to a perceived emergency, our lizard brain is designed to swiftly override our normal cognitive functions. It's spring-loaded and ready to snap instantly into swift action, like a leg trap for catching small animals.

The lizard brain knows only five ways to snap into action. It can make us *flee*, or *fight*, or *freeze*, or *fawn*, or *annihilate*.

*Fleeing* may involve running away, locking our door and refusing to leave our home, or otherwise removing ourselves from the source of perceived danger. But we can also internally flee from danger—by pretending that it doesn't exist, or that it can't harm us, or that the threat is imaginary, overblown, or off in the future. Or we can simply ignore (or try to ignore) it. We can also emotionally shut down, or withdraw into a fantasy world, or turn and look the other way.

*Fighting* is often physical, but it can also involve shouting, or making threatening gestures, or saying, "I'll sue your ass for every penny you're worth." It can also involve calling the police, a security guard, or the store manager for no legitimate reason. (Karen and Kevin,[34] I'm talking about you.)

*Freezing* can mean temporary physical immobilization, but it can also manifest as an inability to think, choose, or discern (a brain lockup); an endless loop of anxiety and hand-wringing; overthinking that creates an endless stream of *what ifs*; or saying to someone, "I have no idea what you're talking about."

*Fawning* involves offering our subservience and surrender to a person, group, movement, or government. It can also involve joining a dangerous but potentially winning team. Think of the Muslims and Jews who converted to Christianity during the Crusades; the Christians and Hindus in Pakistan who are being forcibly converted to Islam today; teenagers who join the M4 gang after being told that if they don't, their parents and siblings will be murdered; or the state and national legislators who formerly supported and protected American democracy but now pledge their absolute fealty to Donald Trump.

*Annihilating* is a severe *fight* response that pushes us to destroy the source of our discomfort—or to obtain a complete, scorched-earth victory over it. *Annihilation* is often physical, but it can also take the form of extreme verbal abuse, making an extreme threat, or filing a big lawsuit.

Should a civil war begin, a great many American bodies will often act in one or more of these five ways.

When you encounter another body and recognize that it is experiencing a trauma response, remind yourself that their

---

34  A *Karen* is a white woman who tries to dominate a body of culture—one who has done nothing wrong—by calling the authorities on them. A *Kevin* is a white male Karen.

cognitive brain is disengaged and their lizard brain is temporarily in charge.

And when you find your own body edging toward a trauma response, use the body practices in this book—especially the five anchors in Chapter 21—to stay present, settle your body, and back away from that response.

## BODY PRACTICE
## YOUR FORMER FREAKOUT

All of us lose our tempers sometimes. And occasionally, each of us just plain freaks out, flipping into a *fight* or *flee* response. It's part of being human.[35]

The body practices in this book won't make you impervious to stress. But they will help you sense when you are getting close to your edge. Sometimes they will help you pause, breathe, stay in your body, hold onto yourself, and back away from that edge.

If and when you do go over your edge, they will also help you pause, recognize what's happening, and bring yourself back to a more settled state. They can also reduce the number of times you tumble over that edge.

As our country slides toward civil war or widespread mayhem and chaos, the stresses you experience may grow exponentially. The practice below will help you temper and condition your body in preparation for these severe stresses.

Find a private, fairly quiet spot where you can be alone. Sit down and get comfortable. Take a few slow, deep breaths.

Then recall a recent incident in which you freaked out and spun into a *fight* or *flee* or *annihilate* response. Relive that incident in your body and mind. What created the stresses or conflict? What did your body experience as the stresses mounted? Did you sense yourself getting close to your edge? How did this awareness show up in your body?

What happened that finally pushed you over that edge? What did your body experience as you went over it? What did you say and/or do as you freaked out? What happened after that?

---

35   I hear your question. Yes, I lose my temper sometimes. And yes, I've freaked out, although it's rare. Every therapist, yoga or meditation teacher, and member of the clergy also loses their temper occasionally and freaks out once in a while. Seriously doubt anyone who claims otherwise.

What did you eventually do that enabled your body to begin to settle? What, if anything, did anyone else do to help you settle?

Soul scribe about this entire experience, from the rising stresses to your eventual settling. For each part of the process, note any:

- vibrations
- images and thoughts
- meanings, judgments, stories, and explanations
- behaviors, movements, actions, impulses, and urges
- affect and emotions
- sensations

## BODY PRACTICE
## EMBODIED SLEEP

Some people imagine that sleep is just our cognitive mind's "off" switch. But sleep is not mere unproductive down time; it's a deeply important body experience. The energy flows of sleep help our bodies to heal, relax, rejuvenate, and metabolize what we experienced while we were awake.

Sleeping well is a profoundly valuable and restorative body practice. To help your body get the most from sleep, follow the suggestions below.

- First and foremost, get enough sleep. Most Americans get too little; some get far too little. The vast majority of adults need between seven and nine hours of sleep each day. Teenagers usually need nine to eleven, young children need eleven to twelve, and infants and babies need much more. You know you've gotten enough sleep when you awake refreshed and relaxed—or when you wake up naturally, without an alarm.

- You don't have to get all your sleep in one continuous stretch. In fact, many people find that their energy and mood improve if they regularly take a nap in the afternoon and sleep fewer hours at night. Some also say that they need less total daily sleep when they nap during the day.[36]

- Don't drink alcohol within three hours of going to sleep. Don't drink caffeine within five hours.

---

36  Napping can even be a form of principled resistance. For more on this topic, check out the Facebook page for the Nap Ministry, at https://www.facebook.com/Thenapministry.

- Set aside all electronic devices at least half an hour before going to bed. If possible, keep phones and computers entirely out of your bedroom.

- Create a daily period of sleep preparation time, during which everything you do is soothing and relaxing. This can be as brief as twenty minutes or as long as two hours. Wind down by reading (a print book, not an e-book, whose electrical energy can inhibit sleep); taking a hot bath; sitting out in the garden or on the front stoop; or doing some of the more relaxing body practices in this book.

- Keep your bedroom cool. Many people find that they sleep much better in a room that is sixty-eight degrees or cooler.

- Wear a separate sleeping outfit. This doesn't have to be pajamas; it can be an oversize T-shirt, a tank top and sweatpants, or anything else comfortable and familiar to your body. Just putting on the outfit will subtly cue your body that it is time to sleep.

# 13

# YOU ARE ALREADY THE ENEMY

*With each passing day, it looks less like we have one nation divided by differing political beliefs and more like we have two warring countries battling each other within shared borders. One side represents and seeks to preserve the United States. The other seeks to destroy it.*

David Rothkopf

*Sometimes people try to destroy you, precisely because they recognize your power—not because they don't see it, but because they see it and don't want it to exist.*

bell hooks

*No body stands outside the consequences of injustice.*

Aurora Levins Morales

*We must always take sides. Neutrality helps the oppressor, never the victim. Silence encourages the tormentor, never the tormented. Sometimes we must interfere. When human lives are endangered, when human dignity is in jeopardy, national borders and sensitivities become irrelevant. Whenever men or women are persecuted because of their race, religion, or political views, that place must—at that moment—become the center of the universe.*

Elie Wiesel

*Your hate makes me stronger.*

LeBron James

Because you're reading this book, you may have already chosen to support justice, liberation, and democracy, rather than the Republican Party's Big Lie and an authoritarian dictatorship.

This choice wasn't cognitive. You didn't think, *Let me weigh the benefits of fascism and a totalitarian dictatorship versus justice and an emancipatory democracy. I'll make a list of the pros and cons of each.* You knew in your body which choice is sane and wholesome and which one is dangerous and dehumanizing. Your body also understands the value of healing from racialized trauma—and the importance of moving through clean pain.

The people who will be activated in the coming civil war also made a noncognitive choice. They know, deep in their bodies, that feralness and authoritarianism—perhaps combined with white-body supremacy and/or evangelical Christianity—are what America needs. And their bodies are committed to denying their racialized trauma, refusing to heal, and creating lots of dirty pain for themselves and others.

These are not two dueling political philosophies. They are two mutually exclusive ways to organize a society and a country. They cannot coexist. If one is to thrive, the other must be pushed aside.

Here is what this means: should millions of Americans violently oppose democracy, justice, and liberation, they will not see you as an opponent to be outmaneuvered. *They will see you as an enemy who must be destroyed.*

If you have a body of culture—especially a Black or Indigenous body—you have probably gotten used to being viewed in this way by the white-body collective.

However, if you have a white body and have never fought in a war, then you probably have no experience of being seen as an enemy who needs to be destroyed. *Your world may soon become much more dangerous—in ways that are outside your experience.*

Here is what else this means: the people who see you as their enemy will pay no attention to your press releases, petitions, pleas for peace, attempts to negotiate a settlement, or questions such as *Why can't we all get along?*[37] There will be no demilitarized zones,

---

37    In Los Angeles in 1991, unarmed Black motorist Rodney King was arrested for speeding, drunk driving, and leading the police in a high-speed chase. The LA police beat him over fifty times with batons, broke his leg, disfigured his face, and shocked him with a stun gun. An onlooker videotaped the incident, which was aired on local television. The video provoked worldwide outrage, and the

no neutral positions, and no sidelines to sit on. You will be forced to pick a side—and then to stand up for it. You may be forced to risk your safety for it. You may even be forced to risk your life.

Somatic Abolitionism will help you choose growth, take a stand, and act from the best parts of yourself.

Once the civil war begins, getting along may not be possible. The United States may have become thoroughly polarized into two groups that cannot be reconciled: (1) people who want to heal from generations of racialized trauma, and (2) people committed to harming other human bodies—and our institutions of democracy and justice[38]—in order to prevent that healing.

People on one side of this divide will, overwhelmingly, have white bodies. People on the other will have bodies that feature the full range of skin pigmentations, including many white bodies.

At some point, the overwhelmingly white-bodied side will insist that the essential conflict being played out is between white bodies and bodies of culture. Yet when you look around, it will be obvious that this is not the case. What you will see instead is powerful white bodies using right-wing media to attempt to falsely frame the conflict in this way.

Pay close attention to this. As you will see in Chapter 40, it will be history repeating itself.

## BODY PRACTICE
## METABOLIZING YOUR ENEMYNESS

Your cognitive brain understands that you will be vilified, targeted, threatened, and possibly attacked for doing what your body knows is right.

For acting out of your humanity—out of the best parts of yourself—you may also be declared less than human.

---

county charged four of the police officers with assault and the use of excessive force. When a jury (none of whom were Black) acquitted all four of the officers, riots broke out in parts of Los Angeles. During these riots, King went on television and pleaded for an end to the violence. He famously said, "Can we all get along? . . . Let's try to work it out." (Later, in a separate federal trial arising from the incident, two of the police officers were sentenced to thirty months in prison. King's civil suit against the county resulted in his being awarded $3.8 million in damages.)

38   Again, we need to recognize that these institutions remain imperfect and, in many ways, inequitable. But they can be made more just and equitable. Plenty of people (including me, and I hope you) are working—and will continue to work—to make them that way.

Now your body needs to metabolize this awareness.

Find a place where you can be alone in front of a mirror. Bring pen and paper with you.

Stand or sit comfortably. Take a few deep, slow breaths. Then ground and orient yourself.

As you look at your image in the mirror, say these words aloud, slowly:

"I am considered the enemy. I am considered less than human."

Pay close attention to what arises in your body as you say and hear these words. Note any:

- vibrations
- images and thoughts
- meanings, judgments, stories, and explanations
- behaviors, movements, actions, impulses, and urges
- affect and emotions
- sensations

Soul scribe what you experience in your body.

Look back at your image in the mirror. Now say these words aloud, slowly and firmly:

"I am not defective. I am not a traitor. I am not subhuman.

"I can act out of my humanity—out of the best parts of myself—no matter what people say about me."

Notice what emerges in your body as you say and listen to these words. Again, note any:

- vibrations
- images and thoughts
- meanings, judgments, stories, and explanations
- behaviors, movements, actions, impulses, and urges
- affect and emotions
- sensations

Once again, soul scribe what you experience in your body.

# 14

# THE WISDOM
# OF YOUR BODY

*I touch my own skin, and it tells me that before
there was any harm, there was miracle.*

adrienne maree brown

*If we allow care, connection, and compassion to unfold
from the wisdom of the body, we become more aligned
with what is righteous, clear, and just.*

Rev. angel Kyodo williams

*Pause.*
What are you experiencing in your body right now?

It's easy to imagine the human body as a very sophisticated machine—a moist robot being controlled by a little CEO inside its head. But this model is deeply inaccurate.

Your body is not an object but a complex system of ever-emergent flows and vibrations. Its fluids, gases, and energies are constantly in motion, constantly interacting. Ask any biologist.

Your body is also the dynamic interaction of elemental structures: earth (bone), water (blood), air (breath), and fire (body heat). These can be further broken down into calcium; hydrogen and oxygen; nitrogen, oxygen, and carbon dioxide; and chemical reactions. Ask any chemist.

Your body comes from—and is an expression of—creation itself. It's an ever-emergent, ever-unfolding process. Ask any physicist.

Your body is also an ongoing source of great resilience, resource, and wisdom, even during the worst of times or your darkest of moods. Ask any somatic therapist.

Your body is also a brilliantly organized system of interacting bells, bowls, diaphragms, and antennae. Ask any physiologist.

Your body, like all human bodies, is fundamentally good and lovable. You might have a hearing loss or a missing hand or chronic illness or a heart defect. But *you* are not defective. Just ask someone who loves you. Or ask me.

Do you begin to see how your and others' bodies are the keys to healing trauma? To preventing—or swiftly ending—a civil war? To creating a living antiracist culture?

Your body—every human body—has an immense capacity for resource.

Resource is not an attribute but a flow. It moves through your body and among multiple bodies when they are harmonized.

Resource is not a strategy we study and learn. Human bodies are born with the ability to access it, and this ability comes naturally to us.

Resource is also something we can grow by accessing the energies in and around us, in any given moment. We'll look at this practice of cultivating resource in detail in Chapter 29.

In order to grow up and heal from racialized trauma, we need to learn to stay with discomfort and settle our bodies. But this doesn't mean that settling is always good and mobilizing is always wrong.

Every human body naturally settles and mobilizes, settles and mobilizes—sometimes in a rhythm, but more often in response to unfolding events and energy flows. We need the ability to do *either one* at any time, based on what emerges in us and around us.

You may know someone who compulsively tries to settle their body, no matter what their situation. They might see this as an important skill or even a virtue. But it's actually a limitation.

We need to respond to emerging events with discernment, compassion, and wisdom—not with an unexamined, reflexive, or habitual response of any kind. Sometimes the wise thing to do is to settle your body. Sometimes the right thing to do is to mobilize it. In many situations, you will need to settle first, then mobilize— then perhaps stop and settle it again.

As you repeat the body practices in this book, you will learn to settle your body, or mobilize it, or move back and forth between the two, whenever you need to.

BODY PRACTICE
## KNEE DROP AND CATCH

Lie comfortably on a mat or carpeted floor, with your knees up and together. Fold your hands loosely across your chest. Take a few breaths. Keep your knees together.

Then, slowly, let both knees, together, fall to one side. At whatever point seems natural, use your leg, hip, and back muscles to catch and stop the fall.

*Pause.* Let your leg muscles hold your knees where they are. Take three slow, deep breaths. Be curious about this spot. Note any:

- vibrations

- images and thoughts

- meanings, judgments, stories, and explanations

- behaviors, movements, actions, impulses, and urges

- affect and emotions

- sensations

Then slowly move your knees back to the center, until they naturally balance without your holding them in place. *Pause* again, and take three more breaths. Now notice any:

- vibrations

- images and thoughts

- meanings, judgments, stories, and explanations
- behaviors, movements, actions, impulses, and urges
- affect and emotions
- sensations

Now slowly let your knees drop to the other side. As before, at whatever point seems natural, use your leg, hip, and back muscles to catch and stop the fall.

*Pause.* Let your leg muscles hold your knees where they are. Be curious about this spot. Take three slow, deep breaths. Note any:

- vibrations
- images and thoughts
- meanings, judgments, stories, and explanations
- behaviors, movements, actions, impulses, and urges
- affect and emotions
- sensations

Repeat this three-part sequence—falling and catching on one side, returning to the center, and falling and catching on the other side—three times.

## BODY PRACTICE
## STAYING WITH DISCOMFORT

If you don't already take a shower every morning, start doing so now. It's a simple and pleasurable way to help you fully experience your body—and to help it settle.

The shower is also where you can do the following body practice, which will help condition your body to accept and stay with temporary discomfort:

Each morning, at the end of your shower, once you're warm and clean but are still standing beneath the water flow, turn off the hot water.

For five breaths—no more—let the cold water flow down your body. No matter how much you might want to leap away, stay under the water—

and stay in your body—for five inhalations and exhalations. (If five breaths is too long, then do it for two or three.)

During these five breaths, notice the following:

- any sensations of cold, wetness, pressure, or pain
- where your body constricts or braces itself
- any impulse to move, or avoid the cold, or block the water flow, or turn off the faucet
- any images or emotions that arise
- any thoughts, questions, or stories that pop into your head (Why the hell am I doing this?, etc.)

If you need to briefly shout, or curse, or gasp, that's fine.

After five breaths, get out of the shower, dry yourself, and warm up.

At first, your five breaths may be quick and sudden—more like gasps. Eventually, though, your breathing will slow down, until you're able to stand under the cold water for five natural breaths with your toes relaxed. Slowly, you will notice things about your bodymind that you do not notice now.

As the weeks pass, your body may begin settling into the cold instead of constricting or bracing itself.

Or it may not. But even if it doesn't, repeat this practice regularly for five breaths (or three, or two) each time, and notice what your body experiences.

Continue with this practice until it becomes a natural part of your daily routine. If you like, soul scribe about it at any time.

# 15

# YOUR BODY BROADCASTS
# AND RECEIVES

*The secrets of the universe are imprinted
on the cells of your body.*

Dan Millman

*Your body isn't just a body. It's an ecosystem.*

Douglas Coupland

We tend to think of the human body as a self-enclosed system. But all evidence and all human experience tell us otherwise.

Every human body is in constant interaction and communication with its environment—and, often, with many other bodies, human and otherwise. As a quantum physicist might add, each human body is also in constant communication with the entire universe.

Your body is a fine-tuned and highly sensitive antenna, as well as a receiver and an amplifier. It naturally picks up on a wide variety of energy flows, then processes and amplifies them.

This is not woo-woo. Most of these energies—such as subtle changes in pressure, speed, direction, temperature, duration, frequency, volume, and tone—can be measured with electronic devices.

Other energies that we can't yet measure electronically—for example, what we often call *vibes*—are very likely different combinations of these elemental flows. Some that currently seem mysterious—for instance, the sense that you're being watched—may turn out to be quantifiable, once we figure out what to measure, how to measure it, and/or what measures to combine. Not that we need to measure such energies with anything other than our bodies.

Your body doesn't just pick up on and amplify *external* signals. It does the same with *internal* signals—informing you of subtle changes in the pressures, temperature, and flows of electricity inside your body. Biologists call this *interoception*.

Nor is all of this a one-way process. Your body also constantly sends signals out into the world, using many of the same organs and processes to broadcast information that it does to receive it.

One of the most important—and most often overlooked—aspects of our body as an amplifier is that it can naturally amplify resource. By *resource*, I mean any source of grounding, flow, settling, courage, commitment, resilience, or affirming energy. We'll dive into the process of cultivating resource in Chapter 29.

A complex system of diaphragms, bells, bowls, chambers, and other biological structures naturally handles all of these functions. Five aspects of this sending and receiving system are especially notable:

- **Our brain** is the center for processing, screening, and routing a variety of signals in all directions.

- **Our skin** is our largest organ. An average-size person is covered with twenty-two square feet of skin—about eight pounds' worth. Our skin is deeply sensitive to subtle changes in pressure and temperature, as well as to a variety of other vibrations and rhythms.

- **Our soul nerve** (also called the *vagal nerve*) is the unifying organ of our nervous system. It reaches into most of our body, including our large and small intestine, our kidneys, our pancreas and spleen, our stomach and liver, our heart and lungs, and our throat. Our soul nerve is where we experience love, compassion, fear, grief, dread, sadness, loneliness, hope, empathy, anxiety, caring, disgust, despair, and many other things that make us human. We'll examine the soul nerve more deeply in Chapter 25.

- **Our gut** has about a hundred million neurons, more than are in our spinal cord. This is why we sense so many things in our belly—and why some biologists call the gut our "second brain." Our gut is where our body experiences flow, coherence, and the rightness or wrongness of things. The largest part of our soul nerve is embedded in our gut. So is most of our soul muscle (see below).

- **Our soul muscle** (also called the *psoas*). This muscle attaches to the spine and helps create the curve that enables us to stand and walk upright. It is highly attuned to the flows of fluids throughout the body. Psoas educator Liz Koch calls the soul muscle "bio-intelligent tissue . . . an organ of perception—juicy, delicate, tender, and responsive." In Chapter 25, we'll look more closely at this deeply important part of our body.

Your power of discernment emerges from your body's ability to receive and amplify signals. Discernment tells you when another body's signals are strong, clear, and consistent; when they are mixed or contradictory; when they are weak and easily subject to change; or when they are actually noise, distractions, lies, or dog whistles. It helps you decide whom to trust and whom not to, what to believe and what not to, and whether a particular body or situation is safe.

When the words someone utters or writes do not match some of their other signals, your discernment will help you pause and look closely at the inconsistency. When your cognitive brain tells you one thing but other parts of your body tell you another, your discernment will prompt you to pause and carefully examine the competing messages.

If you have a body of culture, all of this may seem familiar. To survive in a world suffused with white-body supremacy, many of us learned at an early age to closely read other bodies' vibes, movements, leanings, recoilings, glances, voices, and facial expressions. We *had* to learn these, because they often provided the cues that told us when we were in danger.

That said, everyone can benefit from growing their discernment. And growing discernment goes far beyond just being able to sense potential danger. As you repeat the body practices in this book, you'll cultivate your body's ability to accurately receive, amplify, discern, and broadcast a wide range of messages and energies.

*Pause.*

## BODY PRACTICE
## **YOUR BODY AS A RECEIVER**

Do this practice when you're with someone who is important to you— and when their body broadcasts an emotional or judgmental vibe that doesn't match the words they're saying.

This could be any emotion—fear, worry, contentment, delight, frustration, anxiety, dread, grief, shock, desire, anger, joy, etc. It could be any form of judgment—approval, disapproval, doubt, disgust, or caution.

Their signals might be directed at you—or they might have nothing to do with you. (For example, the person might be talking calmly about their neighbor, while giving off signals of anger and dismay.)

When you find yourself in this situation, *pause.*

For the next few breaths, carefully note what you experience in *your own* body. Note any:

- vibrations
- images and thoughts
- meanings, judgments, stories, and explanations
- behaviors, movements, actions, impulses, and urges
- affect and emotions
- sensations

*Pause* again. What does your body's response tell you about what the other person is experiencing?

On its own, this practice will help you build your discernment and temper and condition your body. But if you sense an opportunity to go deeper, also do this:

Settle your own body. Look the other person in the eye in a curious and nonconfrontative way. Then say, "I hear you. I'm also picking up a sense of *(whatever urge and/or judgment you notice)*. I could be wrong, though; maybe it's my own energy I'm experiencing. What are your thoughts about this?"

Asking this question may open up possibilities. It may also open up potential peril. The person may get angry at you for probing. They may verbally deny the signals you're picking up from their body—perhaps while continuing to broadcast those same signals.

If this happens, *pause* again. Notice what their body is doing. Also notice what you experience in your own body.

Afterward, soul scribe about your experience.

In the future, use this body practice whenever someone's words and actions—or words and body energies—don't seem to align.

# 16

# THE ESSENTIALS OF WHITE-BODY SUPREMACY

*White supremacy cannot be appeased. It can't be bargained with. It can't be convinced. . . . It is America's embryotic fluid. America was born in it and genetically coded by it. No amount of hoping or waiting, coalition-building or Kumbaya can redress that reality.*

Charles M. Blow

*The hard truth is that whichever United States political party has been most rooted in the fears, anxieties, and resentments of white people has never cared much about democracy or the Constitution designed to preserve it. Those who do want to make America a multi-racial democracy must face this fact with clear eyes and stiff spines to repel the ever-escalating threats to the nation's most cherished institutions and values. . . . The party that prioritized protecting white rights has always been more willing to destroy the country than accept a situation where people of color are equal and can participate in the democratic process.*

Steve Phillips

*White Supremacy is this nation's oldest pyramid scheme. Even those who have lost everything to the scheme are still hanging in there, waiting for their turn to cash out.*

Ijeoma Oluo

*White folks have been duped to trade their*
*humanity for their privilege.*

Rev. angel Kyodo williams

*No society can understand itself without*
*looking at its shadow side.*

Gabor Maté

White-body supremacy is in the air we breathe, the water we drink, the foods we eat, the systems and structures that govern us, the institutions that support (and sometimes hobble) us, and the social contracts under which we live. In the United States, and in some other parts of the world, it is almost everywhere we turn and everywhere we look.

Most of all, though, white-body supremacy lives in our bodies—bodies of all skin tones—weathering us, depleting us, and eroding our health and happiness. All of this is what makes WBS not just an idea or a belief system, but a pigmentocracy.

The basic rules of white-body supremacy—WBS—have remained unchanged for the past three hundred fifty years:

- The white body deems itself the supreme standard against which the humanity of all other bodies is measured and judged, both structurally and philosophically.

- Only the white body is fully human. All other bodies, or bodies of culture, are lesser primates—deviants from the human standard.

- The white body—and only the white body—is inherently pure and virtuous.

- The many different types of bodies of culture can be ranked on a vertical continuum. At the bottom are Black and Indigenous bodies.[39]

---

39    At times, this ranking has involved mathematical formulas. In what is known as *the three-fifths compromise* of the 1787 Constitutional Convention, delegates agreed to count an enslaved African or African American as three-fifths of a human being. Until 1900, the US Census included the categories of *mulatto* (half white, half Black), *quadroon* (one-quarter Black), and *octoroon* (one-eighth Black—i.e., someone who had one Black great-grandparent and whose parents and other grandparents were white). Today a racialized numerical formula lives on in very different form—and for very different purposes—in the Indigenous measurement of blood quantum.

- Only white bodies get to define who is fully human and who is not.

- White bodies get to change this definition whenever they please—which they do constantly.

- WBS is a pigmentocracy. Body pigmentation is primary— not identity.

The race question in this country (and throughout much of the world) is actually a species question. Are bodies of culture less than fully human? According to WBS, the answer is yes: every such body is a lesser primate.

The urge to otherize—to divide human beings into separate groups of *us* versus *them*, with *us* as worthy and spotless, and *them* as unworthy and dirty—goes back thousands of years. But the WBS we live with today was deliberately invented by a group of wealthy, powerful white landowners in Virginia in the seventeenth century. The sole purpose of WBS was to enable that small clique to protect, maintain, and increase their already-substantial power and wealth—and to divide and repress any challenge to them.

What these members of the Virginia Assembly did was a quantum leap in othering. They created a work of malevolent genius—and, arguably, history's most successful and enduring scam.

At the time, wealthy Virginian landowners faced a growing rebellion by workers—a rebellion that included people of many skin tones[40] (and for whom those differing skin tones carried few advantages or signals). In response, the Assembly legislated into existence two new classes of human beings: whites and nonwhites—thus creating our modern notion of race.

The Assembly took away certain fundamental rights from nonwhites (Africans, the descendants of Africans, and Indigenous people from North America), while specifically granting those rights to all whites. It also made the marriage of a Black and a

---

40 Indigenous people were not part of this rebellion because very few (if any) worked for these landowners. Instead, large numbers were slaughtered or dispossessed.

white person a crime, with a required prison sentence of six months for both people.

The Assembly and its surrogates then spread this message to poor white Virginians: *You are exactly the same as us wealthy white bodies—and nothing at all like those darker-skinned bodies. Because you are white like us, no matter how poor or miserable you might be, you are better and more deserving than every nonwhite person on the planet.*

*So hand in your French card, your Portuguese card, or your British card. Hand in your laborer card, your farmer card, or your servant card. We're handing you a new card—one that defines you as white. That is now the center of your identity—just like it's the center of our identity as wealthy white landowners.*

This strategy was—and continues to be—spectacularly successful. Very quickly, working-class white laborers began to identify and ultimately side with their wealthy white oppressors and to turn against their enslaved Black brethren. This quickly and efficiently dampened any rebellious impulses in poor whites—and helped to set in motion centuries of enslavement, violence, death, and trauma for bodies of culture. It also sucked some of the humanity out of many millions of white bodies, even as they denied the humanity of millions of bodies of culture.

As Ibram X. Kendi and others have pointed out, our modern concepts of race and speciesness were not primarily the product of hatred, but of greed and self-interest. Nevertheless, these concepts have been used to justify genocide, land theft, colonialism, imperialism, and enslavement. Many generations of trauma, hatred, and violence have been their results and their legacy.

The laws passed by the Virginia Assembly also codified a key aspect of the WBS continuum: Black and Indigenous bodies were deemed the least human, the lowest of the low.

If you are going to kidnap and enslave one group and conquer and steal land from another, this makes a kind of feral and nefarious sense. Why be concerned about the kidnapping, land theft, enslavement, or conquest of animals?[41]

---

41    WBS harms everyone it touches, including white bodies. That said, your place on the continuum tends to roughly correlate with the amount of difficulty and dirty pain that WBS has inflicted upon you. Many people push for reparations for Black and Indigenous Americans, but not for other groups of bodies who have been hurt by WBS, because of the clear placement of Black and Indigenous people at the very bottom of the WBS continuum.

It is therefore no coincidence that, on the North American continent, Black and Indigenous people's struggles for justice and liberation often connect or run parallel.

Now, over three centuries years later, WBS continues to thrive throughout the United States, as well as in much of the rest of the world. It is literally in the expression of our genes, the wombs of mothers, and the sperm of fathers. It is embedded in most of our institutions, our laws, our language, and our codes of behavior. It is ingrained in our habits, our norms, our assumptions, and our expectations. Over the past three and a half centuries, it has killed millions of people and injured or traumatized hundreds of millions more.

Today, WBS continues to express itself in our hearts, thoughts, words, actions, and decisions. We now also know that it embeds itself in many of our bodily structures; in the rhythms, flows, and vibrations of our bodies; and in our very cells. It thwarts and constricts the energy of creation as it moves within us. Yet WBS is so much a part of most of us that it seems entirely natural and innate. This feature of WBS makes it hard to recognize. In fact, to many Americans, WBS is invisible.

It's a widespread misconception that WBS is primarily an attribute held by specific people with bad intentions. Another misconception is that the way for our culture to grow out of WBS is to identify these folks, call them racists, and demand that they do better. Both of these faux solutions largely miss what's really going on. (Actually, both impulses are themselves aspects of WBS. They allow many people to tell themselves, *I'm not a racist, and I have good intentions, so I'm not involved with WBS in any way and don't have to do anything about it.*) [42]

---

42  Have you ever wondered why some white people, when they do or say something racially problematic and are challenged on it, respond immediately with "I'm not a racist!"? Let's unpack this. First, this response distracts people from the actual issue at hand. Second, it recenters the discussion on *the white person* and their identity, not on what they actually might have said or done. Third, the response suggests that their own self-image is more important to them than any harm they may have done to another human being—or any accountability for it. Fourth, it is often a tell that they *do* believe they are responsible (and perhaps guilty) for what they said or did, but want to avoid being held to account. Imagine this scenario: you arrive at the scene of a fender bender. One of the drivers immediately runs up to you and shouts, "It wasn't my fault! I'm a great driver!" What would you conclude? For a quintessential example of such a response, watch or read the testimony of Carolyn Pawlenty, Derek Chauvin's mother, *after* he was found guilty of murdering George Floyd. Pawlenty

Healing white-body supremacy is not primarily about going after sharks. It's mostly about cleaning up and protecting the water we all swim in.

Please don't focus on WBS as just a characteristic of individual people, such as brown eyes, or big ears, or a talent for drawing. Because WBS is all around us, like language and bacteria, calling someone a white-body supremacist—while it may be accurate— misses the point of how WBS operates structurally.[43]

If you have a white body, defending yourself by saying, "I'm *not* a white-body supremacist!" also misses the point. In the same way, your denial takes the focus off the structural aspects of WBS. If my house is on fire, your shouting, "I didn't set the fire!" will not help me. Instead, I need you to help me put out the fire.

WBS is passed down through the generations by what children are taught, how they are raised, and what they watch their parents accept and reject, lean into and recoil from. In 2015, researchers also discovered that WBS can be passed from parents to their children through the genetic expression of their cells.[44]

---

expresses no empathy for George Floyd's family. She does not even acknowledge that her son killed a man. Instead, she tells the court that she believes that her son is innocent, and says, "My son's identity has also been reduced to that of a racist. I want this court to know that none of these things are true and that my son is a good man." Let me be as clear as possible: a jury did not find Derek Chauvin guilty of being a racist. It sentenced him to twenty-two and a half years in prison for murdering another human being. Had Chauvin treated George Floyd fairly, respectfully, and nonviolently—even if he had spent the entire encounter thinking, *Screw you, you N*—then he would have committed no crime and performed his duties honorably. More to the point, George Floyd would still be alive. (In December 2021, Chauvin pleaded guilty to federal charges of violating George Floyd's civil rights by kneeling on his neck as he was handcuffed and not resisting, and then failing to provide medical care.)

43   The exceptions are people with vehement or devout WBS who proclaim to the world, "I'm a white-body supremacist—and proud!" Call these folks racists if you like.

44   *Epigenetics* is the study of inheritable changes in gene expression. A landmark study demonstrating such changes in multiple generations of mice was published in 2014 by Brian G. Dias and Kerry J. Ressler ("Parental Olfactory Experience Influences Behavior and Neural Structure in Subsequent Generations," *Nature Neuroscience* 17 [2014]: 89–96). Two years later, Rachel Yehuda and her colleagues published the first study to clearly show that stress can cause inheritable gene defects in humans (Rachel Yehuda, Nikolaos P. Daskalakis, Linda M. Bierer, et al., "Holocaust Exposure Induced Intergenerational Effects in FKBP5 Methylation," *Biological Psychiatry* 80, no. 5 [2016], 372– 80). For a more interesting and accessible read, I recommend Olga Khazan's October 16, 2018, article in *The Atlantic*, "Inherited Trauma Shapes Your Health," theatlantic.com/health/archive/2018/10/ trauma-inherited-generations/573055. Some background: In the Dias and Ressler experiment, adult male mice were given occasional painful electric shocks. A few seconds before each shock, the mice were exposed to the scent of cherry blossoms. The mice quickly learned to associate the smell with the shock that would follow. After a time, whenever the smell of cherry blossoms was released into their environment, they immediately freaked out. These adult male mice were then bred with female mice, none of whom were exposed to either electric shocks or the smell of cherry blossoms. Their offspring, none of whom had received or witnessed an electric shock, were then sprayed with the aroma of cherry blossoms. They immediately freaked out, just as their fathers had.

Here's how this works: when someone experiences a potentially trauma-inducing event, they may pass on their trauma to their children in multiple ways—women through the biochemicals in their wombs, men through the genetic expression in their sperm, and both through the ways in which they raise their kids. As a result, their children may suffer a variety of physical and mental health issues without anyone understanding why. Evidence suggests that this transfer can continue for multiple generations.

White-body supremacy doesn't just live in white bodies. In the United States, it has thrived for centuries in the tissues and thoughts of the great majority of bodies of all skin hues.

There are six primary variants of WBS:

- the *vehement* variant, which exists only in white bodies

- the *devout* variant, which appears in white bodies almost exclusively

- the *complicit, collective* variant, which is most common in white bodies but can appear in bodies of any skin tone

- the *progressive* variant, which also primarily lives in white bodies

- the *bodies of culture* variant, which appears in most bodies who are defined as nonwhite

- the *Black* variant, which lives in most Black bodies who have been raised on American soil (and some who have not)

All six variants can create an acute awareness of the white body as the supreme standard against which all bodies are judged and measured, both structurally and philosophically. All six variants hold trauma in the body. All six were created by wealthy, powerful white bodies to create and maintain advantages for themselves. All six also provide some advantages for other white bodies. All six emphasize anti-Blackness and Indigenous invisibility. And all six partly block the human body's normal impulse to emotionally grow and mature.

The central internal message of the *vehement* WBS variant is: *White bodies are the only bodies that deserve to live and thrive. All other bodies are dangerous. They need to be deported, segregated, incarcerated, or destroyed.*

The core internal message of the *devout* WBS variant is: *White bodies are the best bodies. White bodies rule and deserve to rule. Being a grown-up means supporting and defending these principles by any means necessary.*

The defining internal message of the *complicit, collective* WBS variant is: *I accept white bodies as the norm and as the default mode of humanity. I'll learn to work with this arrangement, and sometimes around it, as best I can—and I will do little or nothing to change it. This often means keeping quiet when I witness—or am harmed by—brief or subtle examples of WBS.*[45]

The core internal message of the *progressive* WBS variant is: *No body is better than another body. But having a white body grants me advantages, and I accept these advantages without working to extend them to everyone. Being a grown-up means properly performing expressions of concern and agreement with bodies of culture, while protecting—and failing to honestly examine and interrogate—my own white advantage.*

The *bodies of culture* variant makes the sufferer constantly scan for clues about when, where, and how the standard of whiteness is (or is not) present; when and whether to challenge that standard; when and whether to lean into it; when and whether to ignore it; and when that person is safe or unsafe because they are not white. This applies not only to events, situations, interactions, and relationships, but also to the person's own assumptions, ideas, and bodily sensations. Perhaps most notably, it applies to their conflicting desires to assimilate or stand apart; to seek borrowed advantages from white bodies or refuse to engage in such borrowing; to outperform white bodies or refuse to compete

---

45   These folks may declare things like, "I get along with everyone," or "I don't see race," or "I just want to raise my family and get along with my neighbors." They imagine (or pretend) that they are free of WBS by attempting to sidestep the many conflicts and tensions it creates. They thus attempt to also sidestep their own limitations around race and center their own self-declared virtues as standard virtues for any human being. It's a slick move. It also supports their own racial advantage, while denying the existence of (and their participation in) that advantage. But WBS is still in their bodies. They carry it and spread it. And they continue to enjoy all the white-body advantages, while typically doing little or nothing—either individually or in concert with other white bodies—to help turn those advantages into norms for everyone. Until they recognize and address the WBS in their bodies, and until they choose to employ and repeat practices that enable them to heal and grow, such as the body practices in this book, they will pass on WBS to others.

with them; and to define themselves in relation to white bodies or reject the act of defining oneself against others.[46]

Someone with the *Black variant* (which most African Americans harbor *in addition to* the bodies of culture variant) is also constantly on the alert for danger, especially physical and emotional danger. This danger can come from any quarter: white bodies; institutions, laws, and norms; other Black bodies; and the sufferer's own WBS-driven experiences of doubt, inferiority, impostorhood, anger, and/or despair.

In some situations, especially stressful ones, some people may shift from one variant to another. For example, I have watched quite a few white bodies react to the energetic charge of race by moving abruptly from the progressive variant of WBS into the complicit, collective variant—or from the complicit, collective variant to the devout variant.

Underlying these six variants—and supporting and feeding them—is a persistent form of WBS that is present in America's air, water, discourse, norms, and, most of all, our bodies. The primary symptom of this form of WBS is an automatic acceptance of the supreme standard of whiteness—*and* the lack of a clear awareness of that standard. This awareness is usually blurred, unexamined, or otherwise difficult for a person's cognitive brain to access. But it is present throughout their body as a *background rigidity* (and/or constriction or urgency) in relation to race. Although this form of WBS harms everyone, it provides specific advantages to white bodies.

Because this background rigidity is ubiquitous, we experience it as normal. But of course it is neither normal nor healthy. It is like polluted air or water that we take in constantly and also take for granted. Meanwhile, it steadily harms our health and well-being.

In addressing all of these variants, the human body is the key, because the healing of racialized trauma always begins in the body.

---

46  In a not-uncommon mutation of the bodies of culture variant, some bodies of culture form trauma bonds with white bodies (and with whiteness in general). If a particular body of culture's pigmentation is light enough, they may also, implicitly or explicitly, declare themselves to be white. This trauma bond typically goes unexamined. In some cases, it may encourage the body of culture to victimize other bodies of culture, perhaps brutally, in order to demonstrate their whiteness or white adjacency.

We will not end white-body supremacy, or any form of abuse or malevolence, by trying to tear it to pieces—or by turning on each other. Instead, we can offer people better ways to belong and better things to belong to. Each of us can also build our own capacity for genuine belonging.

As you will see in later chapters, Somatic Abolitionism encourages all of these practices.

So who exactly *is* white—that is, human?

You would think that WBS would provide a simple answer to this question. But it doesn't. That is part of its abusive genius.

WBS is made up of two unique but intertwined threads: *body pigmentation* and *identity*.

The *pigmentation* thread is primary. White-body supremacy is a *pigmentocracy*—a hierarchy that assigns differing amounts of power, advantage, and value based on skin tones.[47] According to WBS, anyone without pale skin is by definition nonwhite—and therefore less than human.

But WBS is neither an either/or binary structure nor a gradually sloping continuum. While there is a clear dividing line between human and subhuman, the subhuman portion of the continuum has multiple levels of subhumanness based on pigmentation, with Black and Indigenous bodies at the bottom.

Take one look at me, and you can see that I don't qualify as white. But neither does anyone with East Asian (or what used to be called *Oriental*, a WBS-inspired term) skin or features. Whiteness also doesn't (yet) include people from central Asia—for example, Sri Lanka, India, Bangladesh, Nepal, Bhutan, or Pakistan—even if they have very pale skin. Nor does it (yet) include light-skinned Indigenous Americans.[48]

What about "olive-skinned" folks from Italy, Egypt, Greece, or Morocco? What about Victor Varnado, an African American

---

47   A body's location on this continuum is ostensibly fixed at birth by its pigmentation and unchangeable by that body. Nevertheless, according to WBS, white bodies may change the location of any *nonwhite* group of bodies on this continuum as they please, for any (or no) reason. If you're thinking *WTF?*, that is an excellent question.

48   I'm speaking collectively about Indigenous Americans and people from central Asia. Given the wide variety of facial features and skin tones, a few folks from each group will not be so easy to visually identify as nonwhite. These people may be able to "pass" as white.

standup comedian with albinism, who is extremely pale-skinned? White-body supremacy's answer to all such questions is: *Shut up.*

In the eyes of WBS, because of my body pigmentation, there is nothing I can do to make myself white (or human, or sufficiently virtuous). Ditto for anyone else who fails the pigmentation test.

According to WBS, I am more subhuman than my wife, whose skin is lighter than mine. I am also more subhuman than, for example, Mindy Kaling or George Takei. I am close to the bottom of the pigmentation barrel, along with folks such as Delroy Lindo and Deb Haaland.

But certain aspects of subhumanness are additive. If I were to convert to Islam or Judaism, I would descend still further into a lower subhuman realm.

Colorism has long been an intrinsic aspect of WBS. The principle was simple: the darker you are, the less human you are. For many decades, people used the paper bag test: if your skin was darker than a standard brown paper bag, then you were not white. Period. Unless you were deemed white and had a suntan.

Another such test, the fine-toothed comb test, which was widely used during the twentieth century, had both nothing and everything to do with pigmentation. White bodies used kinky hair as a proxy for Blackness, so if a fine-toothed comb could not be passed through your hair, you did not qualify as white even if your skin was pale. The (often incorrect) assumption was that the kinkiness of one's hair inevitably reflected Blackness in their genes.

The *identity* thread is secondary and even more confusing. Any question of pigmentation aside, according to the devout and vehement variants of WBS, you do not qualify as white—or human—if you are Latinx or if you practice Judaism or Islam.

Let's unpack just a few of the many crazymaking nuances here.

If you're Latinx, even if your skin is quite pale, you are *ipso facto* subhuman. However, the darker your skin, the lower you sink on the WBS continuum. Ditto for your kids (usually), even if they were born and raised in the United States.

But what if, for example, you are Ted Cruz or Marco Rubio, both of whose fathers were born and raised in Cuba? Are you white or not? WBS offers us this guidance: *Shut up.*

According to the devout and vehement variants of WBS, no person who practices Judaism, regardless of their pigmentation, can ever be considered white.[49] Their Jewishness is in their genes, not their religious beliefs—even someone who was raised Christian in Norway and who converted to Judaism as an adult.

Now let's imagine that, later in life, this person renounces Judaism and declares themselves an atheist. Are they forever nonwhite? What about their kids? What if those kids convert to Christianity? WBS has a definitive answer: *Shut up.*

In any case, someone with pale skin who practices Judaism surely benefits from white advantage. Doesn't that make them white? If they don't wear any identifying clothing (such as a kippah), how do you even know if they're Jewish? Does this mean they're nonwhite, or a white-bodied Jew? WBS has this to say about such dilemmas: *Shut up.*

What about someone who otherwise qualifies as white but practices Hinduism, or Buddhism, or Sikhism, or Zoroastrianism, or Baha'i? As WBS explains, *SHUT THE FUCK UP.*

Here is what makes WBS simultaneously so intractable and so slippery:

On the one hand, white bodies insist that only white bodies are fully human. On the other, white bodies constantly change their own definition of white bodies. So, although whiteness equals humanness, whiteness is nothing more than whatever white people say it is at that particular moment.

A century ago, people immigrating to America from Ireland, Italy, Poland, Greece, and some Slavic nations were widely considered nonwhite—and, therefore, less than fully human. (This was not some unspoken assumption. It was how scientists, journalists, and politicians routinely wrote and spoke of these people in public.) The same was true of their American-born children.

---

49  According to the other WBS variants, the whiteness of a particular Jewish person depends on their individual skin tone. Any identity issue is overridden by their pigmentation. Thus there are white-bodied Jews, Black-bodied Jews, Asian Jews, and so on.

As the decades passed, however, and these new immigrants and their descendants assimilated into American culture, they were gradually accepted as white. (David R. Roediger has written an eye-opening book about this process, called *Working Toward Whiteness: How America's Immigrants Became White: The Strange Journey from Ellis Island to the Suburbs*).

Arguably, as I write this chapter in late 2021, white-bodied Jewish Americans are collectively midway through this process of becoming white. You can see this reflected in my discussion (and the conundrums it raises) earlier in this chapter. Of course, to many folks with the devout or vehement variant of WBS, no Jew can ever become white, any more than a dog can become a giraffe.

In contrast, bodies from central Asia—folks of all pigmentations from countries such as India, Pakistan, Sri Lanka, Nepal, and Bangladesh—have collectively not even started to become white. White bodies have not yet begun to collectively permit it. (To be 100 percent clear: I'm not suggesting that this is in any way fair, reasonable, consistent, or logical. I'm just looking at the widely understood but unwritten 2021 WBS schematic diagram.)

CNN commentator John Blake has captured this hot, ever-shifting mess in a single pithy sentence: "The numbers and types of people who are defined as White may change, but the status and power that comes with being White has remained the same."

If you find all of this deeply confusing, impossibly complex, self-contradictory, and insane, you are getting a good sense of just how WBS works—and why it is often so difficult to analyze or discuss.

When Nell Irvin Painter, author of *The History of White People*, was asked by an interviewer a series of questions about whiteness, she responded repeatedly (and with some exasperation), "What do you mean by white?" She was trying to get her interviewer to begin to sense all the confusion, complexity, contradictions, feralness, and insanity that are baked into WBS.

Because of the ubiquity of WBS, the great majority of white American bodies have little acuity or agility when it comes to race. Partly this is because they haven't needed to develop these skills. For centuries, simply by being white, they've been able to rely on the advantages that WBS provides without having to examine, or even recognize, those advantages. For white bodies, this is a cushy deal.[50]

But it's also a form of dirty pain. There is a vicious and costly underbelly to this arrangement. For one thing, accepting the advantages of WBS without examining its effect on others can eat away at your humanity. For another, it's all too easy to grow accustomed to these advantages; to insist on holding onto them, no matter how much they may harm others; to believe that you're genuinely entitled to them; or, when pressed (or faced with losing those advantages), to deny that they exist.

White bodies thus find themselves in a serious moral dilemma, because any effort to seriously investigate their advantages could cost them a great deal—access, approval, friendships, community, prestige, a sense of belonging, and, above all, their long-held innocence regarding race.

It's no surprise, then, that many white bodies with the vehement and devout variants of WBS regularly practice *racialized gaslighting*. This involves creating, embracing, and spreading grossly false narratives that uphold and defend WBS.[51]

These narratives have steadily evolved over the past three centuries. Until the mid-1900s, many of them involved the inferiority of bodies of culture, especially Black bodies. Today, though, most such narratives focus not on bodies of culture but on the actions and intentions of white bodies. Here are some of the most common ones:

- Africans who were kidnapped, trafficked across the Atlantic Ocean, enslaved, and sold to white Americans were "African immigrants."

- Enslavement was a boon to Black bodies, who were happy and relatively prosperous (compared to conditions in Africa) while under the thumbs of their enslavers.

---

50   I'm not suggesting that white bodies don't face barriers, difficulties, bad breaks, struggles, thwarted opportunities, or other aspects of the human condition. Of course they do. All human beings do. But for bodies of culture, WBS compounds every one of these troubles.

51   As I write this chapter in late 2021, many American states, especially those with Republican leaders, routinely racially gaslight children with lessons and textbooks that teach historical falsehoods upholding WBS. Currently, a movement is growing in many GOP-led states to greatly turbocharge this gaslighting; to make the teaching of an accurate history of race in America illegal; and, in some school districts and states, to ban any serious discussion of race from all K-12 public school classrooms. If successful, this movement would transform racialized gaslighting into racialized brainwashing.

- Most people who owned enslaved human beings treated them well.

- The Civil War of the 1860s was a noble effort. Its purpose was to protect Southern moral uprightness, honor, and gentility from Northern aggressors. (This is known as the *lost cause narrative*.)

- The Confederacy was a movement of patriots, heroes, and brave warriors. These people deserve to be honored and celebrated.

- America does not have a history of white-body supremacy. That is a myth created by Black Lives Matter, Antifa, critical race theorists, liberals, and/or socialists, whose fervent desire is to destroy morality, Christianity, democracy, and the American way of life.

- White-body supremacy does not exist now. That is a myth created by bodies of culture, Ivy League universities, George Soros, Jews, and other right-wing targets of blame.

- White bodies are regularly—and unfairly—victimized by all of the folks listed above.

Two other, related aspects of WBS in white bodies are *racial ignorance* and *ignorance as a source of pride*.

Most white Americans don't just lack racial acuity, agility, and grit. They are also profoundly ignorant about much of the history, psychology, and sociology of race in their country. They're equally ignorant about the lived experience of many bodies of culture.

This is largely because they've been gaslighted for many years (or, in some cases, for generations). It's also because they don't *need* to learn much; they can simply coast on their white advantage.[52] In many cases, it's also because of a lack of curiosity and interest.

But there's another, less obvious piece to this. Racial ignorance is embedded in most of our institutions. It is also held deep inside many white bodies. Among some white bodies, this ignorance is a

---

52   Think of all the situations an ordinary American encounters throughout their life, regardless of their body pigmentation. Now ask yourself: For people with white bodies, how many of these contexts require a working knowledge of the history of race in America?

part of their very identity as white people. Indeed, to some white people with the devout or vehement form of WBS, this ignorance is a point of pride.

This pride is a body experience, not a cognitive one—but if it were put into words, it would go something like this: *Because I have a white body, I enjoy a variety of advantages, including not needing to know or think much about race. I'll flaunt these advantages—and my ignorance—whenever I can. This rubs my white advantage in the faces of bodies of culture. If I could get away with it, I'd wear a T-shirt that said,* White, Ignorant, and Proud.[53]

Currently, the Republican Party, with the help of its complicitors, strongly supports and encourages white racial ignorance as a source of pride. It also implicitly (and sometimes explicitly) declares this pride to be a hallmark of patriotism and authentic Americanism.

The false narratives and deliberate ignorance described above soothe white bodies around WBS in multiple ways. In many white bodies, this soothing can become compulsive, so that the mere mention of race may activate an immediate trauma response in them. Such responses are hallmarks of *white fragility*.

In some of these bodies, maintaining personal comfort around race can become all-consuming and all-important. To these bodies, the rights, agency, well-being, safety, happiness, and liberation of bodies of culture may need to be sacrificed in order to maintain this comfort.

Often these bodies conflate comfort with safety. They may tell bodies of culture—or white bodies who have challenged or questioned them around race—"I don't feel safe around you." Translation: *I'm unwilling to grow up, face any discomfort around race, and move through it. So, when something you say or do—or your mere presence as a body of culture—activates my unexamined racialized trauma or results in my experiencing discomfort, I'm going to blame you, insist that I feel unsafe, and brand you an aggressor.*

You already know where this conflation of safety and comfort can lead. We read news stories about it all the time. They all share

---

53   I would not be surprised if, after the publication of this book, someone starts selling just such a T-shirt—and builds a successful business from it.

the same overarching narrative: *A white body became uncomfortable in the presence of a body of culture. The body of culture got hurt, killed, or arrested.*

White-body supremacy has also been described as a virus; a public health threat; a form of group narcissism; a malignant social compact; a massive (and very successful) brainwashing project or form of mass hypnosis; a collective delusion; a widespread lie, fraud, and grift; a racialized form of fascism[54]; a contemporary expression of historical feralness; and an embodied cultural pathology. While it is arguably all of these, most of all it is a failure to grow up.

Which is why it is our responsibility, both individually and collectively, to grow out of it.

As we've seen, the plan of the Republican Party is to activate the racialized trauma in the bodies of people with vehement and devout WBS, and then spur them to widespread destruction and brutality. With the assistance of many of the GOP's complicitors, this plan has been unfolding steadily since early 2021.

However, the same efforts that incite and mobilize these folks will also activate the racialized trauma in *most* Americans' bodies—probably including yours. This will create potential peril but also the possibility of deep healing. If many of us can experience, recognize, and metabolize the racialized trauma that has long been stuck in our bodies, we can begin to grow up around matters of race.

## BODY PRACTICE
## NOT YOUR FAULT, BUT STILL YOUR PROBLEM

I'm writing this chapter in the midst of the COVID-19 pandemic. Throughout this pandemic, each of us has had to face a stark reality:

We did not cause COVID. We did not desire COVID. Yet each of us is responsible for protecting our fellow human beings from it—by wearing a mask, social distancing, getting vaccinated, avoiding large gatherings, and so on.

---

54    As Jason Stanley suggests in his book *How Fascism Works*, all toxic us-versus-them frameworks are, in essence, either forms of fascism or potential precursors to it.

Those of us who refused to shoulder this responsibility put many other people's lives at risk and made the pandemic much worse and much more widespread.

Our situation with WBS is similar. Before we were even conceived, WBS was in the air, the water, the culture, the wombs of our mothers, and the seed of our fathers. We did not create it. We did not ask to harbor it in our bodies. Yet, as with COVID, we must shoulder the responsibility of keeping it from spreading. We cannot say, "It's not my problem." We also cannot allow it continued safe harbor in any of our institutions, norms, or practices. We're all in this together.

*Pause.* Pay attention to your body for your next several breaths. What is emerging in it in response to this awareness? Sorrow? Grief? Anger? Frustration? Impatience? A desire for things to be different?

Note any:

- vibrations
- images and thoughts
- meanings, judgments, stories, and explanations
- behaviors, movements, actions, impulses, and urges
- affect and emotions
- sensations

If your body wants to physically respond—to rock, or cry, or snarl, or wail, or curse, or punch a pillow, or go for a long jog—allow it to, unless doing so might harm you or someone else.

Then soul scribe on your experience with this practice.

# 17

# WHAT ARE REPS?

*If you try something once, it probably won't be perfect, and you have to keep working on it if you want to be good at it.*
Nicole Byer

*Many of us have been running all of our lives. Practice stopping.*
Thich Nhat Hanh

Repeating an activity, over and over, is how human bodies build muscle, endurance, and flexibility. It's also how we build resilience, presence, and discernment. Through repetition after repetition—through *reps*—we learn and grow.

We use this same process to learn to sing, write, dance, paint, and solve equations; create inventions; address problems; become great athletes; and become loving partners or parents.

Each body practice in this book is meant to be experienced, over and over, through multiple reps, until it becomes part of your body's physical memory. Over time, these reps create more and more room for growth and discernment in your body. This sets the stage for good things to happen—not just in your physical body, but in your thoughts and energy fields.

And they may not just happen to you. Over time, as you connect with other people and groups, some personal reps may become communal reps. And when a practice is repeated collectively, with other bodies, its effects can ripple out into the world—and ultimately change it for the better.

The body practices in this book all involve race, though this might not always be obvious at first. Race has a charge, a texture, a weight, a speed, and a direction to it. Through reps, you can begin to develop a container that is able to hold all of these. As a result, when you experience discomfort around race—or, for that matter, anything else—you may be better able to stay with that discomfort instead of bypassing it and flipping into a trauma response of *fleeing, freezing, fighting, fawning,* or *annihilating.*

This ability to stay with discomfort around race is vital for everyone, but it is especially valuable—and especially necessary—for white bodies.

The paragraphs above all speak specifically to the body practices in this book. But every time you do *anything* that helps you remain strong and settled in the midst of discomfort, that's a rep. When you publicly speak up for justice in a potentially perilous situation, that's a rep. When you challenge authority in order to benefit others, even though you know you'll face some blowback, that's a rep. Over time, these reps can help you develop the essential grit of Somatic Abolitionism.

Whenever you act from the best parts of yourself—especially when doing so requires you to accept and move through discomfort—that's a rep. And when you act from the best parts of yourself around a matter that involves race, that's a small step in the direction of Somatic Abolitionism.

## BODY PRACTICE
## NOTING YOUR REPS

Come up with a brief, simple, physical, and *pleasurable* action that you can do each time you complete a rep or a sequence of reps. Some examples:

- Give yourself a quick thumbs-up.
- Rub or pat your belly for two to three seconds.
- Put your hands on your hips; then swivel from side to side two to three times.

- Do a deep knee bend.
- Interlock your fingers, and then push your arms forward, palms outward, into a pleasant stretch.
- Make two fists and raise your arms, in the manner of victorious athletes.

Please *don't* try to keep track of the overall number of reps you do, or otherwise try to quantify them. Reps are not gold stars to be accumulated. They are a lifelong habit of deepening your humanity and your sense of resource.

These tiny embodied rewards will support your efforts to heal and grow up. However, keep in mind that reps are not about reward or relief. They are about tempering and conditioning your bodymind—and acting from the best parts of yourself.

## BODY PRACTICE
## SITTING ON YOUR HEELS

On a carpeted floor or mat, get comfortably on your knees. Keep your legs straight from the knees up. Let your hands rest lightly in front of you, on your thighs. Keep your toes curled under.

Very slowly, let your butt drop toward your heels.

Keep going until your leg muscles tell you that you've reached a natural stopping point, or the stretch begins to be slightly painful, or your butt is resting lightly on your heels. Then stop. If you've only lowered your butt an inch or two, that's fine.

*Pause.* Stay in this position while you take three or four slow, deep breaths. Be curious about this edge. Pay attention to any:

- vibrations
- images and thoughts
- meanings, judgments, stories, and explanations
- behaviors, movements, actions, impulses, and urges
- affect and emotions
- sensations

Now, slowly, raise your butt back to its original position. *Pause* again for three or four deep, slow breaths. Now notice any:

- vibrations
- images and thoughts
- meanings, judgments, stories, and explanations
- behaviors, movements, actions, impulses, and urges
- affect and emotions
- sensations

Repeat this practice three times.

# 18

# TWO TYPES OF REPS

*The more you practice, the better you get,
the more freedom you have to create.*

Jocko Willink

*The more you practice tolerating discomfort,
the more confidence you'll gain in your ability
to accept new challenges.*

Amy Morin

*Something just doesn't pop under your nose;
you have to work for it.*

LeBron James

*Put one foot in front of the other,
smile, and just keep on rolling.*

Kobe Bryant

*Pause.*
What do you experience in your body right now?

Life regularly—and often unexpectedly—presents us with
challenges, most of which are opportunities for growth. These

are usually unwanted, and they will almost always make us uncomfortable. I call these challenges *life reps*.

Each life rep is a chance for you to choose clean pain over dirty pain. Each time you choose clean pain, you will be a bit more able to navigate life's turbulent waters.

You know that you're being offered a life rep whenever you experience emotional discomfort. This is an opportunity to pause, take a few breaths, check in with your body, and anchor yourself. You can then lean into that discomfort rather than away from it—and act out of presence and discernment, rather than fear and avoidance.

Life reps are often urgent situations that push us up against our developmental edge. They ask us to grow or transform. When you lose your job and suddenly have to retrain for a new career, that's a life rep around building your skills and rethinking your life. When you enroll in an in-person coding class, and discover on your first day that you're the only female body of culture in the room—and the oldest student by at least fifteen years—that's a life rep around race, gender, and age.

When your sixty-five-pound dog injures its leg and you carry it to the car for a ride to the vet, that's a life rep for building muscle. Now suppose that a block away, you notice a white policeman aggressively confronting your longtime neighbor Liyana, who is Pakistani American, on her front lawn. You pull over, get out, and say, "Hi, Liyana. Hi, officer. Anything I can help with here?" That's a life rep around race.

Almost any conflict or difficulty involving race can be a life rep. And should there be widespread mob violence in our country, for a time our lives will become one life rep after another.

Life reps force themselves upon us—and force us to grow (or choose to refuse to grow). But we can also be proactive with reps.

*Invited reps* are the challenges—and opportunities for growth—that we deliberately bring into our daily life. When you do curls with a heavy barbell, these are invited reps that build muscle. When you go to work wearing a cap that says *1619* in large numbers—and when people ask you what it signifies, you tell them about *The 1619 Project*—that's an invited rep around race. Most of the body practices in this book are invited reps.

You practice an invited rep when you choose to step forward into clean pain—and into peril and possibility—even when life isn't pushing you to do so at that moment. You practice an invited rep because you recognize that if you don't step forward now, sooner or later your circumstances will force you into a life rep around the same issue or concern. You choose to accept conflict and pain now and deal with it in the present, rather than ignore or deny it and wait for it to bite you on the ass later. Because you know that it eventually will.

Invited reps are bite-sized situations that you can partly control. They help temper and condition you for practicing life reps, which are full meals that you don't ask for—or, in some cases, even anticipate.

Invited reps help you get used to pushing beyond your limitations and leaning into challenges and discomfort, rather than reflexively recoiling from them. They can prepare you for times when, without warning, an opportunity for a life rep appears.

Athletes routinely practice invited reps. I could cite a hundred good examples, but let's use the basketball star Michael Jordan. In his early years with the Chicago Bulls, Jordan realized that he was never going to become the player he wanted to be—and that the Bulls were unlikely to win the national championship—unless he became a different player. So, in addition to the standard grueling practice regimen, Jordan would go back out into the arena after games and practice shooting. He started lifting weights regularly. He put on fifteen pounds of muscle. He spent endless hours watching videos of NBA games. All of these were invited reps.

Jordan understood in his body—and presumably also in his cognitive mind—that the person he was on the basketball court needed to transform into someone who was bigger, stronger, a better shooter, and a better overall player. He also understood that invited reps were the key to this transformation. Eventually those invited reps made all the difference for his career and for the success of his team.

Here are some examples of how you might practice invited reps in your own life:

- You are an activist, and you have sensed growing tension with Gary, another activist you often collaborate with.

But you don't know what the underlying issue is—or even whether the tension is real or imaginary. Instead of ignoring the situation and hoping it will improve on its own—a mild form of dirty pain—you accept the discomfort of directly raising the issue. So when the time seems right, you say to Gary, "Can we talk sometime soon? I want to make sure things are cool between us. If I've caused you any trouble, I want to know about it."

- At your last two extended family gatherings, your sister has made snide remarks about immigrants from Africa. You want to invite her and her husband to your upcoming Thanksgiving celebration, but you also don't want her talking trash at your dinner table. You know that you need to speak with her directly about this—and that doing so might trigger an argument. You call to invite her and her husband to the holiday gathering. But as soon as she accepts, you swallow hard and say, "We have two house rules that we apply to everyone. No smoking inside, but on the balcony or deck is fine. And no ethnic, racial, cultural, or religious slurs. People can think whatever they like, but in conversations in our house, no one gets to demean any group."

- You don't know most of the people on your block very well. Some of them don't seem friendly, though they've never been mean or rude to you. One couple across the street rides Harleys, and sometimes they work on them in their driveway. You'd like to become better acquainted with all of your neighbors. So, even though it causes you some discomfort—and even though you're volunteering to do a fair amount of work—you drop a note in all the mailboxes on your block, asking all your neighbors if they'd like to become part of a block club, and offering to help organize it.

There's another important piece to this. After (or as) you do any of the above invited reps, you also notice what you experience in your body. You might also soul scribe about your body's experience.

Invited reps are never performative. If you practice an invited rep to demonstrate to someone else (or the world) how woke or caring or compassionate you are, it's not a rep at all—it's vanity.

All of us need to practice both types of reps, because they reinforce each other. Some can further strengthen your existing strengths. Others can highlight your limitations and help you push beyond them. Sometimes a life rep may prompt you to pause, consider the situation and the VIMBAS in your body, and do an invited rep that builds on it.

Most of the body practices you've encountered so far in this book are invited reps. But Your Body as a Receiver, in Chapter 15, is a classic example of a life rep. As you'll see, in the chapters to come, you'll have many opportunities to practice reps of both types.

## BODY PRACTICE
## FROM DODGING TO INVITING

Think of a racialized situation, conflict, or problem that you've been avoiding. If more than one comes to mind, pick any one you like.

Now imagine that you can no longer avoid this problem or situation. Assume that you must deal with it right now, in this very moment.

Explore what you experience in your body. Note any:

- vibrations
- images and thoughts
- meanings, judgments, stories, and explanations
- behaviors, movements, actions, impulses, and urges
- affect and emotions
- sensations

If you like, soul scribe about what your body is experiencing.

Take a few deep, slow breaths. Spend the next minute or two grounding and orienting your body.

Now make a *simple* plan to address the actual situation or problem, and decide when you will execute this plan. This should be soon. Then, when the time comes, do it.

When you carry out this plan, you will have completed an important invited rep.

Practice this process at least once every month, each time with a new situation, problem, or conflict—whether racialized or otherwise. It can help you build your discernment and tolerance for clean pain. It may also improve the overall quality of your life—and the lives of others around you.

Even if an immediate outcome is uncomfortable, you will still have completed a rep and added to your body's tempering and conditioning.

# 19

# HOW CAN THIS BOOK HELP
# PREVENT A CIVIL WAR?

*When mass noncooperation is organized and strategic and targeted well, it has shown again and again that it can protect democracy and challenge authoritarianism.*

Hardy Merriman

*Enough committed fleas biting strategically can make even the biggest dog uncomfortable and transform even the biggest nation.*

Marian Wright Edelman

*Change will not come if we wait for some other person or some other time. We are the ones we've been waiting for. We are the change that we seek.*

Barack Obama

Preparation is a form of prevention.

Soon after the gang violence at the US Capitol on January 6, 2021, social media began buzzing with plans for a second round of attacks on January 20. Our country's intelligence professionals monitored many of these conversations closely. As a result, lawmakers who were targeted or threatened were assigned extra security. As January 20 neared, police and soldiers were moved into place to protect Capitols around the country.

On January 20, nothing happened. By preparing for armed attacks, our federal and state governments prevented them.

In the mid-nineteenth century, Karl Marx predicted that the extreme exploitation of ordinary workers by powerful capitalists would lead to mass revolts. These revolts would ultimately destroy capitalism. This is precisely what took place in Russia in its 1917 revolution.

Elsewhere in the world, however, the same capitalists whom Marx predicted would be toppled from power read his writings carefully. Many of these capitalists, sensing that their days in power (and possibly on Earth) were numbered if they didn't at least partly change course, improved the salaries and working conditions of their employees.[55] As Yuval Noah Harari explains in his book *Homo Deus: A Brief History of Tomorrow,* "Capitalists in countries such as Britain and France strove to better the lot of the workers, strengthen their national consciousness, and integrate them into the political system." Because of the changes, these workers no longer experienced as much oppression and had less of an incentive to revolt. Thus, in those countries, Marx's predicted revolutions never took place.

Marx's predictions of the future led to efforts that prevented the very events he predicted—and changed the course of history.

At worst, this book will help you prepare your body, your family, and your community for the Republican Party's planned civil war. In the event of such a conflict, it will also help you and other justice-loving people work *with* one another instead of *against* each other. (The GOP and many of its complicitors will make every effort to drive wedges between you and your compatriots, split you into groups, and incite those groups to rip each other's hearts out. More about this in Chapter 37.)

But if enough people use this book's insights, and its individual and communal embodied practices, their response to attempted mayhem may be swift, courageous, energetic, and resilient. In

---

55  In many cases, workers continued to be exploited and mistreated—but not so badly that they felt compelled to revolt.

the face of such firm resistance and resolve, the attempted gang violence may be quickly thwarted and a full-scale civil war averted.

An even more positive outcome is also possible. Perhaps—because so many people will embrace Somatic Abolitionism, and regularly practice reps—Republican leaders and their complicitors may be compelled to avoid calling for war in the first place.

Better still: perhaps a few party leaders will follow in the footsteps of the influential capitalists who read Marx a century ago. They may read this book, see the danger that lurks in their support of totalitarianism, and instead choose to embrace justice, unfettered democracy, the orderly transfer of power, and the liberation of all Americans.

## BODY PRACTICE
## TAKING THE COMING WAR SERIOUSLY

If our country descends into a civil war or widespread chaos, all of your usual strategies for avoiding and reducing conflict will likely fail.

Should this war occur, it will involve force, violence, and broken bodies. You will not be able to talk to your enemies, or work things out with them, or come to some kind of settlement. Their goal will be to hurt you, capture you, or murder you. Do not forget that in the January 6, 2021 attack on the US Capitol, five people died, and a hundred forty police officers were injured.

If your body still gives you the message, *That won't happen where I live, and it certainly won't happen to me,* please Google "Tulsa race massacre," and read about the incident. Then Google "Duluth 1920 lynchings" and read about those. Then Google and read about "Charlottesville 2017." If you have a white body, this is especially important.

I strongly urge you to put together a "bug-out pack" or "go pack." This is a backpack containing essential items to help you get by in an emergency. Keep this pack in a place where you can get to it quickly and easily. Should you have to leave your home with little or no notice, you can quickly grab your pack and hustle out of there.

Here are some things you might put in your bug-out pack[56]:

---

56    This is of course not an exhaustive list, but a general guide and a starting point.

- a good first-aid kit
- a bag of toiletries
- any important prescription medications or supplements
- acetaminophen, ibuprofen, or some other pain reliever
- photocopies of your driver's license, your passport, and a major credit card
- a few bottles of water
- a spare phone charger (and perhaps a spare phone)
- a powerful flashlight and extra batteries
- a police-band radio
- a few changes of underwear and socks
- a change of clothes or two
- a personal alarm
- one or more weapons that you legally own, for self-protection

If your body is now becoming unsettled or activated, stay with whatever you experience for as long as you can. Notice what you experience in your body, including any:

- vibrations
- images and thoughts
- meanings, judgments, stories, and explanations
- behaviors, movements, actions, impulses, and urges
- affect and emotions
- sensations

If you like, soul scribe about what your body is experiencing right now.

The longer you can stay with any fear, dread, constriction, or quaking, the more you will condition and temper your body for any violence that may later emerge.

# 20

# RACIALIZED TRAUMA

*Achieving Trump's disruptive goals on a national scale might be simpler than we want to admit. An NBC poll reveals Trump commands the loyalty of 87 percent of Republicans—even after the Jan. 6 assault. And his followers have successfully employed a cultural tool so powerful many even deny it even exists: White privilege.*

Malcolm Nance

*If you are silent about your pain, they'll kill you and say you enjoyed it.*

Zora Neale Hurston

*Failing to acknowledge the fact that the original sins have not been atoned for, acting as if the recompense is firmly in the past, adequate and complete, is to perpetuate the injustices and pave the way for future transgression and brutality. Cruelty and bigotry and white impunity are built into the system. And by remaining silent about historical truths, couching them in euphemism, or rewriting them altogether, we ensure that the system will not change.*

Mary L. Trump

> *Trauma has been normalized in the Black*
> *community, but not healing.*
> Charlamagne Tha God

> *The white collective can't*
> *conceive of a free Black body.*
> Rev. angel Kyodo williams

*Racialized trauma* is the body's response to the stresses of white-body supremacy. This trauma haunts hundreds of millions of Americans, and many millions more in other nations.

In America, this trauma has lived in our bodies for at least fifteen generations. During that time, it has destroyed or limited the lives of many, many millions of people of all skin pigmentations.

You didn't ask for this trauma. You don't deserve it. And you didn't create it. But you may be doing things to keep it locked inside your body, and you may be passing it on to others.

If you've ever wondered why the subject of race is a flash point for so much anger, fear, resentment, and defensiveness, it's because these experiences are natural and common trauma responses. Start a conversation around race with someone, regardless of their body pigmentation, and they may soon move into a *flee*, or *fight*, or *freeze*, or *fawn*, or *annihilate* response. Often you can easily observe this emerging in their body—in its movements, constriction, vibes, or tone of voice. You may notice your own body doing the same thing.

Racialized trauma is not a defect, a sin, or a source of shame. Remember, *trauma is a human body's normal response to an experience that it perceives as overwhelming.* Remember, too, that it is an opportunity for healing. It is a way for our bodies to temporarily contain and manage clean pain—so that later, under the right circumstances, that pain can be accessed, metabolized, and healed.

Because trauma lives primarily in our bodies—not mostly in our emotions or cognitive minds—healing from racialized trauma needs to begin in our bodies. The reps that appear throughout this book—especially the five anchors described in Chapter 21—can encourage and support this healing.

Most Americans of all skin tones have at least some racialized trauma lodged in their bodies. This is not because they're bigots, or weaklings, or immature, or dysfunctional. It's because trauma is the body's normal and appropriate response to extreme or long-term stress—in this case, the stress of white-body supremacy.

The most telltale symptoms of racialized trauma in white bodies include a profound lack of racial acuity and agility, high anxiety and/or defensiveness around race, an extremely low trauma-response threshold in any discussion around race, and, in many cases, intense denial about the three previous symptoms. The devout and vehement variants of WBS are of course also symptoms of racialized trauma in white bodies.

The most common symptoms of racialized trauma in bodies of culture are the classic symptoms of trauma in general. Many of these are mostly physical—sleep problems, obesity, heart palpitations, digestive issues, high blood pressure, fatigue or exhaustion, jaw or mouth pain, menstrual cramps, muscle tension, headaches, intense sweating, nausea, and a general weathering of the cardiovascular, endocrine, reproductive, and musculoskeletal systems. Other common symptoms include intense fear or anxiety; a sense of helplessness; a sense of being an impostor, or inherently unworthy or inferior; and/or bouts of racialized shame. Other, somewhat less-common symptoms—such as uterine fibroids and an ongoing sense of urgency—are often not recognized as having racialized trauma as a source. Then there are the collective symptoms, such as lower life expectancy and higher infant mortality rates.

As I observed a few paragraphs ago, you didn't ask for this trauma. You don't deserve it. And you didn't create it. But if you sense that racialized trauma is stuck in your body, only you can take the necessary steps to heal it.

In this sense, racialized trauma is much like an infection. You didn't ask or attempt to become infected. But once you've fallen ill, it is your responsibility to heal—not through some ostensible act of will, but through an embodied, emergent process.

Like all trauma, racialized trauma can manifest as a spring-loaded trap in your body—an urgent stuckness that's ready to instantly activate whenever your lizard brain tells it to. But this isn't just an individual phenomenon. Because we all swim in the water of white-body supremacy, our whole culture is similarly spring-loaded, poised to snap into a sudden, collective trauma response.

As you'll continue to discover, this book is not just a guide to maintaining safety, sanity, and stability under dangerous circumstances. It's also about using emerging moments of peril and possibility to heal our personal and collective racialized trauma.

## BODY PRACTICE
# ENVISIONING PERIL

Most living Americans have not witnessed a serious, widespread attempt to overthrow their government. As a result, many of our bodies—especially white bodies—sense that what is now the United States will remain intact indefinitely. We experience a stability and safety in our bodies that the citizens of Myanmar, Egypt, Iran, Nepal, Sudan, Venezuela, Yemen, and many other countries cannot.

Yet this sense of safety and stability is false. Before you and I were born, on what is now American soil, there were two widespread revolts: the American Revolution, which killed 6,800 people, and the American Civil War, which killed 620,000.[57] (This is of course the same soil on which many millions of Black bodies were enslaved and many millions of Indigenous people murdered.)

I often hear people in the media describe the possibility of another widespread revolt as "unthinkable" or "unimaginable." What they actually mean, though, is *My body hasn't been conditioned to handle the energy of an attempted coup or widespread mob violence.*

The practice below can help your own body become more discerning and less vulnerable.

Go to a safe and fairly busy public place that you've never been to before, such as an unfamiliar shopping area, bus station, food court, or hospital lobby. Bring paper and a pen with you.

---

57  There were also, of course, smaller military operations—some defense operations, some revolts—by Indigenous nations. These were failed attempts to keep their homelands from being stolen and declared American soil. I should also note that in 1775, in what is now Canada, residents faced and vanquished both a rebellion in Nova Scotia and an attempted invasion by Rebel forces—American revolutionaries—in Quebec.

Find a spot where you can sit quietly and comfortably for a few minutes without being in anyone's way.

Orient your body for safety, using the body practice "Orienting for Safety" from Chapter 10.

Pick a nearby entrance or opening; then focus your gaze on that spot.

Imagine that a crowd of white bodies, many of them armed, is charging through that entrance or opening toward you. Everyone is shouting; some are carrying flags. Behind them, filling up all the visible space, are more armed white bodies, along with one Black body that appears to be part of the mob. They see you and head straight for you.

*Pause.* Close your eyes briefly if you like.

What are you experiencing in your body right now? Where does it constrict? What changes do you sense in your breathing, heartbeat, and body temperature? What do you notice shifting, quaking, or activating?

Now open your eyes. Notice what your body experiences now, including any:

- vibrations
- images and thoughts
- meanings, judgments, stories, and explanations
- behaviors, movements, actions, impulses, and urges
- affect and emotions
- sensations

Soul scribe about your body's experience.

Lastly, ask yourself, *If what I envisioned were to actually happen, what would I do?* Write down the answer to this question.

Repeat this practice at least once a month for several months, at a new location each time.

## BODY PRACTICE
## BYPASSING AND OVERRIDING

One of the keys to working with trauma, conflict, or extreme stress is understanding the difference between *settling, resting, bypassing,* and *overriding*. The first two can support growth and healing, while the other two can create problems and dirty pain.

In the heat of conflict, many people try to *calm* their body rather than *settle* it. When their body quakes or constricts, they try to instill calm through meditation, yoga, a mantra, or a visualization. Instead of leaning into whatever pain, quaking, or constriction they experience, they use one of these techniques to dissociate, or move into a trance state, or otherwise bypass their current experience.

If you have long experience with meditation, yoga, mantras, or visualizations, you know that this is a misuse of these practices, which are designed to make bodies more present to whatever is happening, not less. *Only by being present with an experience can we metabolize it.* This is particularly true of experiences involving race, which carry a four-hundred-year-old charge.

Other folks may try to override their pain or discomfort by focusing their attention in a different direction. For instance, if they have a conflict with a coworker, they reflexively leave the room rather than resource themselves and deal with the issue. If they dread making a difficult decision about their dying father's medical care, they binge-watch *Schitt's Creek* instead. If a discussion about race makes their stomach and shoulders tighten, they quickly change the subject.

As you do any body practice in this book, if you find yourself trying to dodge rather than accept what your body is experiencing, *pause*.

Then take three slow, deep breaths. Bring yourself back to the here and now by grounding and orienting your body with the practice from Chapter 3; or using the five anchors from Chapter 21, which follows; or doing one or more of the other practices in this book that your body may call for.

# 21

# THE FIVE ANCHORS

*Slow down, I tell myself . . . slow down. The risk to my neighbors by my rushing to a most certain and final judgment in very uncertain and temporary situations far outweighs the risk to myself. I'm often wrong in the initial assessment of chaotic scenes, and so I try to be wrong silently, allowing my judgment to catch up to my reactions, to allow my perceptions to catch up with my vision. Slow down.*

Patrick Skinner

*Be calm when the unthinkable arrives.*

Timothy Snyder

We primarily experience sensations in our bodies, not our minds. That's why, in order to process and work through any strong emotion—as well as any situation that we perceive as a potential threat—we need to first recognize it in our body. Then we need to fully experience it—and then metabolize it. It's like digesting food.

Of all the body practices you'll encounter in this book, the five anchors are among the most important. I consider them the foundational practice for conditioning and tempering your body, your mind, and your soul.

When you experience a stressful situation or conflict, and strong emotions arise in you, pay close attention to your body.

If you sense that you may fall into a trauma response—that is, you may *fight, flee, freeze, fawn,* or *annihilate*—then use this internal process[58]:

- Soothe and resource yourself to quiet your mind, calm your heart, and settle your body.

- *Pause,* then notice and discern the sensations, vibrations, and emotions in your body instead of reacting to them.

- Accept and tolerate the discomfort instead of trying to flee from it.

- Stay present and in your body as you move through the unfolding experience, with all its ambiguity and uncertainty, and respond from the best parts of yourself.

- Metabolize any energy that remains.

These anchoring practices can help you stay flexible, engaged, and present. They can help you stay aware of your environment, your bodily sensations, your emotions, and your thoughts. They can help you develop grit and discernment. Most important of all, they can help you slow yourself down so you can discern what's happening and make deliberate choices, rather than react in a trauma response.

When you first use the anchors in any new situation, you'll normally employ the first four anchors in sequence. You soothe yourself to calm down and notice what you're experiencing in your body. You become aware of your bodily sensations in order to accept them. You use this awareness as a baseline, so you can pull yourself back to the present when your brain starts to stray. This entire initial sequence may take only a few seconds.

However, once you're moving through the experience, you may find yourself practicing all four anchors at once, or moving back and forth among them.

The more you practice these anchors—the more reps you do—the more capable and comfortable you'll get with using them. The more agility and discernment you build, the more you condition

---

58   These anchors have many progenitors, most notably the Crucible 4 Points of Balance (crucible4points.com), which were devised by one of my mentors, Dr. David Schnarch.

and temper your body. Eventually the anchors will become your natural first response to conflict or difficulty.

Let's look at the anchors in detail, so you can be ready to practice them whenever the heat under you gets turned way up.

**Anchor 1:** Soothe and resource yourself to quiet your mind, calm your heart, and settle your body.

- If you are in imminent physical danger, get to safety as quickly as you can. If there is nowhere safe to go, move your body into the most protected spot or position you can.

- For the next few seconds, don't say anything—no matter how much you might want to, or how much you have to say, or how chaotic the situation is, or how loudly someone is shouting at you. Just breathe.

- If you can, and it's safe to do so, sit down. Put your hands in your lap or on your knees.

- *Pause.* Take a breath—or two or three.

- Mentally tell yourself, *Stay calm* or *Keep it together* or (my own favorite) *Calm the fuck down.*

- If disengaging and leaving temporarily is possible, go to the bathroom. Say, "I need to use the john"; then find a bathroom, go in, and close the door. I know this sounds silly. But in many situations, it's the best way to get two minutes alone to catch your breath and move into Anchor 2.

- If you can't leave, do something else to slow things down. Take a long, slow drink from your water bottle; open or close a window; or slowly put down whatever you're holding.

**Anchor 2:** Notice the sensations, vibrations, and emotions in your body instead of reacting to them.

- Pay attention to what your body experiences in your clothes. Notice how and where your body touches your underwear, your shirt, your pants, your skirt, your socks or stockings, your hat.

- Notice any other body sensations: your back against the chair, your tongue against the roof of your mouth, the wind blowing against your face. Move into and mentally name each sensation: heat, cold, tightness, relaxation, hollowness, looseness, weakness, trembling.
- As thoughts, emotions, images, and urges arise, don't follow them. Stay with your body and its sensations.

**Anchor 3:** Accept the discomfort instead of trying to flee from it.

- When you experience an urge to tamp down or push away the discomfort, don't. Keep your attention focused directly on it. Stay with it.
- When you get the impulse to analyze or think about the discomfort, bring yourself back to the discomfort itself.
- When your mind spits out strategies for what to do next, don't grab onto them. Just stay with the discomfort.
- When thoughts or images about the past or future pop up, let them float past you. Stay in your body.

**Anchor 4:** Stay present and in your body as you move through the unfolding experience, with all its ambiguity and uncertainty, and respond from the best parts of yourself.

- Continue to use the first three anchors to hold onto yourself.
- At the same time, slowly move into the heat, peril, and possibility of the moment. Let yourself go forward into the unfolding unknown, breath by breath.
- If you find yourself focusing on the future or the past, use the first three anchors to bring yourself back to your body and the here and now.
- Find a place in your body where you experience warmth, love, or concern. Focus on that spot.
- Don't try to know what will happen next. You can't.
- Act from the best parts of yourself. As events unfold, you'll sense what these parts are.

Anchor 4 always involves uncertainty—not only about what will happen, but about how long it will take. Events may take only seconds to play out, or they may unfold over minutes or hours. Throughout this process, if you sense that you are starting to become overwhelmed, *pause* again as soon as you can. If necessary (and possible), remove yourself from the situation, *pause* for a time, and return to the unfolding events when you are ready.

**Anchor 5:** Metabolize any energy that remains.

If you watch animals in the wild, you'll see that after a high-stress situation has passed, they'll instinctively discharge their built-up energy. A zebra that has just outrun a lion will vigorously shake itself or ripple the skin along its back. Other animals will roll on the ground, or run in a circle, or pick brief mock fights with each other. They're metabolizing their excess energy.

After you have been in the heat of a conflict, this same kind of energy is bottled up in your body. But we humans need to metabolize it differently than animals do. We need to process it internally by pausing, reflecting on what we have been through, and absorbing what it may have taught us.

This is sometimes done in the moment, but often it happens later. Sometimes it occurs suddenly, in a rush of bodily understanding. More likely, though, it gets metabolized slowly and gradually, over minutes or hours—or even days or weeks—in the same way that a meal digests or a wound heals.

These five anchors are not tactical or technical. Their use is an art, not a science. They are not so much plans to carry out as ways to live into uncertainty in real time.

Using the five anchors can help you move through difficult situations, defuse highly charged encounters, and stay focused and present when the people around you are losing their minds. If our country does fall into civil war, they may even save your life.

That said, don't use the five anchors only during life reps. They are just as useful for tempering and conditioning your bodymind while you do an invited rep—or as *their own* invited rep, which you can add to almost any situation.

Over time, the five anchors will help you develop a protective, thickened skin; a fortified mindset (or, more accurately, *bodymindset*); and a light, malleable heart—one that you and others can readily access.

Compare this with the outcomes of reflexively retreating into dirty pain: a thin skin, a hardened heart, and an unfortified mindset.

Which would you rather have at the center of your life?

## BODY PRACTICE
# LIVING INTO THE FIVE ANCHORS

The five anchors are the foundational practice for conditioning and tempering your bodymind. Plan to use them, time after time, as stresses and conflicts emerge.

In times of great conflict, uncertainty, or peril, you may need to use the five anchors regularly, in one encounter after another. The greater or more frequent the stress, the more important the anchors become, and the more helpful they can be.

The next time your body senses potential conflict—the beginning of a potential life rep—pay close attention to this bodily message. Then use the five anchors to:

- Soothe and resource yourself to quiet your mind, calm your heart, and settle your body.

- *Pause*, then notice and discern the sensations, vibrations, and emotions in your body instead of reacting to them.

- Accept and tolerate the discomfort instead of trying to flee from it.

- Stay present and in your body as you move through the unfolding experience, with all its ambiguity and uncertainty, and respond from the best parts of yourself.

- Metabolize any energy that remains.

The first few times you use the five anchors:

After the encounter has passed, or the situation has simmered down, find a quiet spot to be alone for a few minutes. Mentally review what happened during the encounter. Pay special attention to what arose in your body. Note any:

- vibrations
- images and thoughts
- meanings, judgments, stories, and explanations
- behaviors, movements, actions, impulses, and urges
- affect and emotions
- sensations

If you like, soul scribe about your experience.

# 22

# PLANTATION ETHICS

*America and Afghanistan are the two places I've been where people carrying assault rifles think of themselves as the chosen ones and the rest as subhumans and are committed to the project of destroying a democracy with violence.*

Umair Haque

*If you are Black, you were born in jail, in the North as well as the South. Stop talking about the South. As long as you are South of the Canadian border, you are South.*

Malcolm X

*Too often we hold fast to the clichés of our forebears. We subject all facts to a prefabricated set of interpretations. We enjoy the comfort of opinion without the discomfort of thought.*

John F. Kennedy

*True growth comes when you explore your shadows.*

Devi Brown

On American plantations in the 1600s through 1800s, each plantation owner was the sole local authority. With few limitations, he did whatever he pleased. If you were an enslaved person on a plantation, its owner could legally rape, torture, kill, or sell you or your loved ones at any time. He controlled your body and your choices. He could rape you for pleasure, production, or profit— or simply to dominate you, humiliate you, and make you suffer. He and others had unfettered access to Black bodies. On his land, which had perhaps been stolen from its Indigenous inhabitants, he was a despot and, effectively, a cruel god.

Plantation ethics were not built on justice or morality. They were built on violence, raw power, and racial domination. There was a feralness to them that is echoed more recently by the Taliban, Boko Haram, the Myanmar military, the government of China, and the mass shootings that have become everyday occurrences in America.[59] They were also a more nuanced (and more modern) version of the ethics the conquistadors brought from Europe to the Americas centuries earlier: *We're white people with guns, cannons, lots of other weapons, and the full support of our God. Do what we say, or we'll kill you. We might kill you anyway.*[60]

This was the creed of the plantation owner and his family members: *I do whatever I want, to any Black body I want, whenever I want, using every tool at my disposal: rape, fear, humiliation, rumor mongering, lies, scripture, incarceration, violence, murder. For Black bodies on my land, I am the only authority and the only person who matters. I dominate; Black bodies obey. On my land, white safety, comfort, and leisure are always more important than Black humanness.*

*Furthermore, my complete domination of Black bodies extends beyond the borders of my land. Slave patrols will enforce my claim on any Black body I own—even one who escapes to the North. My influence—*

---

59  My body first sensed that our country was headed for civil war, or something akin to it, after the 2012 mass killing of twenty-six people at Sandy Hook Elementary School in Newtown, Connecticut. The political right's response to these horrifying murders was a call for prayers; a strident call for more guns (American gun sales rose by three million in the four months after the killings); a huge, aggressive, and completely successful push against any form of gun legislation; and an absurd, cruel, easily debunked, yet widely spread and fairly widely believed counternarrative that no one was hurt in the incident, which was ostensibly staged by the Deep State as a plot to advance gun control. As I write this chapter in August 2021, Republican politicians and media figures are spreading multiple equally false, and equally easily disproven, counternarratives about COVID-19. Belief in these false narratives has caused the COVID-related deaths of tens of thousands of loyal GOP followers. Notably, the more deaths these stories cause, the more fiercely many Republican voters embrace those stories and spread them (as well as the virus). It is not too strong to say that the GOP in 2021 encouraged, welcomed, and celebrated death. A widely popular political movement with such a focus can only be disastrous for any country.

60  As Dr. Chanda Prescod-Weinstein has noted, "[A] curious feature of enlightened Europe was the obsession not just with conquering everything, but also with justifying abominable behavior."

*and my right to kidnap and dominate Black bodies—extends north not merely to the Mason-Dixon line but to the Canadian border.*

Plantation owners also dominated the poor whites who worked for them with cruelty and feralness, although poor white bodies had some legal protections that Black ones did not.

In the eighteenth and nineteenth centuries, fewer than 1 percent of white Southerners actually owned plantations. Nevertheless, enslavement and plantation ethics extended far and wide. During the first half of the nineteenth century, a third of all white Southern families enslaved at least one African American; on average, they enslaved and dominated four to five. And the ethics of plantation ownership spread into the bodies of many white Americans.

Built into the creed of the plantation owner and his family was a paradox. At its center was an insistence that the white male owner be the sole authority over his land and the people he enslaved. This very insistence made many plantation owners deeply distrustful of all other forms of authority. The struggle between these two irreconcilable positions lodged deeply in many plantation owners' bodies. We see this same struggle playing out today among many white-bodied Americans, especially white Republicans and many of their complicitors.

Fast forward to today. In 2022, many white bodies continue to live (or do their best to live) by plantation ethics. This is often the case for bodies with the vehement or devout forms of white-body supremacy. It is also the case for former president Trump, who saw the entire United States not as a federation of fifty distinct states, but as his plantation. "I'm the only one that matters," Trump famously said in a 2017 TV interview. Later, he told America's governors, "If you don't dominate, you're wasting your time." On January 6, 2021, he urged his supporters—who were and are overwhelmingly white—to subvert democracy, storm the US Capitol, and commit widespread violence.

Remember the famous 2021 photos of a Texas border agent on horseback grabbing a terrified Haitian who was attempting to cross the US border?[61] Such images, while disturbing enough

---

[61] Here are two of those photos: npr.org/2021/09/21/1039230310/u-s-border-agents-haiti-migrants-horses-photographer-del-rio and nbcnews.com/politics/white-house/biden-says-officials-seen-chasing-haitians-horseback-will-pay-n1280032.

in their own right, evoked strong historical memories of patrols capturing plantation owners' escaped human property.

White-body supremacy is of course the foundational doctrine of plantation ethics. However, built upon that foundation are seven additional deep-seated convictions that folks with plantation ethics hold—and hold dear:

- The safety, comfort, and leisure of white bodies always trump the liberation, interests, needs, and survival of bodies of culture.

- As someone with a white body, I have the right to do whatever I want to any body of culture I want—especially any Black body.

- It is the natural order of things for white bodies to dominate and receive deference from bodies of culture, particularly Black bodies.

- My white body entitles me to every one of the advantages that plantation ethics enforce.

- Law, policing, and authority in general exist to protect white bodies. I have the power to call on them at any time—or to deputize myself as one of WBS's enforcers.

- Bodies of culture—especially Black bodies—are the cause of the constant weight, constriction, and fear that I experience in my own body.

- White-bodied women and children have a special God-given purity that no body of culture can ever possess. This purity must be defended and protected at all costs—with all such costs always borne by bodies of culture. If a body of culture—especially a Black body—fails to show complete deference to a white-bodied woman, or looks at her strangely, or perhaps even meets her eyes, I am entitled to violently punish, or even kill, that body of culture.

The very word *plantation* is an attempt to sanitize a widespread form of historical brutality. American plantations were forced-labor camps where, for generation upon generation, kidnapping and rape were not only legal but standard practices. People were imprisoned there against their will, compelled to toil for long hours growing cotton and other crops, poorly housed and fed, and frequently abused. Meanwhile, they were paid nothing, and others profited from their labor.[62]

Like enslavement, Southern plantations no longer exist as American institutions.[63] But today plantation ethics continue to live on in a great many American bodies and institutions—as well as in bodies and undemocratic governments around the world. Here are two recent examples:

In 2021, in the middle of the COVID-19 pandemic, Democrats in Congress (with zero votes from Republicans in both houses) passed the American Rescue Plan, which provided $350 billion in COVID-related aid to state, local, territorial, and tribal governments. The governor of Alabama, Kay Ivey, convened a special session of her state's legislature to vote on how to use $400 million of this money. Both houses of the Alabama legislature, which are overwhelmingly Republican (and 76 percent white), voted to use the money to build three new prisons and renovate others. It will not surprise you to learn that most of the people in Alabama's state prisons are Black, even though only 28 percent of the state's residents are.

US House Judiciary Committee chair Jerrold Nadler wrote, "Directing funding meant to protect our citizens from a pandemic to fuel mass incarceration is in direct contravention of the intended purposes of the ARP legislation." But it is a near-perfect example of plantation ethics. It simultaneously reinforces (and signals) white bodies' power to dominate, supports the incarceration of more Black bodies, and also hurts poor white bodies (who make

62 Forced-labor camps are not historical artifacts. Today, China operates them on a massive scale. The Chinese government recently rounded up over half a million Uighurs and other Muslims and forcibly relocated them to these camps. These enslaved people now pick cotton under the watchful eyes of security guards employed by the Chinese government, who practice the Chinese version of plantation ethics. Meanwhile, the Chinese government continues to operate a totalitarian regime built on overt Chinese-body supremacy, which views Uighur and Muslim bodies as less than human and the ethnically Chinese body as the supreme standard against which all other bodies are judged and measured, structurally and philosophically. Contemporary America has its own versions of forced-labor camps: state and federal prisons. In these, workers are paid as little as $1 a day, yet the collective value of their labor is estimated at over $1 billion per year.

63 Actually, many plantation sites and buildings do live on today as retreat centers, wedding destinations, and rental halls for parties, conferences, and other such gatherings.

up the majority of the remaining inmates). It also diverts money away from other potentially lifesaving efforts.

Here is a more personal, and more familiar, example of plantation ethics. When Amy Cooper and Christian Cooper encountered each other in New York City's Central Park, Amy was breaking the law by allowing her dog to run free. After Christian asked her to put her dog on a leash, Amy called 911 and announced, "There is an African American man . . . threatening myself and my dog. Please send the cops immediately."

Amy's message to Christian was a pure distillation of plantation ethics: *I'm white, so the laws don't apply to me. I can do whatever I want. And because you're Black, I can bear false witness against you. Now I'm going to have you arrested—and maybe beaten or killed—even though you did nothing wrong and I'm the one who broke the law. Why am I doing this? Because I can.*

In the twenty-first century, one of the most common—and most taken-for-granted—remnants of plantation ethics is often called *the white gaze.* The white gaze can be as simple as a half second of eye contact or as complex as a full interaction. Its core message is *Stay in line—or fall in line—with the rules and expectations of white-body supremacy.* The white gaze always includes an implied threat of punishment, retribution, or physical harm if the other person fails to comply. It is a subtle form of policing, self-deputizing, threatening, and coercion.

The white gaze is meant to be normalizing and controlling. Its purpose is to coerce people into policing themselves to conform to WBS, by activating their own internalized WBS.

The white gaze is widely used by people in authority, such as teachers, judges, police, security guards, bus drivers, and store managers—but also, sometimes, by sales clerks, cashiers, bank tellers, restaurant servers, baristas, and bartenders. As we'll see in Chapter 41, it is also commonly employed during potential conflicts, when a white body deputizes another white body to control a body of culture. Sometimes a white body will deputize themselves for this purpose.

The white gaze is also used by white bodies on other white bodies, typically to enlist (or demand) their help in controlling one or more bodies of culture. (I'll say more about this in Chapter 41.)

A cousin of the white gaze is what I call *protective vibing*, which is a look that one body of culture may give another. Through this look, they attempt to protect the other body of culture by wordlessly encouraging them to stay in line and not challenge white authority. The underlying message is, *Neither of us is safe right now. For our own protection, we need to temporarily follow the demands of white-body supremacy. So, for your sake and mine, you need to toe the line.*

It's not hard to see how the white gaze has evolved from the watchful and suspicious gaze of the plantation overseer. It can also be traced back to the scrutiny of white sentries, who stood guard in forts built to maintain control of land that was, in many cases, stolen from Indigenous people.

In situations where white bodies experience discomfort, or realize they are at a disadvantage, they will often spontaneously deploy the white gaze in an attempt to enforce WBS. Karens and Kevins routinely use the white gaze in this way. So did Amy Cooper—although she turbocharged it.

## BODY PRACTICE
## YOU AND YOUR KIND

No one wants to be targeted as an enemy. Yet creating multiple classes of enemies—what therapist, mediator, and lawyer Bill Eddy calls *fantasy villains*[64]—is at the heart of every authoritarian's attempt to seize power.

Find a quiet, safe spot where you can be alone for a few minutes. Bring pen and paper with you. Sit quietly and comfortably as you take a few deep, slow breaths.

Imagine that you are in a relatively busy commercial area, walking down the sidewalk alone. Suddenly, a large, muscular white man comes charging out of the door of a shop, scowling. He walks quickly up to you and blocks your path. Then he leans toward you and begins shouting: "You and your kind are destroying America! *Get the fuck out of my country!*" He points a finger in your face. "I'm not kidding. Your people's days are numbered. The storm is coming. You can leave, or you can die." He glares at you for another moment, then pushes past you and hurries away.

---

64    The term *fantasy villain* is from Eddy's very relevant and timely book, *Why We Elect Narcissists and Sociopaths—and How We Can Stop!* As Eddy explains, these fantasy villains are blamed for a *fantasy crisis*—in this case the ostensible stealing of elections from their rightful Republican victors.

Note any of the following as they arise in your body right now:

- vibrations
- images and thoughts
- meanings, judgments, stories, and explanations
- behaviors, movements, actions, impulses, and urges
- affect and emotions
- sensations

Soul scribe about your body's experience.

### If you have a body of culture:

As you do this body practice, pay special attention to any memories that arise, and notice how your body responds to each memory.

If you begin to become overwhelmed, or sense that you may soon slip into a *fight* or *flee* response, *pause*. Stand up and end this body practice. Later, when you sense that you have greater access to resource, do this practice again.

# 23

# PRIMAL REPS

*Repetition is based on body rhythms, so we identify with the
heartbeat, or with walking, or with breathing.*

Karlheinz Stockhausen

*Life is about rhythm. We vibrate, our hearts are
pumping blood, we are a rhythm machine.*

Mickey Hart

*Rhythm . . . is related to the pulse, the heartbeat, the way
we breathe. It rises and falls; it takes us into ourselves;
it takes us out of ourselves.*

Edward Hirsch

*Pause.*

In Chapters 17 and 18, you read about life reps and invited reps. There's also a third type of rep, which I call *primal reps*. These are small, simple movements that make us more aware of our body—and of the energies that move through it.

Primal reps can be done almost anywhere at almost any time. Some of them can be done in groups or pairs, as well as individually.

Primal reps are not New Age practices developed by a yoga or meditation master. They're exactly the opposite. They're practices built into our bodies that are older than the human species. They're also built into the very fabric and flows of creation itself.

Primal reps are very brief and very basic. You practice them almost solely with your body, with minimal cognitive direction.

Most of these primal practices are things your body already does naturally, at least on occasion. For instance, if you're like most people—and most dogs, cats, apes, and many other mammals—you automatically stretch parts of your body when you first wake up or get out of bed. That's a classic primal rep.

In fact, as you'll see, many primal reps are things that many living creatures do, from lower primates to fish to single-cell organisms. These practices tie us back to creation. Each time you do a primal rep, you express the universe and your full participation in it.

As you've moved through this book, you've done some primal reps already. For example, the body practices of curling and uncurling (from Chapter 1), stretching (from Chapter 2), and wiggling (from Chapter 3) are all primal reps.

Here are some general guidelines for doing primal reps:

- Do any primal practice you choose for three breaths at a time, while noticing what you experience in your body. Three breaths equals one rep.

- One rep should give you enough time to pause, focus, and notice what your body is experiencing. But if your body wants to do more than one rep—and if that engenders greater resourcing or energy—then by all means do more.

- Do primal reps often.

- Don't do any primal rep in a situation where it might disturb or distract others. Don't curl up like a fetus at a funeral or sway your hips back and forth while making a presentation at work.

- Do primal reps for as long as you live.

Below are eleven different primal reps. Try all of them. After that, do whichever practices your body wants to do, when it wants to do them, in whatever ways it wants.

- **Swaying.** Using your hips—and while staying balanced—sway from side to side, or forward and backward.

- **Touching.** Place your hand gently on any part of your body that asks to be touched. Let your hand rest there for three breaths. Notice what you experience in that body part, in your hand, and in the rest of your body.

- **Squeezing.** Gently squeeze any part of your body with your hand or with two or more of your fingers; hold the squeeze for three breaths; then release. As a variation, gently curl your fingers into relaxed fists.

- **Pushing and pulling.** While maintaining your balance, gently push against a wall or table; then gently pull yourself back toward it. Or plant your feet shoulder-width apart, and then make pushing and pulling movements into the space around you.

- **Stretching.** Stretch out any body part that wants to be stretched, in any direction that your body wants to stretch; hold for three breaths; release.

- **Softening your face.** Relax all the muscles in your face and head. Let your eyelids droop (but not close). Let your jaw hang. Let your tongue fall to the bottom of your mouth.

- **Softening your eye muscles.** With your eyelids open, relax the muscles around your eyeballs, so that you are not holding them in place, but letting them simply rest in their sockets. Then *pause* for a few breaths, and notice what changes you experience in your body. (This is not about focusing your gaze but about resting the muscles that surround your eyeballs.)

- **Pumping.** Using your hips and knees, gently pump your body up and down.

- **Standing curl and uncurl.** Push out your chest and belly, curling your spine forward. Then pull your spine back and your shoulders forward, so that your upper body curls in the opposite direction.

- **Humming.** Take a deep, slow, full breath. For five seconds, simply hum, at whatever pitch and volume your body wishes. Notice what it experiences at the beginning of the hum, during the hum, at the end of the hum, and after the hum, when silence reappears. Then, for five seconds, take another breath and try a different pitch, or a different volume, or a different amount of air. Over five breaths, vary your humming in whatever way you wish. For each breath, notice what you experience in your body at each of the four parts of the hum.

- **Working with your joints.** Move your head in a few slow circles; repeat in the opposite direction. Do the same with any or all of these joints, one by one: shoulders, wrists, hips, knees, ankles. If you like, do this with your thumbs and then each finger, one by one.

At first, you may have questions about primal reps such as these: *Which ones should I do? In what order should I do them? How fast or slow should I go? How many different primal reps should I do each day? Can I do more than one type of primal rep at once? Should I spend ten minutes a day doing them, or twenty, or thirty? Which ones are best for someone with neck issues? How do I know if I'm doing a primal rep correctly? Are ten reps better than two, or are ten reps too many?*

The answer to each of these questions is the same: do what your body prompts you to do.

Approach these primal reps with openness and curiosity. Notice what arises, emerges, or gets released as you do each practice. You may discover that certain practices help excavate and release trauma that has gotten stuck somewhere in your body.

Primal reps are *not* physical or spiritual exercises; forms of relief from physical or emotional ailments; forms of self-improvement or self-actualization; things to perform in front of others in order to demonstrate your wokeness or spiritual advancement; things to become a supposed expert in; things to lead special workshops on; and/or things to "teach" and charge money for.[65]

Over time, with enough reps, many of these practices will naturally become parts of your life. In the process, they may also steadily deepen your sense of resource.

## BODY PRACTICE
## YOUR ELEMENTAL BODY

The ancient Africans and Greeks—and, surely, some other ancient peoples as well—spoke of the universe being made of several basic elements, including earth, air, water, and fire.

---

65   If you do any of these things, people will call you an asshole—and they will be right.

Our bodies are made of these same elements. Our bones are calcium, the fifth most abundant element on our planet—and a part of the Earth's crust. Our breath is the constant inflow and outflow of air. Our blood is an ongoing, enormously complex flow of water. And our entire body, like that of every warm-blooded creature, is a 24/7 furnace.

Below are some very simple primal reps that will help you condition and temper your bodymind in subtle ways. I recommend doing all four in the sequence below, spending five or six breaths on each element.

**Earth/bone:** Lightly tap some parts of your body where the shapes of bones are visible—your jaw, your ankles, your elbows, your knuckles, your forehead.

**Air/breath:** Follow the air as each new breath moves into your nose, down your windpipe, into your lungs and belly, and back out again.

**Water/blood:** Place your attention on your heart as it squeezes and releases in your chest. See if you can sense the flow of blood radiating from your heart into the rest of your body.

**Fire/heat:** Place your attention on your skin. First, notice any heat or coolness in the environment outside you. Then shift your attention slightly, and notice any heat that emerges from inside of you.

Do this body practice often. It may seem very basic, but you may be surprised at how much it can expand your awareness.

## BODY PRACTICE
# GROANING, MOANING, GROWLING, AND GRUNTING

Before humans invented languages, we vocalized through low-frequency vibrations that came from deep in our throats and bellies. Today, in a world of well over six thousand languages, our bodies continue to naturally groan, moan, grunt, and growl.

Take ten deep, slow breaths. Each time as you exhale, let your body grunt, moan, growl, or groan as it wants to—loudly or softly, briefly or at length.

Notice what you experience in your body with each exhalation.

# 24

# WHITE BODIES AND THE ENERGIES OF RACE

*Fighting racism requires stamina, strategy, but most importantly love: a love greater than the hate. It requires a sense of shared humanity that is bigger than the fear engendered by those who use racism as a diversionary tactic from their own mortal failings, greed, and ineptitude. . . . Together, we rise.*

Sarah Bellamy

*The great fraud of the construct of whiteness is that it has coerced and convinced most white folks to no longer see their own oppression.*

Rev. angel Kyodo williams

*There's nothing that makes white Americans more uncomfortable than discussing race.*

Newt Gingrich

*There is no need for white people to fall into guilt or despair because the structures we were born into ensured the pervasive message of the superiority of white people. It is no one individual's fault. There is, however, a desperate need for white people to identify the workings of Whiteness and make daily choices that fracture the domination and exclusion it asserts.*

Jacqueline Battalora

*Don't let your past create your future. Everyone can change.*

Nipsey Hussle

Race has its own unique charge, texture, weight, and speed. The ability to hold and work with these energies isn't inborn. It needs to be acquired through effort and practice. It's like learning to play the guitar or make potato salad without raisins.

Most bodies of culture acquire this ability when they're young. We have to, because it's so closely tied to our survival. Some of us learn it purely through the hard knocks of life. Others, like me, are more fortunate: our parents and other elders carefully coach us in a variety of racial survival skills. We also learn it by observing the actions of our elders—especially what we watch them lean into and recoil from.

In contrast, most white American bodies have little agility, acuity, or grit around race. This isn't because of some ability they lack. Most white bodies simply haven't had the opportunity or need to learn to work with the energies of race—or, in most cases, an interest in doing so. Throughout their lives, they've been able to fall back on white advantage—and to simply ignore or turn away from issues involving race.[66] Unfortunately, as a result, racialized trauma stays stuck inside their bodies, day after day,

---

66    One reason why George Floyd's murder reverberated around the world was that the multiple videos of his slow, tortuous death could not be ignored by white bodies. The videos were everywhere, and anyone who watched one of them could not dismiss the evidence of their own eyes and ears. That said, I'm writing this about sixteen months after Floyd's murder. In real time, I'm watching as many white bodies who were formerly engaged in and committed to antiracism efforts begin to relapse into a familiar pattern of racial apathy and inaction. Also, Floyd's murderer, Derek Chauvin, is appealing his conviction.

year upon year. It also gets transmitted to later generations as an accepted, standard, and morally acceptable way of being.

Because most white bodies haven't built this agility, acuity, or grit, when they encounter strong energy or stress around race, their racialized trauma can easily get activated. They may then shift into *fight, flee, freeze, fawn,* or *annihilate mode.* Often this means becoming anxious, or angry, or defensive, or tearful. All of these are forms of dirty pain. They may then try to blow this pain through other bodies—especially bodies of culture.

As I said earlier, America will not upend WBS by simply blaming white bodies for this and calling them racists. It's true that, as my brothas and sistas say, sometimes you gotta check a fool hard. But this alone will never be sufficient.

How many white people do you think will respond to being called out with words like these? *Oh, shit—you're right. What I just said or did was racist. How could I not have realized it before? My mistake—and my apology. I now see that I need to dedicate a part of the rest of my life to interrogating my own white-body supremacy, studying its effects on the world, and helping myself and my fellow white-bodied human beings to grow out of it. Thanks for the wake-up call!*

Most white bodies simply have not interrogated their own racialized trauma and metabolized the energy stuck inside it. And WBS cannot be dissolved until a great many white bodies practice this interrogation.

If you have a white body, now is the time for this interrogation, and the potential healing and growth it offers. This book will provide the guidance you need to begin—though, as you'll see, the process requires a lifetime commitment.

You won't—and can't—do this on your own. Together, white bodies also need to develop a *collective* container that can hold the charge, weight, speed, and texture of race. This collective container will be essential for passing on the energies of Somatic Abolitionism from body to body and generation to generation. This book also provides some guidance for beginning that process.

Right now, many white bodies—perhaps many more than you realize—have the right intentions and aspirations for creating a living, embodied antiracist culture. But their bodies aren't yet prepared to turn those aspirations into reality. These white bodies will first need to be tempered and conditioned through reps.

Reps make the difference between good intentions and wise, concerted action—and between losing steam and pressing forward. Without enough reps under your belt, you may have a strong burst of energy for a time. But when the going gets tough— which we both know it sometimes will—you're likely to give up or slow down. However, if you've been practicing enough reps, day after day and month after month, you'll have built the stamina and resilience and grit to keep moving steadily forward.

Please don't confuse a lack of preparation with a lack of ability. If you have a white body, you are already fully equipped with everything you need for its tempering and conditioning around race.

This process of interrogating, tempering, and conditioning will involve some pain, some failure, some discouragement, and some taking of Ls.

Black people often speak about taking Ls—taking losses. But there are two other, equally important Ls that white bodies need to take—the L of learning and the L of leaps of integrity. There's also the L of leaving a legacy. (I'll say more about this in Chapter 30.)

This process may also bring you joy, success, and gratitude— and the development of compassionate humility.

If you have a white body, *pause*.

How is your body responding to the idea that it already has everything it needs to become conditioned and tempered around race?

How is it responding to the recognition that it is fully capable of practicing Somatic Abolitionism—and that SA isn't just for bodies of culture and white progressives?

How is it responding to your awareness that you cannot dodge the challenge of Somatic Abolitionism?

Do not pretend that you are unable to rise to the challenge of SA. You can either accept this challenge, and sometimes make mistakes or fail, or choose to not to take it up at all and accept the consequences of turning away from your own growth and liberation.

When I and my colleagues run workshops and classes on the healing of racialized trauma, we tell participants at the outset, "All kinds of things might emerge in your body. Traumatic energies will probably get released, and they'll need to be worked through. Some of what you experience may be intense, or sudden, or unexpected. Temporarily, you may experience a lot of clean pain. *Pause* and stay with it. You're safe here. We'll support you in moving through the clean pain. Please don't turn it into dirty pain by trying to blow it through other people."

Most participants experience things such as anger, grief, fear, dread, anxiety, shock, panic, constriction, release, shaking, sobbing, sudden recollections of long-forgotten incidents, and a wide range of impulses. But they use the five anchors, stay with what they experience, metabolize the traumatic energies, and begin to heal.

Sometimes people freak out for a short time before settling into the clean pain. Occasionally they'll run out of the room, walk around the block a couple of times—or spend five minutes weeping in the rest room, or go to the nearby Whole Foods and get a giant cookie and a latté (or a big bowl of unspiced kale)—but then they'll return and resume the process. I always welcome them back. Although I don't always say so aloud, I appreciate their resilience and commitment. (At the same time, I also recognize that dissolving WBS requires a great deal more from them—including ongoing resilience, commitment, and the development of a living, embodied antiracist culture among white bodies.)

But occasionally a white body flips into a *fight* and/or *flight* response—and stays there. In front of everyone, they lean into their Karen or Kevin underbelly. They tell me and my colleagues that what we're doing is dangerous or insensitive or unprofessional, that they "feel violated" or "are devastated," that they're going to report us to a therapists' oversight board, and so on. Then they storm out and don't return.

Other white bodies simply leave, and I experience their Karenhood or Kevinhood later. They send me long, accusatory letters and e-mails, citing various authorities, walking me through a list of their own credentials (PhDs they've earned, conference presentations they've done, etc.), and letting me know how righteous and offended they are, and how abominable I and my colleagues are.

Both variations are classic *fight/flight* combinations. The person's body can't contain the energy of racialized trauma that has gotten released, so they freak out, weaponize that energy against my colleagues and me, and disappear.

Yet even this can be the beginning of healing.

Let's recall those folks who fled, then cried their eyes out in a toilet stall, or chowed down on a cookie and a latté, but who came back and picked up where they left off. That demonstrates grit, and it's an important step toward healing.

Now let's look at the people who bailed and didn't come back. They are not defective or failures. They have not declared themselves Kevins or Karens for life. They have not burned any bridges. Like the folks who slipped out to the coffee shop or rest room, they can always return to the healing process. They may no longer want to work with me or my associates (and/or vice versa), but their journey is not over.

This process doesn't have to involve me or one of my associates. Lots of good therapists assist in the healing of trauma, and some specialize in working with racialized trauma.

But the people who bailed and didn't return do need to learn to pause and stay with clean pain. And they need to recognize that their healing will take time, commitment, and lots of practice. Day after day, they will need to get their reps in.


Earlier in this chapter, I wrote that white bodies need to develop a collective container that can handle the charge of race. Creating this collective container will also require time, commitment, and practice—and plenty of trial and error.

I don't know how long this container will take to create. But we need to think in terms of generations, if not centuries. White-body supremacy has been circulating in American bodies—and has been intrinsic to American life—for well over three centuries. That cannot be quickly undone.

My best guess—and it is only a guess—is that it will take roughly nine generations for white Americans to grow a living, embodied antiracist culture, and for the great majority of

Americans of all skin pigmentations to fully live into that culture. If this can be done more quickly, wonderful. But plan on being an early traveler on a long collective journey.

If you have a white body, know that you may not see profound positive results in your lifetime. That is no reason to turn away from the task of individual and collective healing. Regardless of how long the work may take, it begins—or continues—right now, in your own body.

You are not doing this just for yourself, or for me, or for any particular person or cause. You are doing it because you don't want to pass on the cruel legacy of WBS to your children, or to your children's children, for generation upon generation.

The efforts you make will not only support your own healing and growth. They can support the lives of all the people you encounter, whatever their body pigmentation. They can create more room for growth in the bodies of your children, your grandchildren, and their descendants. And, year by year, generation upon generation, they can transform the energies of race into energies of liberation.

## BODY PRACTICE
## RACE AND YOUR MAJOR LIFE EVENT

Pick an important event from your past that was marked by a public ceremony—such as your wedding, your graduation, your confirmation, or the funeral of someone close to you. Then find a group photo of most or all of the people who attended the event.

As you look at this photo, ask yourself, *What percentage of the people are white?* Once you know the answer, notice how your body responds to that degree of whiteness.

Next, ask yourself, *What percentage of the people are bodies of culture?* Notice how your body responds to the answer to this question.

Now ask yourself, *How and why was it that the bodies struck this balance—or imbalance?* Again, note how your body responds to your answer to this question.

If you like, soul scribe in response to this body practice.

*Important:* This practice is not about right versus wrong. It is about noticing what your body experiences.

## BODY PRACTICE
# BLACK BODIES AND WHITE COMFORT

### *If you have a Black body:*

Recall a recent incident in which someone with a white body asked you to comfort or protect them. Mentally relive that incident; then answer these questions:

- What did your body experience when they made the request?
- Did you say yes or no? Why? Did you say anything else?
- What did you experience in your body when you said yes (or no)?
- If you said yes, what was the result of your comfort or protection? What did the white body say and do? How did your body respond to the incident?
- In retrospect, was your comfort or protection genuinely necessary? Was it helpful? Or could the person have soothed or protected themselves?
- If they *had* soothed or protected themselves, how might the situation have evolved differently?

Afterward, soul scribe about your body's experience. Note any:

- vibrations
- images and thoughts
- meanings, judgments, stories, and explanations
- behaviors, movements, actions, impulses, and urges
- affect and emotions
- sensations

### *If you have a white body:*

Recall a recent incident in which you asked someone with a Black body to comfort or protect you. Mentally relive that incident, and then answer these questions:

- What did your body experience that encouraged you to make the request?
- Why did you make the request of that particular body?
- Did the person say yes or no?

- What did you experience in your body when they said yes (or no)?
- If they said yes, what was the result of their comfort or protection? How did your body respond to it?
- In retrospect, was their comfort or protection genuinely necessary? Or could you have soothed or protected yourself?
- If you *had* soothed or protected yourself, how might the situation have evolved differently?

Afterward, soul scribe about your body's experience. Note any:

- vibrations
- images and thoughts
- meanings, judgments, stories, and explanations
- behaviors, movements, actions, impulses, and urges
- affect and emotions
- sensations

## 25

# YOUR SOUL NERVE
# AND SOUL MUSCLE

*I have seen, over and over, the connection between tuning in
to what brings aliveness into our systems and being able to
access personal, relational and communal power.*

adrienne maree brown

*The soul nerve is where we find our sense of belonging and
connection with others. . . . We can use our soul nerve to calm
ourselves, feel comfort and activate when needed. We can work
with our soul nerve to be a powerful tool in perceiving, feeling
and regulating ourselves for comfort and not distress.*

Paula Mangum Sheridan

*The vagus nerve's tendrils extend to many organs,
acting like fiber-optic cables that send instructions to
release enzymes and proteins like prolactin, vasopressin,
and oxytocin, which calm you down.*

Jordan Rosenfeld

*[A] lush psoas conducts electrical and neurological
impulses that can inform, orchestrate, and sustain
your vitality for the long haul.*

Liz Koch

168

In Chapter 15, we saw how the human body naturally receives, amplifies, and broadcasts a variety of physical and energetic signals. Although your entire body participates in processing and sending these signals, two of its organs[67] play a central role: the *vagal nerve* (which I and others call your *soul nerve*) and the *psoas* (which I and others call your *soul muscle*). These two structures are essential to our physical and emotional health, our connection with other bodies, and our body's ongoing interactions with the cosmos.

Your soul nerve unifies your entire nervous system. Your psoas connects the top and bottom halves of your body and is instrumental in maintaining and regulating the energy flows between the two.

Until the final years of the twentieth century, the roles and functions of these two structures were not well understood. However, thanks to the pioneering work of Dr. Stephen Porges (with the soul nerve), Liz Koch (with the soul muscle), and the many talented people who stand on their metaphorical shoulders, we are steadily learning more about both.

These two interactive structures are profoundly intelligent. They help our bodies to mobilize—and, when necessary, immobilize. They are where we experience resonance, dissonance, connection, disconnection, a sense of rightness, and a sense that something is off. They are also gateways to cultivating, experiencing, and deepening resource of all kinds.

Separately and together, both structures support the metabolization of clean pain, the healing of trauma, the process of growing up, and the practices of Somatic Abolitionism. Both naturally express who we are and what we experience. Both resonate with the signals we pick up from inside our own body, from other bodies, from our surroundings, and from the present moment as it unfolds.[68]

---

67  Because these are both physical body structures, they are technically known as organs. However, a more accurate description of each one—and of the human body itself—would be *an ever-emergent biological process.*

68  If you'd like to learn more about these wise and complex body processes, I encourage you to visit the websites of Dr. Stephen Porges (stephenporges.com and polyvagalinstitute.org) and Liz Koch (coreawareness.com).

In *My Grandmother's Hands*, I described the soul nerve this way[69]:

> When your body has an emotional response, such as when your stomach clenches, your voice catches, your pulse races, your shoulders tighten, your breathing quickens, your body braces for impact, or you have a sense that danger is lurking, that's your soul nerve at work. When you feel your heart opening or closing down; when you feel anxious in the pit of your stomach; when you sense that something wonderful or terrible is about to happen; when something feels right or wrong in your gut; when your heart sinks; when your spirit soars; or when your stomach turns in nausea—all of these involve your soul nerve.
>
> When your body feels relaxed, open, settled, and in sync with other bodies, that's your soul nerve functioning. When it feels energized, vibrant, and full of life, that's also your soul nerve. When it feels tight, constricted, and self-protective, that's your soul nerve, too. And whenever you have a *fight, flee, freeze, fawn,* or *annihilate* response, that involves your soul nerve as well. . . . Another purpose is precisely the opposite: to receive and spread the message of *It's okay; you're safe right now; you can relax.*
>
> Your soul nerve is vital to your health and well being. It regulates your breathing, heart rate, and blood pressure. It helps prevent inflammation. And it can reduce pain, improve your mood, and help you manage fear. We also know that your soul nerve is intimately involved with how your body interacts with other bodies, and with how your body makes memories. Without your soul nerve, you literally would not be human.

Your psoas—your soul muscle—is equally vital to your well-being. While your soul nerve generates and responds to electrical signals, your soul muscle responds to the flows and movements

---

69   I updated the second paragraph of this quotation from *"fight, flee,* or *freeze"* to *"fight, flee, freeze, fawn,* or *annihilate."*

of your body's many fluids. A healthy psoas is itself very fluid, supple, and juicy.

Your soul muscle helps your body to experience a sense of coherence, integrity, and safety—or, when something is wrong, the lack of these. It locates your body in space and time. (The body practice of grounding and orienting from Chapter 3 invokes the wisdom of your soul muscle.) It is your body's central messenger of connectivity.

Separately and together, your soul nerve and soul muscle are where you build your resilience, grit, discernment, tolerance for clean pain, and racial acuity and agility. They are where you store your ability to slow down, pause, and pay attention. As you get in your reps with multiple body practices, they are where much of your tempering and conditioning will unfold.

With some attention and patience, you can learn to work with your soul nerve and soul muscle—deliberately relaxing, settling your body, sensing your environment and situation, and soothing yourself during difficult or high-stress situations.

Over time, you will also learn to mindfully tend what I call *resonance* and *dissonance fields*. These are the energetic and electromagnetic fields that are naturally generated and broadcast by our bodies.

Please don't dismiss these fields as New Age fantasies. They are real, physical, and measurable. Your heart, for example, is the most powerful generator of electromagnetic energy in your body, creating a field that is sixty times stronger than the electrical activity in your brain. This field extends well beyond your skin and interacts with the energy fields generated by other bodies nearby. Other, similar fields generated by your body involve sound, pressure, pulses, other vibrations, scents, and other measurable energies.[70]

---

70    Human beings are not alone in generating these fields. Animals and plants routinely generate them. So do nonliving objects and processes. So do atoms. Our entire universe is one immense welter of overlapping vibrations. As Tam Hunt, of the University of California, Santa Barbara META (Memory Emotion Thought Awareness) lab, explains, "All things in our universe are constantly in motion, vibrating. Even objects that appear to be stationary are in fact vibrating, oscillating, resonating, at various frequencies. . . . And ultimately all matter is just vibrations of various underlying fields. As such, at every scale, all of nature vibrates. Something interesting happens when different vibrating things come together: They will often start, after a little while, to vibrate together at the same frequency. They 'sync up,' sometimes in ways that can seem mysterious. This is described as the phenomenon of spontaneous self-organization."

When fields from multiple bodies align, they can create a *resonance field* that supports the well-being of all the bodies involved, and that invites the presence of other bodies with similar fields. When fields from two or more bodies conflict, they create a disalignment—a *dissonance field*.

It's not the case that resonance fields are inherently good and dissonance fields are inherently bad. A Ku Klux Klan rally, for example, is one immense, perfectly aligned resonance field of hatred and rage. Now imagine that one of the rally's participants goes to work at his dentistry office the next day. An hour later, when you walk into that office for the first time, you sense that something isn't right, but you can't put your finger on what it is. The dissonance that your body experiences is deeply valuable information.

Through tempering and conditioning, your body can learn to recognize and tend to these fields, and then *work* them. Over time, as you do more and more reps, this process can become more and more nuanced. It may also prove hugely valuable, especially in situations that are stressful, ambiguous, or confusing. In a perilous situation, your ability to work resonance and dissonance fields could even save your life.

Until now, you've been doing the body practices in this book on your own. Now it's time to begin doing some of them with others. This might involve one or two other people, or perhaps a larger group. You might do your reps with the same people time after time—or you might do them with a variety of different people. You might decide to organize some rep sessions in your church, mosque, synagogue, or spiritual group, or at your high school or college. (It's fine to be an organizer and temporary leader, but please don't claim to be an official Somatic Abolitionism teacher or authority figure.)

You'll discover that these practices will have different resonances—and, sometimes, different benefits and outcomes—when you do them with others. As you do the reps together, you'll experience multiple energetic and electromagnetic fields, not just your own.

This doesn't only apply to the body practices that follow. From now on, I also encourage you to do some of the earlier practices in this book both on your own *and* with other bodies.

For the most part, it doesn't matter how a group that practices reps together functions or is organized. But three things *do* matter a great deal:

First, keep each group simple. Spontaneously invite over a friend. Meet your sister and brother-in-law for breakfast and reps before work on Friday mornings. Hold brief rep sessions in your church basement on Tuesday evenings. Make it very easy for people to show up, do reps together, and leave.

Second, never stop doing some reps on your own. While there is unique value in doing these body practices with other bodies, there is *also* unique value in doing them solo. Experiment to find your own ideal balance, while keeping in mind that this balance may change over time.

Third, *do not do reps in groups that mix bodies of culture with white bodies. This is essential.*[71] Remember, most white American bodies have little agility, acuity, or grit around race. As a result, when bodies of culture and white bodies do reps together, it often doesn't take long—perhaps only two or three meetings—before someone with a white body has their racialized trauma activated, slips into a *fight* or *annihilate* response, and creates a problem. People then become hurt and angry; the group disbands; and the racialized trauma in people's bodies only grows. For everyone's protection, don't go down this road. You may think that this won't happen with your group, especially if it's only two or three folks, or if all the people are longtime friends. But—trust me—the potential peril is bigger and more likely than it may seem.

I know how counterintuitive this separation may sound, especially if you have a white body. Deliberately segregating white bodies from bodies of culture—particularly in the name of racial healing—may seem absurd and ironic. But we create similar group separations all the time, for a variety of practical reasons. Many schools separate genders for sex education instruction.

---

71   I'm writing this in late 2021. Perhaps by 2030, or at some point thereafter, Somatic Abolitionism will have evolved—and enough white bodies will have done enough reps—so that the perils I describe above are less likely. If so, use your discernment to decide whether to heed, modify, or ignore this instruction.

Some cultures—and some American schools—separate genders for *all* instruction. Many separate students according to projected levels of ability (or current levels of achievement). When we take group photos, we put short people in front and tall folks in back— not because short people deserve special treatment, but to make sure everyone's face is visible.

What about further separating different types of bodies of culture—for example, having separate groups of Black bodies, or Asian bodies, or Latinx bodies do reps? My experience suggests that there's nothing wrong with this. However, I do suggest that white-bodied Muslim and Jewish people—who, according to some folks with the devout or vehement variants of WBS, don't qualify as fully human—do group reps with other white-bodied people.[72] As we've seen, although identity is a significant secondary aspect of WBS, body pigmentation is the center of its definition of humanness.

## BODY PRACTICE
## EXPLORING YOUR SOUL NERVE AND SOUL MUSCLE

Sit comfortably, by yourself, in a fairly quiet spot. Keep pen and paper nearby.

Take a few slow, deep breaths. Then think back to a time when you experienced strong grief. Briefly recall what led up to this grief. Then recall a moment when your grief was at or near its peak.

*Pause.* Focus your attention on your body's experience of grief. Where do you experience it? What are its physical qualities and nuances? Is there constriction? Heat? Cold? Some other sensation?

*Pause* again. Stay with these sensations for a few more breaths.

Now, soul scribe about your experience by focusing on the physical sensations. Describe the qualities of each sensation and exactly where in your body you experience it.

---

72   If you're Muslim or Jewish, you may find the body practices in Chapter 26, Untangling the Energies of Race, particularly valuable.

Each time you do a new rep of this body practice, pick a different emotion from the list below:

- joy
- fear (or, if your body can handle it, terror)
- dread
- profound relief
- excitement
- disappointment
- disgust
- loneliness
- pride
- horror
- delight
- anger (or, if your body can handle it, rage)
- anxiety
- hope

As you work through this list, you will begin to become familiar with how your soul nerve and soul muscle express important emotions. You will also begin to create an internal map of both structures.

When you have worked your way through the entire list, for your next rep begin again with joy.

# 26

# BECOMING A
# SOMATIC ABOLITIONIST

*If you are neutral in situations of injustice,
you have chosen the side of the oppressor.*

Desmond Tutu

*If you don't like the way the world is, you
change it. You have an obligation to change it.
You just do it one step at a time.*

Marian Wright Edelman

*Sometimes you gotta create what
you want to be a part of.*

Geri Weitzman

*Don't just do enough to get by; do what is required
of you so that you will make it better for your people,
your peers, and the next generation.*

Angela Rye

*When you get to a place where you don't go for what
you can get, but you go for what you can give, you
gonna see your life change tremendously.*

ET, the Hip Hop Preacher (aka Eric Thomas)

The embodied practices and insights in this book point to a way of being that many people call *Somatic Abolitionism.*

*Somatic* simply means *centered on the body. Abolitionism* was the widespread (and also widely opposed) movement to end enslavement in America during the nineteenth century.

Somatic Abolitionism is an individual and communal effort to free our bodies—and our country—from their long enslavement to WBS and racialized trauma. It is an individual and collective form of growing up.

Somatic Abolitionism is a living, embodied, ongoing effort that requires—and helps to build—endurance, stamina, and discipline.

An essential part of Somatic Abolitionism is the repetition of embodied antiracist practices. The practices are body experiences. That's why most of them involve moving, touching, holding, releasing, sensing, or protecting. Over time, these reps will temper and condition your body, your mind, and your soul. Through repeating these practices—particularly the five anchors—you can grow your discernment, your resilience, and your grit around matters of race. You can also deepen your sense of resource and grow your ability to stay with clean pain.

Somatic Abolitionism requires a genuine commitment. It can't be a hobby or a pastime. To practice it, you must commit to studying the impacts of racialization on your and others' bodies—and then to growing up and out of the trauma embedded in your own body.

We practice Somatic Abolitionism as an expression of our shared humanity and of creation itself—not as a performance or demonstration. Please don't put "Somatic Abolitionist" on your résumé, your sweatshirt, or the bumper of your car.

Somatic Abolitionism involves the resourcing of energies that are already (and always) present in your body, in our collective body, and in creation itself. And, as you will experience, what begins in your body will often ripple out to other bodies and then into the world.

The racialized trauma that now percolates in our bodies are inherited energies that our ancestors couldn't metabolize. Part of the work of Somatic Abolitionism is to complete this metabolization. This helps to heal us and the world. It also saves our children and grandchildren from having to complete the actions that we and our ancestors could have completed but chose not to.

Healing racialized trauma and growing up out of white-body supremacy begin with your body, but they do not end there. Somatic Abolitionism (SA) is collective as well as individual. We cannot individualize our way out of three hundred fifty plus years of white-body supremacy. Over months, years, and generations, you , I, and many others will build a communal container that can collectively hold the charge of race. Separately and together, we will metabolize that charge—and, over time, create a genuinely antiracist culture. This will necessarily include embodied social activism.

For now, Somatic Abolitionism—and the practices in this book—can help you , me, and others develop communal glue. As SA spreads, those of us who have made a lifelong commitment to creating a living, embodied antiracist culture can begin to find each other, work together, and learn from one another.

As in all communities, though, the people in your Somatic Abolitionism community will change over time. Think of your SA community not as the people you may have started with, but as the people you end up with. Some of these people may continue the efforts and practices of Somatic Abolitionism long after you have died.

Above all, Somatic Abolitionism is emergent. As you get in reps with the body practices in this book, you usually won't know where they will take you. Over and over, you will experience what emerges—without knowing what will happen—and then move into the next moment with as much integrity as you can.

Here's what Somatic Abolitionism is *not*:

- Somatic Abolitionism isn't a club, an organization, or a movement you can formally join.

- Somatic Abolitionism is not about accumulating accolades or merit. It offers no medallions to win (or confer on others) and no levels of accomplishment to achieve. All such measurements are beside the point. No one gets a medallion for ten years as a mother or earns a black belt as a wise and beloved elder. Ditto for SA.

- The practices of Somatic Abolitionism are not mere strategies, tactics, tools, weapons, or "courageous conversations." These are all insufficient. So is attending (or setting up) a group to discuss this book, or Somatic Abolitionism in general. Like putting up a Black Lives Matter sign, it's fine—but at most it's just a starting point. It's like registering for a class but not yet attending it.

- Somatic Abolitionism is not just an idea, or position, or ideology. It always involves action. Sometimes, though, that action begins with a deliberate pause. Sometimes it involves stepping back, discerning, and only then moving forward.

- Somatic Abolitionism is not new and innovative. It's exactly the opposite. It reclaims the age-old wisdom of human bodies and the ways in which each body already knows how to respect, honor, and resonate with other bodies.

Do not declare yourself to others as a Somatic Abolitionist. Such declarations are counterproductive. If you have a white body and say to a body of culture, "Hi! I'm your ally and a Somatic Abolitionist," they will immediately know that you are neither. And they will be right.

Whatever your body pigmentation, don't say, "I'm a Somatic Abolitionist" to a white body, either. In the racialized tension of an imminent or unfolding civil war, such an announcement could get you injured or killed.

Although I'm a vigorous promoter of Somatic Abolitionism, I am not its leader, guru, or commanding officer.[73] No one is. If anyone claims such authority, they are trying to scam you—and they are probably a narcissist, a sociopath, or a Russian bot.

There's no formal threshold to cross to become a Somatic Abolitionist. It's like the process of becoming wise, or humble, or loving. With enough reps and enough time, you simply grow into it.

No one will award you the title of Somatic Abolitionist or publicly declare that you have earned it. (If they do, they're

---

73    Resist any urge to become my disciple or admirer or groupie. That urge is white-body supremacy in disguise, trying to distract you from facing the clean pain that Somatic Abolitionism requires you to experience. (Also, for the record, I can be an asshole sometimes. My family members can attest to this.)

scamming you.) Nor can you legitimately confer that title on yourself. (If you do, you're scamming yourself.)

It's essential that Somatic Abolitionism not be beholden to any person, institution, movement, spiritual tradition, political party, profession, or system. Trying to retrofit SA into anything—whether it's your religion, your yoga or meditation practice, or your Twelve Step meetings—will only limit it. If you wish, by all means continue to practice your religion, or yoga, or meditation, or the Twelve Steps. But don't force it and SA together. Indeed, doing so may turn both forms of nourishment into poison.[74]

In the run-up to the civil war, right-wing media may declare Somatic Abolitionism to be a form of critical race theory—or, perhaps, the new outrage-inducing replacement for it. The creation of this outrage will be its sole point. Whatever the GOP and its propagandists say about Somatic Abolitionism, all it actually means is the high-decibel, repeated shouting of the N word.

Somatic Abolitionism *is* a movement that has begun to catch on. As with all such movements, it will attract some predators and scammers, who will vigorously wave its banner to con money, sex, or subservience from people. Be alert for these folks, and use your growing discernment to weed them out.

As civil war nears or unfolds, some pro-autocracy people will likely pose as Somatic Abolitionists and do their best to infiltrate and undermine pro-democracy groups. Keep an eye out for these folks as well.

This book will help you sink your toes into Somatic Abolitionism. But it will not chart your course for you.

Here are a few other highly accessible doorways into SA:

- Read *My Grandmother's Hands* and do the body practices in it. If you don't have time to read it, get the audiobook. If you can't afford a copy, borrow one from your library or an acquaintance.

- Take the free five-session online course in racialized trauma that I created for the Cultural Somatics Institute: courses. culturalsomaticsinstitute.com/courses/cultural-somatics-free-5-session-ecourse.

---

74   If you discover that Somatic Abolitionism genuinely conflicts with something else you do or believe in, then don't try to ignore or sidestep the conflict. You will need to choose one and let go of the other.

- If you have a white body, read "100 Ways White People Can Make Life Less Frustrating for People of Color" by Kesiena Boom, and follow its guidance: vice.com/en/article/ne95dm/how-to-be-a-white-ally-to-people-of-color.
- Visit the Libraries for Liberation website, and read some of the books it recommends: librariesforliberation.com/which-books.

If you have a white body, there is one other regular practice that becoming a Somatic Abolitionist requires. You'll discover this practice in Chapter 35.

When your body wants something—food, sleep, touch, sex, warmth, safety, relief—it wants it right now.

But you cannot just will yourself to become a Somatic Abolitionist. You can only grow into it, rep by rep, moment by moment. Over months and years, you can build a Somatic Abolitionist bodyset and mindset.

Similarly, we cannot just will an antiracist culture into being. We can only create it, rep by rep, person by person, moment by moment, over years and generations.

We can build this embodied antiracist culture. We can grow it. We can nurture it. We can forge it. But it will take time.

Know all of this in your body. Know the hope and the possibilities. But also know that building an antiracist culture will take much effort and multiple generations.

Eric Hoffer, the great philosopher (and winner of the Presidential Medal of Freedom), wrote that "every great cause begins as a movement, becomes a business, and eventually degenerates into a racket." To delay the hijacking and degeneration of Somatic Abolitionism as long as possible, I've provided the above list of what SA is not, and what constitutes a tell that someone is trying to appropriate, misuse, or misdefine it for their own purposes.[75]

---

75  A good example of such a misappropriation, misuse, misdefining, and racketeering is the word *self-esteem*, which is now a part of most Americans' everyday vocabulary. The word brings to mind the *Saturday Night Live* character Stuart Smalley, created and played by Al Franken. Smalley spent much of his time telling himself what a good and likeable person he was. Franken's caricature grew

Some people—including some who will review this book—may say that Somatic Abolitionism has *already* degenerated into a business or a racket. Others will say that it *began* as a racket. Still others will point to this very chapter—perhaps this very paragraph—and use it to claim that I've *admitted* to its being a racket. Bullshit. Troll away, folks. I'm onto you.[76]

Like an effective government or a thriving business, Somatic Abolitionism will need to continually evolve and reinvent itself. Importantly, it will—it *must*—not do so under my guiding hand, but through the efforts and energies of many, many human bodies of all skin pigmentations.

There may come a time—perhaps not for generations, perhaps in just a few years—when Somatic Abolitionism does turn into a racket. If and when that happens, please disavow it and work to help a new and more authentic great cause to emerge. Assuming that I'm still alive, I plan to be right there with you.

## BODY PRACTICE
## **WILLINGNESS**

### *If you have a body of culture:*

Place a pen and paper near you. Then slowly read the list of statements below, either silently or aloud:

- I am willing to reclaim my power in order to help heal racialized trauma.

- I am willing to challenge my racialized limitations.

- I am willing to address any colorism, racial shame, self-doubt, or sense of fraudulence or impostorhood that lives in my body.

- I am committed to paying attention to what happens in my body.

---

out of the bogus idea that self-esteem is primarily about self-talk—or, in some cases, self-gaslighting. The entire self-esteem movement of the 1990s and 2000s was a classic case of a useful psychological principle getting hijacked, twisted into a new and dysfunctional shape, spread far and wide, and turned into a racket. You may wish to read the foundational book on the subject, *Self-Esteem: A Family Affair* by Jean Illsley Clarke, which was published in 1978. You may be shocked to discover that it is a bullshit-free book for *parents* about parenting and has almost nothing to do with telling yourself what a great person you are.

76 My work is not for everyone—nor do I want it to be—and I am arguably an acquired taste. That said, I am a healer, not a grifter.

- I understand that my body may reflexively constrict in order to protect itself from truth. I commit to moving through and past this constriction in order to live into truth.

- I will practice the five anchors, and other body practices from this book, in order to keep myself present, settle my body, build my discernment, and temper and condition my body.

- I will heal my trauma, including my inherited trauma.

- I believe that responsibility for dismantling white-body supremacy lies in the hands of white people. I may choose to assist with these efforts, but it is not my obligation.

- I admit that notions of white primacy and white-body supremacy live in my body.

- I am willing to search inside myself to recognize all the ways I have been impacted by white-body supremacy.

- I am willing to experience the pain of dismantling white-body supremacy.

- I am committed to helping build a living, embodied antiracist culture that will be sane and loving, and will provide everyone with a sense of belonging.

What did your body experience as you slowly read this list? Soul scribe, noting any:

- vibrations

- images and thoughts

- meanings, judgments, stories, and explanations

- behaviors, movements, actions, impulses, and urges

- affect and emotions

- sensations

Now ask yourself: *Am I willing to commit to everything on the list above? If not, what am I willing to commit to?* Then express and solidify that commitment by speaking it aloud.

### If you have a white body:

Place a pen and paper near you. Then slowly read the list of statements below, either silently or aloud:

- I am willing to be challenged.
- I am willing to be humbled.
- I am committed to paying attention to what happens in my body.
- I am willing to take my Ls—my losses, leaps, and learnings.
- I understand that my body may reflexively constrict in order to protect itself from truth. I commit to moving through and past this constriction in order to live into truth.
- I will practice the five anchors, and other body practices from this book, in order to keep myself present, settle my body, build my discernment, and temper and condition my body.
- I will heal my trauma, including my inherited trauma.
- I believe that responsibility for dismantling white-body supremacy lies in the hands of white people.
- I admit that notions of white primacy and white-body supremacy live in my body.
- I am willing to address any white guilt and white fragility that live in my body.
- I am willing to search inside myself to recognize all the ways I have been advantaged by white-body supremacy—and all the ways in which bodies of culture have been harmed.
- I am willing to experience the pain of dismantling white-body supremacy.
- I am willing to give up my power as a white-bodied person in order to help heal racialized trauma.
- I am committed to helping build an antiracist culture that will be sane and loving, and will provide everyone with a sense of belonging.

What did your body experience as you slowly read this list? Soul scribe, noting any:

- vibrations
- images and thoughts
- meanings, judgments, stories, and explanations
- behaviors, movements, actions, impulses, and urges

- affect and emotions
- sensations

Now ask yourself: *Am I willing to commit to everything on the list above? If not, what* am *I willing to commit to?* Then express and solidify that commitment by speaking it aloud.


BODY PRACTICE
# UNTANGLING THE ENERGIES OF RACE, PART 1

*If you have a white body[77]:*

This body practice is specifically for white-bodied people who may be marginalized, subjugated, or discriminated against because of their identity—for example, if they're female, Muslim, Jewish, trans, gay, non-cisgender, non-binary, foreign-born, disabled, very short, etc. These folks receive advantages from white-body supremacy, yet are also vulnerable for different reasons.

If the above description fits you, your body carries inside it energies of both the oppressor and the oppressed, the victim and the perpetrator. Because the two energies are intertwined, it may be very difficult for you to work with either one. As a result, you may be (understandably) conflicted about matters of race.

The body practice below can help you disentangle these opposing energies and begin to metabolize them.

Find a quiet place where you can sit comfortably and alone at a desk, table, or other flat surface.

Keep a pen and paper beside you.

Place your elbows together, and entwine the fingers of both hands. Then, keeping your elbows on the desk or table, point both your forearms and hands straight up.

For a few breaths, notice the energy that's present in your hands. Don't try to explain or identify this energy. Just experience it.

---

77   If you have a biracial body, you may wish to do this body practice—or you may prefer to do the practice that follows, Untangling the Energies of Race, Part 2.

*Pause.* Take a few more breaths. Notice any shifts or energy surges that might emerge in the rest of your body.

Now, slowly, over three or four breaths, unhook your fingers, and separate your two hands. As you do, pay attention to what the rest of your body experiences.

Keep one hand and forearm upright. (It doesn't matter which one.) This hand holds the energies of white-body supremacy—the energies of colonization, oppression, and discrimination. Slowly lower the other hand, which contains the energies of marginalization and victimhood, to the table or desk.

Focus your attention on your upright hand. For ten breaths, just stay with this hand and its energies. Don't try to visualize or imagine anything. Don't try to move anything or hold it still. Just pay attention.

Then say aloud, slowly, three times: "I am the oppressor."

What moves in your body? What emerges? What grows? What locks down? What does the hand do or want to do? What does the rest of your body do or want to do? Note any:

- vibrations
- images and thoughts
- meanings, judgments, stories, and explanations
- behaviors, movements, actions, impulses, and urges
- affect and emotions
- sensations

Now, slowly, lower this hand, and rest it on the desk or table. Then, keeping your other elbow on that surface, slowly raise the other hand, and hold it upright.

For ten breaths, focus on this hand and its energies of marginalization and victimhood. Again, don't try to visualize, imagine, or move anything. Just pay attention.

Then say aloud, slowly, three times: "I have been subjugated."

What moves in your body? What emerges, or grows, or locks down? What does this hand do or want to do? What does the rest of your body do or what to do? Note any:

- vibrations
- images and thoughts
- meanings, judgments, stories, and explanations
- behaviors, movements, actions, impulses, and urges
- affect and emotions
- sensations

Lower this hand; then pick up the pen and soul scribe. Write down what your body experienced during this practice, in the order in which it experienced it.

Notice if, at any point while you do this practice, you experience an urge to center your white advantage.

BODY PRACTICE
# UNTANGLING THE ENERGIES OF RACE, PART 2

*If your body pigmentation determines that you are not white:*

This body practice is specifically for bodies of culture who may be marginalized or discriminated against not only because of their skin tone, but for one or more other reasons—they are female, Muslim, Jewish, trans, gay, disabled, non-cisgender, non-binary, foreign-born, very short, etc.

If this describes you, the body practice below can help you disentangle these energies and begin to metabolize them.

Sit comfortably at a desk, table, or other flat surface, with a pen and paper beside you.

Place your elbows together, and entwine the fingers of both hands. Then, keeping your elbows on the desk or table, point both your forearms and hands straight up.

For a few breaths, notice the energy that's present in your hands. Don't try to explain or identify this energy. Just experience it.

*Pause.* Take a few more breaths. Notice any shifts or surges of energy that emerge in the rest of your body.

Now, slowly, over three or four breaths, unhook your fingers, and separate your two hands. As you do, pay attention to what the rest of your body experiences.

Keep one hand and forearm upright. (It doesn't matter which one.) This hand holds the energies of marginalization or discrimination because of white-body supremacy. Slowly lower the other hand, which contains the energies of other forms of marginalization or discrimination, to the table or desk.

Focus your attention on your upright hand. For ten breaths, just stay with this hand and its energies. Don't try to visualize or imagine anything. Don't try to move anything or hold it still. Just pay attention.

Then say aloud, three times: "I have been victimized."

What moves in your body? What emerges? What grows? What locks down? What does the hand do or want to do? What does the rest of your body do or want to do? Note any:

- vibrations
- images and thoughts
- meanings, judgments, stories, and explanations
- behaviors, movements, actions, impulses, and urges
- affect and emotions
- sensations

Now, slowly, lower this hand, and rest it on the desk or table. Then, keeping your other elbow on that surface, slowly raise the other hand, and hold it upright.

For ten breaths, focus on this hand and its energies of the other form of discrimination or marginalization that you experience. As before, don't try to do anything with the hand. Just pay attention.

The say aloud, three times: "In some ways, I have hurt other bodies of culture."[78]

---

78    Please note the important distinction between the energies in Part 1 and Part 2 of this body practice. The energy in Part 1 involves *vertical wounding,* in which an oppressor body wounds a subjugated body. (This is sometimes called *punching down.*) The energy in Part 2 involves *horizontal wounding,* in which one subjugated body wounds another.

Now what moves in your body? What emerges, or grows, or locks down? What does the hand do or want to do? What does the rest of your body do or what to do? Note any:

- vibrations
- images and thoughts
- meanings, judgments, stories, and explanations
- behaviors, movements, actions, impulses, and urges
- affect and emotions
- sensations

Lower this hand; then pick up the pen and soul scribe. Write down what your body experienced during this practice, in the order in which it experienced it.

## 27

# QUAKING

*You have to get over the fear of facing the worst in yourself. . . .*
*Do not fear the opportunity to do better.*
Ijeoma Oluo

*Take chances, make mistakes. That's how you grow. Pain nourishes*
*your courage. You have to fail in order to practice being brave.*
Mary Tyler Moore

As efforts to destroy our democracy unfold—and as you do the practices in this book, rep by rep—at some point a quaking will begin in your body. This might happen once; it might happen several times; or it might happen repeatedly over months, or even years. (Happening only once, or not at all, is pretty rare.)

Although this quaking might seem frightening and unfamiliar at first, consider it a very encouraging sign. It tells you that something significant is happening in your body. It may also begin to reveal to you what is possible—or what you need to do.

No one, not even you, can say when or how this quaking will begin, how or where in your body it will manifest, or how long it will last. But when your body starts to quake, you'll know it.

The first time your body quakes, you may become afraid and have a reflexive urge to grasp for comfort. This urge is normal. But following that urge inhibits growth. So, instead, be as curious about the fear as you are about the quaking. Stay with what your body experiences. Notice what it does when you don't respond reflexively. If necessary, remind yourself that both the quaking and the fear are temporary.

You won't know what will happen when the quaking emerges. Maybe you'll cry. Maybe you'll laugh, or scream, or shake, or start doing one type of primal rep after another. Maybe you'll have the urge to blame someone for your quaking—or for not saving you from it. You might experience terror, or joy, or rage, or all three— or no emotion at all, just physical sensations. Let your body do whatever it wants or needs to do (so long as it doesn't harm you or another body). Open yourself to the experience, and pay attention to your body's movements and energies.

After the quaking ends, don't try to find someone (such as a therapist or spiritual leader) to explain or interpret the experience for you.[79] *The meaning of the quaking is the experience itself,* not whatever story you or someone else might tell about it.

And don't confuse your quaking—a highly physical experience—with a spiritual awakening, a revelation, or a message from God. Even if you wound up writhing on the floor and shouting at the top of your lungs (highly unlikely, but possible), this is a sign of voltage, not significance.

I need to mention four caveats.

First, if your body starts to quake in a public setting, such as a religious service or dinner with your in-laws, you may need to get up and leave for a time. If you can't leave, then you may need to try to temporarily override the quaking, so that you don't freak out anyone or cause them to think that you've lost your mind. (If this doesn't work, and your body shifts into a trauma response, leave the situation immediately no matter what else is occurring, unless doing so is physically impossible or dangerous.)

Second, if the quaking simply becomes too much for you, no matter how much you try to accept and experience it, do what you can to get out from under it. Take a brisk walk. Let your body repeat whatever primal practices it wants to. Take a shower. Sing at the top of your lungs for a minute or two. But the next

---

79    To be clear: it's fine (and may even be wise) to talk about your experience of quaking with a trusted therapist or spiritual guide. Just don't ask them to provide a cognitive explanation or interpretation for it. That moves the experience out of your body and into your head. It's also a distraction.

time the quaking begins, try to stay with it throughout the entire experience. Ditto for the time after that. And the one after that.

Third, if your quaking begins to create potential harm for you or anyone else, disengage as quickly as you can. Follow the guidance above for cutting short the experience. If necessary, leave and go to a different, safer place.

Fourth, remind yourself that the source of this quaking may be the four-hundred-year-old charge of race. This is a lot of energy for any body to metabolize.

If you find yourself overwhelmed by quaking more than once or twice, consider enlisting the help of a somatic therapist. You can locate somatic therapists through *Psychology Today's* therapist directory (psychologytoday.com/us/therapists/somatic), or through the directory of "culturally sensitive" therapists at Trucircle, mytrucircle.com.

Quaking is ultimately about disaligning, realigning, and moving into any extra room that emerges in your body.

As you grow and heal, some of your body's energies will disalign for a time and then later realign. *Disalignment* typically occurs when a belief becomes uncomfortable, a norm is cast aside, or a long-held assumption or belief is proven false, and you allow your body to fully process that experience. *Realignment* takes place when your body's energies find a new way to flow in the wake of this change. This realignment can deepen your sense of resource. Sometimes, but not always, a cognitive insight will accompany this realignment.

Whatever happens, plan to get used to quaking. It is something your body needs to do, and it is a natural part of healing and growing up.

That said, quaking is not a threshold to cross, a bar to clear, or a sign of progress or achievement. Don't try to encourage your body to quake—and don't try to prevent or discourage it, either. It's just your human body being human.

BODY PRACTICE
# LIVING INTO QUAKING

Quaking is a life rep that can create room for more emergence in your body. It can't be invited or activated, but it can (and eventually will) activate you.

Nevertheless, you can prepare yourself for quaking by keeping in mind the instructions below:

When the quaking begins, don't try to stop it, explain it, or understand it. Simply be curious about it. Whatever form it takes, let yourself experience it fully. Use the five anchors from Chapter 21:

- Soothe and resource yourself to quiet your mind, calm your heart, and settle your body.
- *Pause*, then notice and discern the sensations, vibrations, and emotions in your body instead of reacting to them.
- Accept and tolerate the discomfort instead of trying to flee from it.
- Stay present and in your body as you move through the unfolding experience, with all its ambiguity and uncertainty, and respond from the best parts of yourself.
- Metabolize any energy that remains.

As soon as you can after the quaking ceases, soul scribe about it. Write about the experience from beginning to end, noting any:

- vibrations
- images and thoughts
- meanings, judgments, stories, and explanations
- behaviors, movements, actions, impulses, and urges
- affect and emotions
- sensations

# 28

# WOKENESS, ALLYSHIP, AND COMPLICITY

*Wanna-be allies, do your own work. . . . Stop asking us to validate*
*you. Stop asking us to educate you. Stop being lazy. Do better.*
*If you wanna be a true ally, do the damn work.*

WOC and Allies

*Intentions are irrelevant. . . . And we need to let go of our*
*intentions and attend to the impact, to focus on that.*

Robin DiAngelo

*Pause.*

Suppose you have a white body. At your request, I agree to
meet you for lunch and conversation at a convenient restaurant.

Soon after we sit down, I begin telling you about the many
white friends I have. I mention that my brother is married to a
white woman, and I laud the comedic talents of Bill Burr, Patton
Oswalt, Tina Fey, and Paula Poundstone.

When the server comes to take our order, I ask for a roast beef
sandwich with mayonnaise and tell him, with a big smile, "I *love*
mayo—but I can't eat a lot of it. It's just too spicy for me." After
he leaves, I lean forward and say to you, "Man, those shoulder-
length blonde locks of his are amazing, aren't they? I almost asked
if I could touch them, but I know better."

At what point in my monologue did you begin to question my authenticity? At what point did you sense that I was performing or pandering? At what point did you begin to wonder what was wrong with me? Did you begin to give up on ever getting to know the real Resmaa?

If you're a progressive with a white body, do the moves I made seem familiar? They should, because white progressives make similar moves with me—and other bodies of culture—all the time. They trot out their racial résumés, ostensibly to let me know that they're on my side—that they're my ally, that they're woke, that they're not racist, and that I can trust them. Sometimes they literally say the words "I'm an ally" or "I'm not a racist."

But I'm not stupid. I know a performance when I see one. I can also see whom the performance is for—and it isn't me. It's for the performer. They're demonstrating to themselves what a good, nonracist, well-intentioned white person they are. It's a distant cousin of obsessive name dropping—and a form of magical thinking and equally magical self-talk.

Here is what these orations communicate to me and to other bodies of culture:

*I'm enacting the progressive variant of WBS. As soon as I set eyes on you, my racialized trauma was activated. I experienced guilt, a fear of being called out, and an urge to protect my self-image. I'm unwilling to interrogate and heal my racialized trauma, which was passed down to me by my ancestors and which is reinforced by structures that advantage me. Because of my unwillingness, I reflexively flipped into a* fawn *response. Now I can't stop myself from telling you a story about what a decent, trustworthy, body-of-culture-respecting white person I am. I have little or no racial acuity, agility, or grit, but I still want your acceptance and approval—and your tacit agreement that you won't call me out or hold me accountable. Okay?*

No. It's not okay. It's a form of dirty pain.

If you have a white body, *please* don't tell me—or any other body of culture—that you're their ally. Everything else aside, no one will believe you. If a stranger (or a distant acquaintance) walks up to you and announces, "I'm your friend!" your first thought will probably be *No, you're not.*

No grown-up automatically believes what other people declare about themselves. (In fact, there's a name for the folks who do: suckers.) Any adult body of culture—indeed, any grown-up of any skin tone—will judge your trustworthiness and commitment by your actions, not your declarations of being independent from other white folks and free of WBS.

I can't tell you how many racial résumés I have watched white bodies perform. I *can* tell you that each performance is painful to watch. And boring. And exhausting. And sometimes pathetic. And very difficult to deal with.

When a white body with the devout or vehement variant of WBS sets eyes on me, their racialized trauma and background rigidity quickly get activated. Because they're unwilling to interrogate and heal that unexamined (and very likely inherited) trauma, they instantly dislike and distrust me. Usually, though, they'll quickly—and often very directly—let me know what they think about me. This isn't too hard for me to deal with because I know precisely where I stand with them.

But with folks who have the progressive variant of WBS, almost anything I say or do in response to their performance will be counterproductive. Calling them out directly may flip them from a *fawn* trauma response into a *fight* response. (I'll say more about this in Chapter 43, which focuses on white rage.) Giving them a frown or a stern look may cause them to extend their performance ("My best friend in high school was Black," etc.). If I just hold up my hands and say, "Come on, man—enough," they may ask for—and expect—an extended lesson in what they did wrong and how to become more woke, as if I'm suddenly their unpaid private tutor. They might start to cry.

To all white progressives reading this chapter, please listen carefully: When you try to tell me that you're woke, or an ally, or not a racist, you actually communicate the opposite. You show me that I cannot, should not, and dare not trust you. You show me that you care more about your own self-image than you do about me. You show me that I cannot have an authentic relationship with you. And you show me that you think of me first and foremost not as Resmaa, but as a Black body.

So if you have a white body, and you notice that you're starting to perform your own racial résumé, immediately *pause*. Stop talking. Stay a second or two in silence. Then smile and say, "Scratch that."

Then take the focus off yourself. Begin to have an actual conversation. Be curious about the other person or people. Ask them some questions about themselves. Later, after the interaction ends, do some invited reps.

This doesn't just apply to interactions with bodies of culture. Put white progressives together, and they'll sometimes perform their racial résumés for each other, trying to impress one another with their wokeness. Sometimes they'll try to out-woke each other. If you catch yourself doing this, *stop*. Please. Later, when you can, do some invited reps.

We human beings need to trust one another. But there's a reason why we don't walk around carrying signs that say, "I'm not a pedophile," "I'm not a thief," "I promise I won't murder you," "I'm a virgin," or, for that matter, "I'm not a virgin." We don't decide whom to trust based on signage, proclamations, or performances. We watch how someone interacts with other human beings, and then we apply our discernment. Think of the many aphorisms that speak to this, such as *Don't trust anyone who is nice to you but rude to servers and baristas.*

So if you have a white body and want to be an ally, or woke, *pause*. Right now. Seriously. *Pause* again.

There is no such thing as an ally. There is no such thing as wokeness. Really. They're both bullshit—and both irrelevant.

Here are some things that *are* real: acting from the best parts of yourself. Holding onto yourself when you experience pressure and heat. Letting yourself stay with clean pain. Metabolizing trauma. Healing. Using your discernment. Acting with wisdom and compassion. Treating other human beings as human beings. Relating with other people instead of performing in front of them.

Don't try to get me—or anyone—to think well of you. Instead, *act* well. Not *act* as in *perform for an audience*, but as in *bring the best of yourself to each moment*. And get your reps in.

If you consistently act well, you won't need to chase after anyone's trust and respect. You'll have naturally earned them.

One more point: if our country does go to war with itself, and you merely *perform* when a situation requires you to *act*, your performance could cost you your life.

Now let's explore another subtle and little-discussed—but deeply pernicious—aspect of white-body supremacy. This one shows up in both the progressive and the complicit, collective variants. It's embodied rather than conceptual, but if it were put into language, it would go like this:

*It's important to be nice and respectful to everyone, regardless of their body pigmentation, unless they become disrespectful themselves. It's also important to show up with good intentions.*

No sane person would argue with this. But here's what else WBS wraps together with it:

*Niceness, kindness, respect, and good intentions are sufficient. If I'm nice, respectful, and well-intentioned, then I'm absolved if I hurt someone or if I fail to intervene on their behalf when someone else attempts to hurt them.*

*In addition, if someone challenges me about what I've done or failed to do—especially if that person is a body of culture—then the whole deal is off. I'll consider them deeply disrespectful, so I'm entitled to yell at them, accuse them of aggression, or call the manager or the police on them.*

Niceness, kindness, and respect are important. The world needs more of all three. But niceness, kindness, and respect alone are inadequate. They are not justice. They are not compassion. They are not genuine caring. They are not movement toward liberation. And they are not supportive action.

If kindness, niceness, and respect are all that you can offer me (or all that I can offer you), we can only have a transactional relationship. No structures of trust, and no relationship glue, will be created between us.

And if your niceness, kindness, and respect are actually a thin veneer that you believe you're entitled to rip away whenever you're under stress, then they are only a performance—and you will uphold and spread WBS.

Mere awareness is also not enough.

Lots of people with the progressive variant of WBS are very aware. They know their history, their antiracist writers, and the current racial issues in the media. But they don't actually *do* anything to help build a living, embodied antiracist culture. At most, they join or create a book club or discussion group, and stop there.

If you're trying to grow a garden, you don't just buy the seeds and let them sit in your basement. If you want to learn Portuguese, you don't just get the teaching app and never open it. If you want to build strength, you don't go to the gym and simply hang out.

Learning or accomplishing anything requires commitment, effort, the cultivation of grit and self-discipline, and, above all, practice. You must get your reps in.

When it comes to justice or liberation, anything less—mere awareness, or performance, or niceness and respect—are forms of complicity with injustice and the status quo.

Here is perhaps the most pernicious aspect of WBS: if you don't actively work against it, it will wash over you, through you, into other human bodies, and out into the world.

## BODY PRACTICE
## I NEED TO BRING THIS UP

*If you have a white body:*

One of the more subtle, but common ways in which white bodies perpetuate white-body supremacy is by failing to call it out when they witness it. Especially when they witness it in someone else who is white—and whom they care about and trust.

Calling out WBS in a stranger isn't that difficult or uncomfortable *(The woman to my right was here before me. Please serve her first;* or *Excuse me, but why are you following that customer around the store? Is it because he's young and Black?).* It can be much more uncomfortable to call out a white friend, partner, or family member, because it might affect your relationship—or even put it at stake. And whenever you call out another white body, it may cost you something.

But you also know that, going forward, this is something you'll need to do at times, in order to keep the commitment you made at the end of Chapter 26.

This body practice has two parts. The first is an invited rep; the second is a life rep.

**Part 1**

Think of someone you're close to, whom you trust, and who is white—such as a partner, friend, or family member. Now imagine that, while you're with this person, they say or do something that supports white-body supremacy.

This should be something that fits their personality—something you can reasonably imagine them doing or saying. This doesn't necessarily mean insulting anyone or deliberately causing them harm. It might involve putting another human body at risk unintentionally or out of ignorance. Maybe the person turned away from a potentially fraught or escalating event. Maybe they simply remained passive when a situation called for them to stop, pay attention, and step in.

Now envision yourself speaking to this person about their action or inaction. Start with these two phrases: *I need to bring this up. Here's what I just noticed. . . .* Then imagine yourself explaining what you observed, how and why it supported white-body supremacy, how their action or inaction could have harmed another human being, and how you hope they won't do such things in the future.

As you do, pay close attention to your body. Note any:

- vibrations
- images and thoughts
- meanings, judgments, stories, and explanations
- behaviors, movements, actions, impulses, and urges
- affect and emotions
- sensations

Soul scribe about what you experienced in your body as you did this practice.

**Part 2**

The next time you notice a white friend, partner, or family member do something that supports WBS, don't let it slide. Say or do something. Let them know that they have potentially put another human being—or multiple human beings—in harm's way.

If the situation warrants it, you may also need to step in to deflect that harm or assist any potential victim.

There's no one-size-fits-all script for what to say to your friend, partner, or family member. Depending on your relationship and the situation, you might be firm or gentle, curious or confrontative, loud or restrained.

If the person you care about acted in support of WBS unintentionally, or out of ignorance, or by simply remaining passive in the face of an injustice, begin by acknowledging this: *I know you weren't try to hurt anyone, but. . . .* Or, *You probably didn't realize this, but. . . .* Or, *You know those people outside the hardware store that you walked right past? Did you notice that. . . .*

Depending on the circumstances, it may seem right to call out the person on the spot, or it might be wise to wait until later. Perhaps your words will be more effective when the two of you are alone, or when there are fewer distractions, or when the other person seems to be in a more receptive mood. Use your discernment. But don't let calling them out slide for too long.

There's no way to know how such a conversation will unfold. The other person may be grateful, or embarrassed, or angry—or perhaps even all three. The discussion may bring you closer together, or it may push you apart. Peril and possibility.

As soon as you can after this discussion ends, soul scribe about your experience. Notice what you experienced in your body during the conversation. Also pay attention to what your body is experiencing right now. Note any:

- vibrations
- images and thoughts
- meanings, judgments, stories, and explanations
- behaviors, movements, actions, impulses, and urges
- affect and emotions
- sensations

## BODY PRACTICE
# FRAUDULENCE, IMPOSTORHOOD, AND SHAME

*If you have a body of culture:*

According to WBS, all nonwhite bodies are subpar, insufficient, inadequate, deviant, less than fully human, and, above all, defective. For centuries, this message has been passed from person to person and generation to generation, damaging every body (especially any body of culture) that absorbs it. This message has been reinforced through our institutions of education, religion, medicine, criminal justice, government, and many, many others.

As a result, many America bodies of culture are caught in self-doubt or self-recrimination. Some struggle with impostor syndrome, in which they doubt their own skills, talents, and accomplishments and live in fear of being exposed as frauds. Many routinely discount or ignore their own needs and experience, while attending to those of others. Some let other people take credit for their work, their insights, and their achievements.

I don't just see this in my therapy office. Even being a mega-celebrity doesn't necessarily extinguish it. At times, Oprah Winfrey has struggled with self-doubt and with putting other people's needs above her own. In 2018, shortly after the publication of her best-selling memoir, Michelle Obama said, "I still have a little [bit of] impostor syndrome. It doesn't go away, that feeling that you shouldn't take me that seriously."

Michelle Obama and Oprah Winfrey are not defective. Neither are you. Any inferiority, worthlessness, or self-doubt you experience is not personal. It's structural.

The body practice below will help you and one other person shed this lie.

Do this practice with another body of culture you trust. It's best to do it in person, but you can also use Zoom, Skype, FaceTime, etc. If it's not possible for you to do this practice with someone else, you can be your own witness.

Sit silently in a quiet room together—just the two of you—for about ten breaths. (If you're reading this during a pandemic and you are not both vaccinated, wear masks, and sit at least six feet apart.)

You will speak first; your companion will be your witness. While you speak, they should simply watch and listen. They can nod or grunt or say *umm-hmm,* but they should not coach you, speak to you, or touch you.

Say to them loudly, clearly, and firmly: "I am not defective."

*Pause* for a few seconds. Then say it again, but add your name. For example: "I, Angela, am not defective." Pay attention to your body as you speak. Experience the vibration of the words throughout your body.

*Pause* for a few more seconds. Now cover your ears with your palms and press down lightly. Say the words once more—for example: "I, Angela, am not defective." Experience the vibration throughout your body again.

Remove your hands from your ears. Nod to your witness. They now say to you, clearly and firmly, "You are not defective," and they add your name. For example: "You are not defective, Angela."

Sit together in silence for five more breaths.

Now switch and repeat the entire practice, with your companion speaking and you becoming their witness.

Afterward, if you like, soul scribe about what you experienced in your body. Note any:

- vibrations
- images and thoughts
- meanings, judgments, stories, and explanations
- behaviors, movements, actions, impulses, and urges
- affect and emotions
- sensations

# 29

# CULTIVATING RESOURCE

*Make good use of your own suffering.*
Janice Bad Moccasin

*Being engaged and fighting for one's future and trying
to make a difference is actually a resource that is
protective for at least some mental health outcomes.*
Dr. David R. Williams

Resource is anyone or anything that promotes growth and healing. It can be a person, process, relationship, experience, memory, or energy flow. Wherever it comes from, it is always tied to creation itself.

Every one of us is blessed with a giant goodie bag full of resource. Yet most of us focus on only one corner of our goodie bag and rarely look beyond it.

This is actually a cause for celebration. It means that you have many more places to turn—and many more options to explore—when the heat gets turned up under you.

Let's review your most familiar and obvious forms of resource:

- family members, friends, and other human beings who care about you

- helping professionals—healthcare workers, therapists, counselors, life coaches, massage practitioners, and so on

- spiritual leaders, coaches, and advisors
- trustworthy mentors, elders, and teachers
- spiritual community
- informal and formal support groups of all types, from Twelve Step meetings to weekly breakfasts with trusted acquaintances
- meaningful written texts[80] of all types—from brief aphorisms to multivolume works
- helpful apps
- talks, podcasts, videos, interviews, and in-person presentations featuring wise and compassionate people
- workshops and classes led by people you trust
- inspiring music and art
- a regular contemplative practice such as meditation, prayer, yoga, chanting, singing, mindful walking, or Mindfulness-Based Stress Reduction. (However, keep in mind the potential peril of bypassing, as I discuss on page 138.)
- time spent in nature—walking, cycling, swimming, bird watching, collecting mushrooms, or watching sunrises
- time spent quietly alone, deliberately not doing any task
- time spent with animals—a beloved pet, the pet of a friend or family member, or wild animals in a park or nature preserve
- an enjoyable art, craft, skill, or hobby—taking photographs, cooking, painting, dancing, restoring your home, playing chess, or creating a new and helpful app
- keeping a journal
- the many body practices in this book, my other books, and my Somatic Abolitionism blog
- principled, compassionate activism—working for a valued cause

---

80    By *texts*, I don't mean brief messages sent from your cell phone. I mean written messages of all types and lengths, from graffiti to books to websites to the contents of openlibrary.org.

- pausing and paying attention
- any other activity that you find meaningful

Now let's investigate four ways to explore your resource toy box that many people overlook or don't recognize as valuable:

1. Add more soft things to your life. Take regular naps. Take relaxing baths. Spend three minutes a day stretched out on the floor, listening to your favorite music. Go dancing. Download and use a stress-reduction or grounding app. Hug and kiss your family members twice as much as you do now. Spend more time playing with your grandkids, your pets, or both. Get massages.

   *Pause.* Before you read any further, write down at least three soft things not on the above list that you can easily add to your life.

   Then *pause* again and notice a couple of deeply important things. First, at any time, you can select and access a resource from the list of soft things two paragraphs earlier, or the longer bulleted list I provided two paragraphs before that, or the list of soft things you just created. Second, notice that, at any time, you can pause and add more soft things to your list.

   The brief, simple processes we just walked through— identifying, selecting, and accessing different forms of resource—are what I call *cultivating resource.*

2. Consider all the people who care about you. We naturally see partners, relatives, and friends as forms of resource. But there are many other people in your life who can help or support you. Don't dismiss them as resources just because you're not close to them.

   If you have early-stage prostate cancer and you're torn about what to do, reach out to your colleague at work who had it a few years ago. If you're beginning to have doubts about the trustworthiness of your minister, speak with two or three other people in your congregation. If you're worried about letting your sixteen-year-old son drive your car, call or e-mail the couple down the block, who now have three kids in college. Your shared interest or experience—and your familiarity as an acquaintance—may be enough to bring the two of you together around your particular concern.

*Pause.* Before you read any further, write down the names of at least three acquaintances who might serve as resources for you—and how you think they may be able to help.

3.  Connect with your elders and ancestors. Each of your ancestors may have wisdom, experience, or information that can guide you. Talk with your parents, grandparents, aunts, uncles, and other respected elders about their lives and about the generations that came before them. Ask them to show you old photos and films. Explore your memories of any ancestors who might provide you with insight or support. Even an ancestor you despise may be able to teach you something, by helping you recognize what *not* to do—and by enabling you to be grateful for having chosen a different path.

    *Pause.*

    The paragraph above lists some ways to reach out to your ancestors and elders. But there is much more to your relationship with them. *Your ancestors are already communicating with you.* Their experience resonates through the family you grew up in and through the ways in which you were raised. Your ancestors taught important lessons—either directly to you or to some of your other relatives. Their DNA is expressed in your own cells. Your body's six intelligences can help you and your ancestors communicate. You'll read an example of this later in this chapter.

4.  Embrace silliness and cuteness. Here is some serious advice: watch videos of cute and goofy animals, cute babies and kids, and pets and their owners doing silly

things. Watch silly comedies.[81] Don't think of these as guilty pleasures, but as forms of resource. They can help you relax and settle your body. They can make you laugh, and they can help you relax. These are both worthwhile outcomes.

Two caveats:

First, if something is funny but cruel or dangerous, it's not resource. Madea and Monty Python are both types of resource, but videos of foolish people or animals injuring themselves are not. Mean-spirited comedians who focus on humiliating others are not, either.

Second, embracing silliness and cuteness doesn't mean using it as an excuse to avoid growing up. You still need to fulfill your daily responsibilities and be an adult, and you still need to get your reps in. If you find yourself spending a lot of your time with silliness and cuteness, reread my cautions about bypassing on page 138.

When you access any resource, pay close attention to what shows up in your body. Remember the VIMBAS from Chapter 6:

- vibrations (the charge or energetic quality that your body picks up about a person or situation)

- images and thoughts (memories, ideas, visions, fantasies, etc.)

- meanings (explanations, stories, comparisons, connections, cognitive judgments, etc.)

- behaviors, impulses, and urges (what your body does, plus what it wants to do that you don't act upon)

- affect and emotions (fear, joy, disgust, delight, anxiety, pride, grief, longing, etc.)

- sensations (pressure, tightness, release, heat, cold, numbness, etc.)

If you like, whenever you access resource, soul scribe by writing down your body's experience with the VIMBAS.

---

81  I regularly do all of these. I also regularly read comic books and sometimes watch cartoons.

As you cultivate resource more and more often, you will eventually discover that resource and discernment often work together and build on each other.

Necessity is the mother not only of invention but of recognizing resource. For many of us, it's only when we get in serious trouble that we allow ourselves to access forms of resource that we always had available but previously ignored.

From 2011 to 2013, I lived on a military base in Afghanistan and traveled throughout the country, managing the wellness and counseling services for civilian contractors on fifty-three US bases. I watched bombs fall, people die, and other people lose their minds. I witnessed more terror and brutality than any human being should ever have to.

When I came back to the States, I was no longer whole. Like many other people who had spent years in war zones, I regularly fantasized about killing myself. To keep myself going, I used as many of the standard-issue resources as I could from the most familiar, therapist-approved corner of my resource toy box. Although I regularly reached out to my wife, I did so in the ways in which we'd always communicated. But it wasn't enough to keep me from slowly coming apart.

It was then that words and images of my ancestors—especially my grandmother—began coming to me. I'd see a flash of my grandmother Addie's face with a smile, or an open and questioning look, or a nod of love and support. I'd recall a long-forgotten phrase that she said to me when I was small, sometimes combined with a gesture or a movement or a smile.

Over time, I was able to access more and more images of her. Soon a variety of vibes and urgings began to emerge as well. I imagined that I was like a spider, standing on a web that spread out across the generations, vibrating with the energies of Addie and my other ancestors.

Eventually I got their message: these ancestors could help me, if only I would reach out to them and accept their wisdom and guidance.

Grandmama Addie had passed away a few years before, so I reached into my memories of her, asked for her help, and opened myself to her responses. She did not magically appear to me with a knowing smile, like Obi-Wan Kenobi at the end of *Return of the Jedi*. But, one by one, memories of her resurfaced—most of them suffused with love, concern, and important lessons. These helped me to reconnect with the person I had been before I flew halfway around the world to make a war zone my temporary home. When I was the most broken, these memories would keep me going for the next minute, or at least the next few seconds.

Then I reached out to my mother, Amanda, who was (and is) still alive and well. I shared my pain with her. She listened without judgment, and at my request she told me stories—about my growing up, about her and my father's marriage and divorce, about her own parents and grandparents. She helped me to experience a web of ancestral love, connection, and context. Her stories reminded me that the troubled young man I once had been still lived inside me—but no longer defined me, made choices for me, or needed to protect me.

Then I did something that, at the time, was deeply difficult for me. I shared with my wife, Maria, all my fear, panic, and despair—and my desire to die. I knew that this would forever alter our relationship and that it would open both of us to unknown peril and possibilities. She listened, and listened some more, and understood. I wasn't even sure what I needed from her—but, somehow, *she* understood, and she provided it.

The "it" wasn't something static. Sometimes she just held me for hours. Sometimes she simply listened while I described some of the horrors I'd witnessed. Sometimes she sat me down at the kitchen table and said, "Here. Eat this fruit salad, and drink this coffee." And sometimes she said, "I love you, baby. Now get your ass up from in front of the TV and take the dog for a walk. And when you come back, go to your office and get to work."

Somehow, with the love and support and memories of these three women, parts of the man I once had been—the person they all loved—began to be re-membered. Small step by small step, my bodymind metabolized the traumas from Afghanistan. Day by day, I healed—and continue to heal.

Each of us, at all times, no matter what our circumstances, has access to a multitude of types of resource. I mean *no matter what our circumstances* quite literally. Here's an example:

Perhaps you've heard of Albert Woodfox, the author of the book *Solitary: Unbroken by Four Decades in Solitary Confinement — My Story of Transformation and Hope*, which was a finalist for the Pulitzer Prize and the National Book Award. Woodfox, a former Black Panther, was convicted for the 1972 murder of a prison corrections officer. The evidence for this conviction was dubious, and during Woodfox's initial trial, potentially exculpatory evidence was withheld. The murder victim's own widow believed that Woodfox was innocent. Nevertheless, he was found guilty, sentenced, and placed in solitary confinement for over four decades. Eventually, after forty-two years, Woodfox's case was overturned by the US Court of Appeals.

For all of those years, Woodfox lived alone in a small cell in Louisiana's Angola Prison. It is hard to imagine a situation in which someone would seemingly have less access to resource.

But Woodfox was able to cultivate multiple types of resource. He borrowed and read law books from the prison library. He did legal work for other prisoners. He taught a fellow prisoner to read. As he wrote in *Solitary*: "I had transformed my cell, which was supposed to be a confined space of destruction and punishment, into something positive. I used that space to educate myself, I used that space to build strong moral character, I used that space to develop principles and a code of conduct, I used that space for everything other than what my captors intended it to be."

But perhaps Woodfox's most important resource was his mother's memory. Beginning about a year after she died in 1994, Woodfox heard his mother's voice in his head. He wrote in *Solitary*, "It was like her voice echoed through the years to speak to me."

In the months and years that followed, Woodfox continued to reach out and connect with his mother's memory. Even though she had passed away—and even though he spent twenty-three hours of each day alone in a prison cell—she became a consistent, reliable resource for him.

This resource was not imaginary. Woodfox accessed his mother's actual words, actions, and energies—and his memories of their interactions together—and made meaning from them.

Woodfox also realized that an image or a memory can connect to all six of the body's intelligences. It can have physical sensations, emotive qualities, vibrations, significant meaning, and a good deal more.

Over more than four decades, Woodfox was able to maintain and grow his sanity, his humanity, his compassion, and his sense of justice by regularly cultivating resource.

Cultivating resource isn't just an emergency measure—something to turn to when life becomes stressful and painful. The practice of cultivating resource can benefit you at all times—not just when the chips are down. Whatever your situation, it can add meaning, wisdom, compassion, insight, and stability to your life.

I hope it's also clear that cultivating resource isn't something you do once and then forget about, like tightening a loose screw. It's something to practice over and over until it becomes second nature—so that your body learns to do it automatically when it needs assistance or support.

Elsewhere in this book I mention the value of a *settled* body. But what's even more valuable is a *well-resourced* body—one that, anytime and anywhere, is prepared and able to cultivate resource.

Being able to settle your body is like owning a car and knowing how to drive it. Being able to cultivate resource is like *also* having a reliable GPS, a travel agent, and years of using many different travel websites.

You can support your practice of cultivating resource by creating your own personal set of *resource icons*. These are images, symbols, and phrases that quickly remind you of specific resources. A resource icon is essentially a shortcut on your internal computer screen that you can quickly locate and click on.

Imagine that you had a teacher in high school who was an important mentor. She died a few years ago, but her words, actions, and lessons still live on inside you. Her photo from your high school yearbook can be a resource icon for all your memories of her and everything you learned from her.

Suppose that your uncle David was a major role model when you were growing up. You have a particular memory of him holding onto your forearm as you practiced learning to ride a bicycle. That memory of his firm and confident grip can become a resource icon. Simply recalling that grip can enable you to quickly access all your learnings and memories involving him.

Here are some other examples of resource icons:

- the way your sister used to call your nickname to announce that supper was ready

- the warmth of your dog's belly on your hand as she sleeps beside you

- the coolness of the night air when you first step outside after dark

- a still image on your phone's home screen from your favorite cat video

- a quote from Angela Rye posted on your refrigerator door

- your best friends from high school or college telling you how proud they are of you

- the business card of the person who hired you for your first meaningful job

- a tweet from Charlamagne Tha God reminding you that your mental health is just as important as your physical health

One of your most valuable forms of resource is a healthy bodymind. You will be far more able to stay with clean pain, metabolize it, heal, and grow if you take good care of your health. Here are a few of the most important things you can do:

- Keep active. Exercise regularly. Even light exercise— walking, biking, skating, swimming, dancing, or playing touch football—can support your health and happiness.

- Eat healthy foods. In particular, avoid eating a lot of processed sugar, which can play havoc with your energy flows. Soft drinks contain large amounts of processed sugar, often in the form of corn syrup—so drink tea, flavored (but sugarless) carbonated water, or sugar-free soft drinks instead.

- Drink plenty of water—probably more than you drink now. This is much more important than most people realize. Most Americans are seriously dehydrated most of the time.

- Eat foods that lower inflammation, including berries, fatty fish (such as salmon, sardines, herring, mackerel, and anchovies), broccoli, avocados, peppers, mushrooms, grapes, turmeric, extra virgin olive oil, dark chocolate (not milk chocolate), tomatoes, and cherries. Drinking green and/or white tea can also help lower inflammation.

- Avoid using tobacco, alcohol, or recreational drugs as forms of support to relax or get through the day.

- Get as much sleep as your body requires. Maintain a regular sleep routine, with uninterrupted sleep cycles. (See the body practice in Chapter 12 for more detailed guidance.)

- Regularly—or at least occasionally—discuss your thoughts, emotions, and experiences with someone you trust.

The body practices that follow will help you make cultivating resource a regular part of your life.

### BODY PRACTICE
## CULTIVATING RESOURCE 101

Here is a very simple, foundational way to cultivate resource:

Sit comfortably and quietly for a minute or two, breathing normally. For ten breaths, follow the air as it enters and leaves your body.

Bring your attention to the bottoms of your feet. Sense the ground beneath them, supporting you. Stay focused here for a few breaths.

Then move your attention to your back. Experience the chair or sofa supporting you, doing what it was designed to do.

Now think of a resource icon—a person, animal, or place that gives you a sense of safety and security. Imagine that you're with that person or animal or in that safe place. Let yourself experience that safety and security for a few breaths.

Notice what your body experiences throughout this practice. Pay attention to any:

- vibrations
- images and thoughts
- meanings, judgments, stories, and explanations
- behaviors, movements, actions, impulses, and urges
- affect and emotions
- sensations

If you like, soul scribe about your experience with this body practice.

## BODY PRACTICE
# YOUR GOODIE BAG OF RESOURCES

Set aside twenty minutes to be alone with your thoughts. Have pen and paper nearby.

Make a list of all the types of resource you can think of. Use the lists and suggestions from the first several pages of this chapter as a guide.

In addition, mentally review all the important things that you have lived through, learned from, and worked on—and the people, connections, skills, and awarenesses that these have brought into your life.

Just remember, a resource must be real. It can't be something you only wish for, hope for, or aspire to.

After twenty minutes, stop. Then slowly review the list from top to bottom. If you like, pause at any time to smile or to be grateful for any resource on your list.

Keep this list in a place that's easy to access. Whenever you like—or whenever you need a boost—take out this list, pick one or more of the resources on it, and connect with it.

Once a month (or more often if you wish), quickly review this list. Then spend ten minutes adding to it.

BODY PRACTICE
## CONNECTING WITH YOUR ANCESTORS AND ELDERS

Find a quiet place where you can sit comfortably by yourself for ten to fifteen minutes. Keep a pen and paper nearby.

Take a few deep, slow breaths. Then ask yourself these questions:

- In what ways do my ancestors and elders communicate with me?
- In what ways are they communicating with me at this very moment?
- Which of my body's intelligences are they using to communicate with me?
- How can I sharpen these intelligences to deepen this resource, connect further with my ancestors and elders, and better discern their guidance?

Sit quietly for a few minutes. Pay attention to what emerges in your body. Note any:

- vibrations
- images and thoughts
- meanings, judgments, stories, and explanations
- behaviors, movements, actions, impulses, and urges
- affect and emotions
- sensations

Soul scribe about your body's experience with this practice.


BODY PRACTICE
## YOUR LIFELONG TRIAD

The body practice described below is for bodies of culture. I discuss and describe a parallel body practice for white bodies at the end of Chapter 35.

### If you have a body of culture:

Find two other bodies of culture whom you know and trust. Ideally, their pigmentation is similar to yours, but this isn't a requirement. A triad might include three Indigenous bodies, or three Black bodies, or three brown bodies with very different identities, or a mixture of types of bodies of culture. (But white bodies need to form their own triads with other white bodies, as I'll explain in Chapter 35.)

Make this agreement with the other two folks in your triad:

*The three of us will get together weekly to work toward ushering in a living, embodied antiracist culture. Separately and together, we will practice, read, research, study, discuss, challenge each other, figure things out, and act from the best parts of ourselves.*

*This process will involve growth, discovery, and generative emergence. It is not a grim duty or an act of racial health maintenance. Together and separately, we will grow our discernment, expand our sense of resource, and explore joy.*

*We may meet in person; through Zoom, Skype, FaceTime, or some other video connection; or in some combination.*

*We'll each do a lot of listening. But we won't just meet and converse. Individually and collectively, we'll also act—though we won't always know what forms those actions will take.*

*We know that, along the way, we will face peril and possibility, make mistakes, learn from those mistakes, and keep going. Our path forward will be unknown and uncharted. We will not follow a playbook; we will write our own.*

*This process will force each of us up against our edges and limitations. When this happens for one of us, we will support them as they examine those edges, move through any discomfort or pain, and metabolize the energy inside it.*

*We know that we must be humble. We will often need to follow in others' footsteps.*

*If one of us leaves the group for any reason, we will find another body of culture to join us, and we will continue.*

*We will do this for the rest of our lives. When all three of us are gone, the group will live on with different bodies of culture.*

Each time you meet in your three-person group, spend some of your time in what I call the resource triangle. This involves three positions: the sharer, the witness, and the observer.

The three of you will take each position in turn, so that each of you spends a few minutes in each position.

The sharer says whatever they wish to say. As they speak, they silently note what they experience in their own body—any movement, stuckness, contraction, expansion, freezing, releasing, trembling, quaking, etc.

The witness listens closely to what the sharer says, without commenting, verbally judging, or interrupting. They also pay close attention to the sharer's body, voice, movements, energy, and vibe as they speak. After the sharer is done speaking, the witness tells the other two people what they witnessed about the sharer.

The observer also listens closely to what the sharer says, without commenting, verbally judging, or interrupting. Then they also listen closely to what the witness says. Throughout it all, they pay close attention to the movements, energy, and vibe of the group as whole, including themselves. After the witness is done speaking, the observer shares what they observed about this three-person communal body.

What will the three of you do during the rest of your time together? I don't know. That's up to you. But don't just chat. Do some of the other body practices together. Commit to taking specific positive action out in the world. Then hold each other accountable for taking that action.

What will each of you do to help usher in a living, embodied antiracist culture outside of these meetings? That's up to you, too.

Each of you has a circle of influence—people you know; relationships you can leverage; opportunities you can take or create or provide; and authority you can wield. Use them to build such a culture.

This might mean instituting (or lobbying for) changes in your workplace. It may mean having a discussion with an elected official. It might mean volunteering for an antiracist cause. It could mean bringing bags of food and bottles of water to a public demonstration. It might mean hiring someone, or firing someone, or changing jobs, or changing neighborhoods.

You may have specific questions. Here is my answer to all of them: This is a process. The three of you will have to live into it. No one can predict it. Just pay attention and act out of the best parts of yourselves.

If enough bodies commit to this foundational practice—and stay committed, year after year and generation after generation—perhaps in nine generations (or eight, or ten) our descendants will be born into a living, embodied antiracist culture.

This is a foundational body practice. If you're not meeting regularly in triads with two other bodies of culture, you may (or may not) be of service to others, but you're not fully practicing Somatic Abolitionism.

Please do not look at this body practice as the ultimate resolution tool—or a rigid container that can hold and process every experience. It's simply one body practice among many. Like all human inventions, it's not perfect, and it shouldn't become static. Please leave room for emergence and change.

This is particularly important for bodies of culture. When we find something that brings us a bit of relief, we can be tempted to idolize it or over-rely on it. Instead, we need to practice it in tandem with other body practices, other forms of resource, and our own discernment.

# 30

# NO FAILURE, ONLY PRACTICE

*I never lose. I either win or learn.*
Nelson Mandela

*Through failure we can re-examine how
to complete the task we just failed.*
David Goggins

*Every defeat, every heartbreak, every loss,
contains its own seed, its own lesson on how
to improve your performance the next time.*
Malcolm X

*Mistakes are a fact of life.
It is the response to error that counts.*
Nikki Giovanni

*No matter how slow you go,
you are still lapping everybody on the couch.*
C. T. Fletcher

*Do the best you can until you know better.
Then when you know better, do better.*
Maya Angelou

*We have to really allow ourselves to create some space for people not knowing, not understanding, just saying stupid things. I mean stupid as in ignorant. That's going to happen, and we have to figure out how to create room for that, rather than policing each other, so that people can actually get into the conversation.*

Rev. angel Kyodo williams

*If you're afraid to fail, then you're probably going to fail.*

Kobe Bryant

When you were a tiny child, the first time you tried to stand up, you fell. The second time you tried, you fell. The fortieth time, you fell. But sometime after your hundredth attempt, you were able to stand up for a breath or two.

Today, unless you're ill or very elderly, or need to use a wheelchair, you can probably walk across the room. Maybe you can run a mile. Perhaps you regularly run marathons.

When you first begin anything new, you'll usually suck at it. But if it's something worth doing—like standing up and walking on your own two legs—you'll naturally keep attempting it. After you succeed once, you'll keep practicing it, getting your reps in until you're good at it. And then you'll keep getting your reps in, because you'll want to keep getting better at it, or at least keep doing it well.

In short, if something is worth doing, then it's worth trying, failing, trying some more, and failing some more. It's worth continuing to do it wrong, do it better, make more mistakes, try new approaches and variations, and eventually do it well. (And even after you've gotten good at it, you'll still make mistakes sometimes.)

In this process, you don't just master an activity; you also develop grit, resilience, stamina, and discipline in your bodymind. You build a habit of perseverance—of being willing to try something new, to fail at it, and to keep trying until you succeed.

This process applies to many of the body practices in this book. It also applies to Somatic Abolitionism in general; to demonstrating; to building and maintaining alliances; to growing up; to acting out of the best parts of yourself; to healing trauma; to creating culture; and to preventing or ending a civil war.

So far, most of the body practices in this book probably haven't been physically difficult for you. That's because they build on movements, habits, and awarenesses that you've already practiced for years.

Other body practices—especially the ones that require you to stay with clean pain—may have been emotionally or energetically difficult at first. But the more you do them, the more embodied they will likely become, and the more natural they will seem.

A few of the body practices in this book may scare the bejeezus out of you at first. A few might activate a strong flight response in your body. This isn't abnormal, unusual, or a problem.

When you come upon a practice that you just can't bring yourself to do, then don't do it. If you begin a practice and have to stop partway through, then stop.

But later—maybe the next day, maybe after five months— come back to that practice and try again.

And then keep coming back, time after time. As you do, you can develop acuity, nuance, and patience—not only in relation to the particular practice, but to your whole life. At the same time, without even trying to, you will also develop more compassion— both for yourself and for others.

This is one of the reasons why soul scribing is so important. It provides a simple written record of what you've done and where you've been, and of what you have earned and what you have yet to earn. Periodically, you can look back at what you wrote a week, a month, or a year earlier. You can then quickly see how much your body has been tempered and conditioned, how much you've grown, and how much you've been able to discern.

In Chapter 24, I mentioned the taking of Ls, or losses. Paradoxically, taking Ls—often lots of Ls—is a necessary part of growth, transformation, and eventual success. Taking Ls may also make room in your body for something new and important to emerge.

As you get more reps in, you'll also experience three other Ls:

- **Leaps of integrity.** One life rep after another will force you to make a choice: either leap into the unpredictable and unknown future, while acting from the best parts of yourself, or step backward into dirty pain.

- **Learnings.** As you do more and more reps, and dive deeper into Somatic Abolitionism, you will learn things about yourself, your past, your family, your country, and its history that you might otherwise not have encountered.

- **Legacy.** The more you grow, act out of the best parts of yourself, and heal from racialized trauma, the more room you may create in your body for resource—and the more love, support, and healing you can pass on to your children, grandchildren, and beyond. Healing creates a legacy that ripples out, not only across the world, but down through many generations.

Here is one of the many paradoxes of white-body supremacy: The advantages that WBS grants to white bodies puts those bodies at a *disadvantage* when it comes to experiencing something new—not only when it comes to race but in general.

In white bodies, WBS gets in the way of emergence. Because WBS also blocks white bodies from them seeing this, they usually aren't bothered by it.

Encoded deep within WBS is this message for white bodies: *You shouldn't have to endure discomfort and clean pain. Instead, you can blow that pain through bodies of culture. And you don't need to learn anything new, different, and potentially challenging. You can stop trying to be better, either individually or collectively; stay exactly as you are; and let yourself be soothed, protected, and cared for by your white advantage.*

This is a powerful and seductive message, and it encourages many white bodies to give up on racialized challenges too quickly or easily. More tragically, it encourages some white bodies to not begin at all—and to not grow up.

WBS also sends white bodies this message about race: *Closely examining issues of race will cause you pain or discomfort, so it's better to not examine them at all. Plus, if you grapple honestly with these issues, you will probably make some terrible mistakes, and experience embarrassment, and perhaps shame. You might offend people, become the target of their righteous anger, and get called out and shot down. You might be called a racist, or a race traitor, or both. All of this will be painful and humiliating. It's better to just keep your head down; stick with the complicit, collective form of WBS; and hope to get by.*

Attached to these two pernicious messages is a third: *I can't possibly develop racial agility and acuity and grit, because I'm white. This means that, as a group, white bodies can't develop collective racial agility, acuity, and grit, either.*

If you have a white body, please take this message to heart:

Of course you can grow your racial acuity and agility and grit. Do you really imagine that white bodies are inherently inferior to bodies of culture when it comes to matters of race? That's absurd—and bullshit. That idea keeps you racially immature and small, as well as complicit in all the harm that WBS perpetrates on bodies of all skin pigmentations.

You do not get to avoid growing up by telling yourself, *I can't do it. It's beyond my abilities. It's too hard. It's too much for me.* No one does.[82]

And if you have a white body and are Muslim, or Jewish, or gay, or non-binary, or trans, or female, or a member of any other often-marginalized group, please note this as well:

Your process will involve some confusion and some conflicting energies. But you can do this. In fact, you're already committed to doing it, or you wouldn't still be reading this book. You don't get to avoid growing up by latching onto the marginalized part of your identity and ignoring the part that is white. Of course the marginalization you face is real, but don't use it to distract yourself (or others) from the task of building a living, embodied antiracist culture. If your whole block is on fire and you see your neighbor's six-year-old child about to jump from a second-story

---

82    I often hear white bodies say, "I want to transform" or "I want to be (or do) better." But in many cases, they're not willing to actually do it. Instead, they want to magically *become* transformed—like being kissed by a prince or touched by a magic wand—without doing the necessary reps and metabolizing the required clean pain. They want to grow while bypassing the process of growing. This simply can't be done. It's like saying you want to be faithful to your partner while having an affair or hoping to build muscle by buying a set of free weights and never actually working out. The way to transform is to do the work of transforming, not to just talk about it, ask for it, or yearn for it. Somatic Abolitionism is not cotton candy. Over and over, you will need to fall down—and sometimes get knocked down, and occasionally knock yourself down—and then get back up, pause, and resume moving forward.

window, you don't say to her, "Hey, my house is burning up, too." You run over to catch the child.

As you live into Somatic Abolitionism, you *will* make mistakes—maybe some big ones—around matters of race. *Go ahead and make them.* You will learn from them. You will grow from them. Sometimes you will fail repeatedly or make the same mistake time after time. Keep working at it until you succeed or get better.

Yes, you will have setbacks. You will become discouraged. You will repeatedly experience clean pain—and, sometimes, dirty pain. *Stay with that pain or discomfort.* It will teach you discernment. Be curious about it. It won't kill you.

All of this will be worth it. All of it will help you act from the best parts of yourself, time after time.

Sometimes, when you make mistakes, you may anger some bodies of culture. Let them be angry at you. Apologize for any mistake you make or harm you did. Human beings have apologized to each other for many thousands of years, and for all of that time it has proven greatly helpful.

Don't be afraid of being called out. It's part of the process. There's no shame in listening, considering a rebuke, discerning that it's legitimate, and saying, "Now I understand. I was wrong. I'm sorry." Depending on the context, you might add, "Do you need me to make amends? If so, what do you suggest?" Most people will respect you for this.

There's also no shame in listening, considering a rebuke, discerning that it might not be legitimate, and saying, "Thank you. I hear you. I need to consider it some more. You may be right, but I'm not sure yet. I promise you that I'll take it seriously, grapple with it, and consult with people I trust about it."

Sometimes, when you are not making mistakes—indeed, *because* you are not making mistakes—you will piss off some white bodies big-time. Then they may threaten you or punish you, because that's what bullies do. Expect to encounter some of this.

Above all, know this: *You are capable of practicing Somatic Abolitionism. You are able to rise to every challenge in this book. Many* other white bodies have risen to those same challenges. Many are rising to them at this very moment. You will be in good company.

Also know this: some of these other white bodies are making big mistakes at this very moment. So when you fuck up, you will still be in good company.

If you have a body of culture, especially a Black body, WBS has this equally powerful, seductive, and pernicious message for you about race: *You are stuck in a conundrum. White bodies have disappointed you time after time when it comes to matters of race. If you put energy and effort into the body practices in this book, you may be disappointed and betrayed by white bodies yet again. All your efforts will then have been wasted. But if you don't put energy and effort into those practices, you'll be branded a cynic. Meanwhile, through your inaction, you'll be complicit in maintaining white-body supremacy, which will continue to harm you and many others.* It seems like a lose/lose proposition.

If you have a body of culture, please take this message to heart:

What looks like a conundrum isn't actually one at all. That's just another of the many lies that WBS tells us.

What white bodies do, or don't do, has nothing to do with the value of this book's body practices. These practices will benefit you—and the people you love, and your descendants, and all of humanity—even if every white person on the planet refuses to do even one of them.

These practices are opportunities for healing and growth. With a few exceptions (all of which I've clearly noted), they were not devised primarily for white bodies. Most were created for all human beings. I also created some solely (or especially) for bodies of culture.

I don't ask you to have faith in white bodies. No such faith is required. Let the practices in this book sink into your body and serve you. Then, as your discernment warrants, use what you learn to serve others. Trust or distrust each particular white body on a case-by-case basis, based on their actions and the energetic messages they broadcast.

Yes, in the past, many white bodies have disappointed you around matters of race with their fear, ignorance, and avoidance. Many will surely do so in the future. Maybe you've read Dr. Martin Luther King Jr.'s 1963 *Letter from a Birmingham Jail*, in which he decried white apathy, obstruction, and preference for order over liberation.

But this doesn't mean that white bodies are incapable of developing agility, acuity, or grit around race—only that, in the past, most of them have been unwilling.

One of the many subtle and contorted aspects of WBS is that it tells people of all skin hues that white people are too weak or entitled or foolish to ever learn to hold the charge of race. That lie allows white bodies to turn away from growth, embrace denial, and fall into the comforting arms of white advantage. It also encourages bodies of culture to fail to hold white bodies accountable, by imagining that they are incapable of growing up.

But all of us are able to grow up, both individually and collectively. That process is encoded in our genes—and embedded in the energy flows of creation and the cosmos.

## BODY PRACTICE
## WHEN FAILURE WASN'T FAILURE

Think back to a time when you tried something new and different—and you failed. But then you tried again, and again, and yet again, and eventually you either succeeded or improved quite a bit.

Briefly review this entire process, from your initial failure through your success or notable improvement. Pay close attention to your body. Note any:

- vibrations
- images and thoughts
- meanings, judgments, stories, and explanations
- behaviors, movements, actions, impulses, and urges
- affect and emotions
- sensations

Soul scribe about what your body experienced throughout this process.

Now think back to when you tried something else new. In this case, though, not only did you fail the first time, but you never succeeded or notably improved. So you stopped trying.

But you didn't quit learning. Instead, you attempted something completely different. Maybe it was a different method for reaching the same goal. Maybe it was a different skill that produced similar results or gave you an equal amount of satisfaction. And, by taking this alternate route, eventually you succeeded or notably improved.

Briefly review this process, from your initial failure, through your continued failure, to your shift to a new direction, to your success or notable improvement. Pay close attention to your body. Note any:

- vibrations
- images and thoughts
- meanings, judgments, stories, and explanations
- behaviors, movements, actions, impulses, and urges
- affect and emotions
- sensations

Soul scribe about your body's experiences throughout this process of learning and growing.

# 31

# PERIL AND POSSIBILITY

*I'd rather regret the risks that didn't work out
than the chances I didn't take at all.*

Simone Biles

*I am no longer accepting the things I cannot change.
I am changing the things I cannot accept.*

Angela Davis

*Bring your best to the moment. Then, whether it fails
or succeeds, at least you know you gave all you had.
We need to live the best that's in us.*

Angela Bassett

*Be as courageous as you can.*

Timothy Snyder

If civil war breaks out, every moment will become rife with potential peril—and potential possibility.

*Pause.*

Why am I so sure about this peril and possibility? Because every moment of life—including right now—is *always* rife with potential peril, potential pain, and possibilities for growth and transformation.

Peril is not always what we imagine it to be. What looks like peril or disaster may turn out to be a blessing, an opening, or a deepening—or vice versa.

At other times, events may unfold into both disaster and opportunity at once. Sometimes, possibility may follow peril, or vice versa, in quick succession. Sometimes one leads to (or turns into) the other in a slow, emergent process.

When we're hurting or confused, we want to be safer and more secure in order to be able to take a risk. But life doesn't operate that way. In fact, it's just the opposite. Security, safety, and transformation come *after* taking a risk, not before.

Taking a risk always involves moving forward into the unknown.

Don't think about the future too much. That can easily become a fool's errand, a rabbit hole, a dodge, or a *freeze* response. More importantly, it distracts you from being present in the unfolding moment.

It's wiser to acknowledge that you can never perfectly predict the future. No one can. But you *can* live into it with as much courage, compassion, and discernment as you can muster.

Don't try to control the future, either. You can't. Nobody can.

As events emerge, stay present and in your body. *Pause* if it's safe to do so. When you know in your body what to do, do that.

If you don't know, stay with your uncertainty and your clean pain. *Pause* again (or some more) if it's safe to do so. Use your discernment, moment after moment. If and when your body tells you to mobilize, follow its guidance.

At all times, act from the best parts of yourself.

## BODY PRACTICE
## WHEN PERIL BECAME POSSIBILITY

Recall an incident from your past when you had to make a choice. One alternative seemed potentially perilous but was more ethical or compassionate. The other seemed safer, but also less ethical or more cowardly. Nevertheless, you chose the more potentially perilous option.

Review this incident from beginning to end. Pay close attention to what your body experienced, from when you first faced the choice, to making the choice, to the events that emerged as a result. Note any:

- vibrations
- images and thoughts
- meanings, judgments, stories, and explanations
- behaviors, movements, actions, impulses, and urges
- affect and emotions
- sensations

Then answer these questions about what happened:

- Did the peril you feared come to pass?
- If not, what happened instead? Was this outcome helpful or harmful to you? Was it helpful or harmful to anyone else involved?
- If the peril you feared *did* occur, was the outcome as bad as you thought it would be?
- If not, was it better or worse? How much better or worse? Why?

Soul scribe about your experience with this body practice.

## BODY PRACTICE
## **WARNING AND WARDING**

Some primal reps are built into our bodyminds, yet most of us rarely need to use them. This body practice will introduce you to some of these reps. Animals use their own versions of these reps to protect themselves and ward off potential threats.

Do each of the following three times:

- **Straighten and raise up.** Make yourself larger and more imposing by straightening your spine, raising your shoulders, and standing on your toes for three breaths.
- **Raise your voice.** Say, "Yes, what is it?" in your normal voice. Then repeat the same phrase in a much louder, stronger, and deeper tone.
- **Bare your teeth.** While keeping your teeth together, separate your lips as much as you can. Hold your lips there for three breaths. If you like, do this in front of a mirror. (On most people, this looks surprisingly fearsome.)

- **Growl.** Do this loudly, from the bottom of your belly as well from as your throat.

- **Widen your eyes.** Raise your eyebrows and bug out your eyes. Hold them in this position for three breaths. Do this in front of a mirror as well.

- **Collapse.** Sit comfortably in a chair. Then slowly lean forward and go limp, so that your whole body deeply slouches forward. Stay this way for three breaths. (This is similar to what a cat does when you put a hand under it and pick it up.) Although this may look like a gesture of surrender, it is actually protective, because it makes your body much more difficult to lift or drag away.

If you like, soul scribe about your experience with any or all of these primal reps.

Every few weeks, return to this chapter and practice each of these warning and warding gestures three more times. If you find yourself facing potential violence, you may find some of these reps very useful—and perhaps necessary.

## 32

# ONCE IT'S CLEAR WE'RE AT WAR

*There can be no compromise in a culture war.*
*There can be no splitting of differences at Armageddon.*
Michael Gerson

*Threats of violence against public officials are now simply part*
*of the Republican repertoire. . . . So they'll do what they can to*
*protect that mob, condemn its targets (whatever they are), and find*
*any excuse they can to portray themselves as the courageous and*
*oppressed. The result is likely to be more mobs and more violence.*
Paul Waldman

*There is light in darkness,*
*you just have to find it.*
bell hooks

In the first American Civil War, eleven states seceded from the United States and formed their own would-be country: the Confederacy. The Confederate government raised over a thousand regiments of more than seven hundred fifty thousand fighters. Soldiers were paid salaries and given uniforms, weapons, and ammunition. Generals created strategies, which were then implemented by lower-ranking officers and soldiers.

None of this will happen in the war that may follow (or precede) the election of 2022 and/or 2024. There will be no initial strategy beyond attempting to incite widespread, uncontrollable havoc.

Wannabe dictators thrive on chaos and blood. In the beginning of this war, Republican leaders, their media surrogates, and most of their other complicitors will try to provoke as much of both as possible. Their goal will be to create a terrified, confused populace. They will want most Americans to not know what is true, what is a lie, whom to trust, what to do next, or where to turn.

In short, *they hope to create a nationwide traumatic freeze response*, so that a despot—in 2024, probably Donald Trump—can step into the void and take over. This despot will promise law, order, safety, clarity, predictability, and stability—and they will claim that they, and only they, can deliver these things.[83]

*This promise will be a lie.* Instead, if they rise to power, they will do their best to deliver widespread murder, terror, destruction, and domination. This is the plan that nearly all would-be dictators and their followers have followed for centuries.

The problem with inciting a riot—or hundreds or thousands of riots throughout a very large nation—is that no one is in charge. Anything can happen. When eight hundred people stormed the US Capitol, five people died, a hundred forty police officers were injured, and someone smeared human shit on one of the Capitol's interior walls. Had Officer Eugene Goodman not led many of the thugs away from the Senate chamber, our country's vice president and multiple senators might have been murdered.

Now imagine similar lawlessness and violence in three thousand locations at once.

*Pause.*

*Hold the pause* for thirty seconds.

Stay with these words: *lawlessness and violence in three thousand locations at once.*

What is your body experiencing right now? Note any:

- vibrations
- images and thoughts

---

83   As I write this paragraph in late 2021, that despot-in-waiting appears to be Donald Trump. But, especially if Trump's health declines, it could turn out to be someone else—for example, Florida governor Ron DeSantis (whose name is already appearing on Trump DeSantis 2024 shirts), Texas governor Greg Abbott, or perhaps Tucker Carlson.

- meanings, judgments, stories, and explanations
- behaviors, movements, actions, impulses, and urges
- affect and emotions
- sensations

If you like, soul scribe about your body's experience.

In the Civil War of the 1860s, the Confederacy was united by a military, a shadow government, and a clear chain of command. Should there by a second civil war, 21st-century militants will not be led by any of these. Instead, they will be united by rage, resentment, and white-body supremacy.

As Al-Qaeda demonstrated, you don't need a government, or buildings, or even a military to perpetrate violence, mayhem, bloodshed, and terror. Al-Qaeda had sleeper cells—unconnected small groups of people—ready all over the world. These secret groups were armed, trained, and waiting for instructions to spring into action and attack. The groups were largely unaware of each other, but united under a single philosophy and goal.

As I write this in December of 2021, that is exactly what the white nationalist and pro-authoritarian movements in America look like. That is what they looked like in September 2020, when then-President Donald Trump told the Proud Boys, other white-body supremacists, and right-wing militia to "stand back and stand by." That is what they looked like at the beginning of 2021 when, from their bully pulpits in the White House, in Congress, on the Ellipse, and in their command center at the Willard Hotel, Donald Trump and his complicitors encouraged thousands of Americans to riot at the Capitol.

The November 2021 verdict in the Charlottesville trial levied judgments of $26 million against some WBS-oriented organizations and leaders. Presumably, this will eventually lead to the bankruptcy and dissolution of some of these organizations. But the judgment did not (and could not) do anything to weaken the philosophical alignment—the collective philosophical personality—of millions of angry white bodies. As was the case on January 6, 2021, there are many (probably thousands) of small, armed, Al-Qaeda-like groups waiting for the signal to attack.

Will Trump, the GOP, and/or their complicitors give that signal? If so, when? Or will they encourage and demonstrate restraint? What does the recent past suggest?

Beyond this initial chaos and possible bloodshed, no one knows how the war will play out. Some of your relationships will surely shift. Some of the white-bodied people you believed were your friends—or at least your peaceful acquaintances—will join or support the coup attempt, and you will need to cut them out of your life. The same may be true for some of your relatives—even siblings, parents, or children.

New relationships will begin as well because you have created more room for them. You may discover some unexpected compatriots. You may come to rely on people whom you meet for the first time or who were previously anonymous faces in the background of your life.

Here is the most important thing to remember once (and if) the war begins: *There is a tried-and-true method for resisting attempted coups and insurrections.*

George Lakey and Stephen Zunes have studied coup and insurrection attempts around the world, and both have written and spoken widely on the topic.[84] Both Lakey and Zunes tell us that these attempts can often be successfully resisted if people do (among other things) the following:

- Stand strong together. This isn't a mere metaphor, and it involves zero kumbaya. It means standing or marching together in public, perhaps with arms linked. It may mean placing yourself in physical danger. It may mean doing all of this day after day, for weeks or months.

- Practice collective nonviolence. When citizens watch opposing groups actively fighting each other in the streets, they tend to stay home and lock their doors. But when they see a public show of collective nonviolent strength, resolve, and resistance, they tend to flock to the sides of the resistors.[85]

---

84  I recommend some of their books, and provide links to some of their other work, in Chapter 50.

85  It's important to make the distinction between *collective* nonviolence and armed self-protection.

- Learn how to physically defend yourself. Take a self-defense course and/or martial arts training. Learn how to repel an attacker using everyday objects or your own body. Encourage your adult and teenaged family members to also learn physical protection techniques. Perhaps take a class in gun use and safety. (I'll discuss this subject in more detail in Chapter 36.)

- Cultivate structures of trust, and build alliances across divides. In successful resistance movements, people reach out to people of all skin tones from a wide range of backgrounds and professions—including, in some cases, police officers and soldiers.[86] They tell these folks about the importance of the moment and how much they can help by joining the resistance. They stress that resistance is not about politics (liberal versus conservative, etc.), but about justice, equality, and a democracy that includes and supports everyone.

- Don't let anyone conflate resistance with politics. When someone calls you a radical, a liberal, a socialist, a traitor, or anything else, shake your head and say, "I'm doing this as an American. This isn't about politics. It's about standing up for justice and an unfettered democracy."

As the conflict unfolds, and as you become involved in resisting the forces of authoritarianism, here are some things to keep in mind:

- Before you join any public demonstration, use the five anchors (or some other body practice) to settle your body and nervous system.

- Help others where and as you can.

---

Depending on where in the United States you live, it may be wise to carry (and learn to use) a handgun and/or to keep one in your home to protect yourself and your family. But don't bring a gun—or a weapon of any kind—to a public demonstration.

86  Use your discernment—and listen closely to your body—when engaging with soldiers and police. On the one hand, when citizens see uniformed soldiers and police supporting the resistance, many will be inspired to join you. On the other, when a solider or police officer goes rogue, switches alliances, or turns out to be a plant who secretly sides with coup supporters, that person may be exceptionally dangerous.

- After any demonstration or similar event, soul scribe if you experience an urge to. If you like, talk with someone you trust about what you experienced.

- If you experience a traumatic, difficult, or high-stress incident, expect (and set aside) a recovery period afterward.

- At all times, do what you can to respond from the best parts of yourself.

- If you become a frequent activist, take classes in CISM (critical incident stress management), basic first aid, CPR, and/or psychological first aid. I've provided some resources on CISM and psychological first aid in Chapter 50.

If you have a body of culture, or if you live in an area with a great deal of unrest or violence, consider buying and wearing a body camera. Get a body-mounted model so that your hands can be free at all times. If possible, set it up so that it regularly (and automatically) uploads into the cloud. That way, even if the camera is destroyed or taken from you, what it has recorded can still be retrieved.

Wear this body camera in a highly visible spot on your body whenever you leave your home.[87] This serves two purposes: first, the camera can record any dangerous or illegal encounter and thus provide solid evidence of what actually transpired; second, the mere presence of this camera may discourage some folks from getting violent with you. A good body-mounted body camera costs between $100 and $150, which is a small price to pay for the potential added security and safety.

At its best, activism is a form of healing. It is a way to learn, and a way to express regard, caring, compassion, and love. Please bring as much of these to your activism as you can.

---

87    Even if a civil war is averted, regularly wearing a body camera may be a good idea for many bodies of culture. Imagine if Christian Cooper had not carried his phone with him, had not had the foresight to video Amy Cooper in Central Park, and had not had both hands free to do it. Perhaps Amy would have succeeded with her con. Also consider this: had multiple bystanders not video-recorded Derek Chauvin's murder of George Floyd, Chauvin might never have been charged with a crime. In the absence of video evidence, when bodies of culture are harmed, perpetrators are often not held accountable, because the conflicting verbal accounts of the people involved frequently lead to "he said, she said" stalemates.

## BODY PRACTICE
# WHAT WE FACE

Find a quiet place where you can sit comfortably, alone, in front of your computer or smartphone. Have pen and paper ready.

Take a few slow, deep breaths.

Google "January 6 riot." Then click on the Videos tab near the top of your screen. A long list of links to videos will appear.

For the next thirty minutes, click on the links, and watch the videos they lead to, one after another.

Afterward, soul scribe about your body's experience. Note any:

- vibrations
- images and thoughts
- meanings, judgments, stories, and explanations
- behaviors, movements, actions, impulses, and urges
- affect and emotions
- sensations

Take a few more deep, slow breaths. Then, say aloud: "This is what our country is facing. This is what it has always been facing."

# 33

# MOVING YOUR BODY INTO THE STREET

*Protest can be organized through social media,*
*but nothing is real that does not end on the streets.*
Timothy Snyder

*Be calm and focused: when things get most intense,*
*react to danger or warning signs sooner, not later.*
"Safety During Protest," Amnesty International

*Do whatever you legally can now, before it's too late,*
*while something can be done.*
Brynn Tannehill

If our nation descends into civil war, or if upheaval is widespread, few of us will have the privilege of watching the conflict from the sidelines. You, I, and many millions of others may need to mobilize. This will mean getting our bodies out into America's streets, town squares, and other public places. And we may need to do this time after time, day after day.

If you are an internet "warrior," it will not be sufficient for you to post videos, spread news and information, make comments, petition elected officials, and otherwise be an online "activist." If you do not put your body where your convictions are, you could be complicit in the death of American democracy.[88]

Let's flip that statement over. *If you put your body on the line for equity, justice, the right to vote, liberation, and an emancipated democracy, you will help provide these for your children, your grandchildren, and their descendants.*

The details that follow will help you stay safe, focused, and settled, from the time you commit to demonstrating until the time you return home afterward. They will also help your participation be as valuable as possible. (For information on many other useful and more detailed guides to demonstrating, as well as other forms of social action, see Chapter 50.)

That said, if the situation unfolding around you appears dire, you may need to immediately hurry outside and join with other justice-loving Americans, ignoring some of the specifics below, in order to promptly and firmly push back against chaos and imminent autocracy.

## Things to Keep in Mind

- Some demonstrations may be carefully planned, organized, and scheduled well in advance. Others may be spontaneous or put together on the fly. Be ready to drop what you're doing and mobilize quickly. You'll have many opportunities to sign up for texts from organizers that will tell you where and when to show up.

- Because the situation may shift rapidly and profoundly, stay on top of local developments as best you can through social media, reliable news sources, and people you trust.

- Depending on what unfolds in your locale, you may need to demonstrate *in support of* local authorities or—in cases where local leaders side with rioters—*against* them. In some spots, this situation could flip 180 degrees (and perhaps back again).

- Remind yourself that speakers and leaders at any demonstration may be young, old, or in between. Suspend

---

88   I'm not asking anyone to do the impossible. If you've got a disability that keeps you homebound, or if you cannot get to a location where you can make a positive difference, do what you can from wherever you are. This can of course be quite a lot.

any judgments you may have about someone's age. A nineteen-year-old may have five years of organizing and activism under their belt.

- Remember that when you demonstrate, you stand together with other Americans in support of democracy, justice, and equality. The woman standing on one side of you may hold a sign that says, "I Support Liz Cheney and Voting Rights." The man on the other side may carry one that says, "Democracy, Yes—Capitalism, No." Remind yourself that, in this war, both people are on your side. Stand with them both. When the war ends, either or both of these folks may become your political opponents. For now, however, they are your compatriots in support of our country's survival.

- Follow all instructions and directions. This is vital, as it keeps demonstrations from devolving into chaos. If you have questions or need further instructions, look for *marshals* (or *stewards*), who are trained to give directions and maintain safety and order. Typically, marshals wear yellow or orange vests, or brightly colored hats (usually green), or signs or banners that say "Marshal" (or "Steward").

- There will often be embedded agitators whose job is to create drama and sow chaos. Stay alert for these folks. If you think you've spotted some, quickly move away from them, find a marshal, and let them know about the potential agitators.

- Nonviolent solidarity is essential. If a demonstration devolves into chaos or violence, leave as swiftly and safely as you can.

## What to Do in Advance

- Consider buying a burner phone to take to demonstrations. This phone should have little or no important information on it. You'll use it mostly to call and text people and perhaps access the web. If this phone gets lost, destroyed, or taken away from you, you will have lost very little. *Keep this phone fully charged.*

- If possible, arrange to go with at least one other person—ideally, two to four others. Stay together with this posse as much as you can, so that as a group all of you can look out for each other. If one person gets into trouble, the other group members can quickly step in and assist them.

- Make sure that everyone in the group has all the phone numbers of everyone else. Remember to give out your burner phone number.

- Memorize the phone numbers of one or two people whom you can contact in case of an emergency. These might or might not be posse members. If you're not good at memorizing numbers, write their names and phone numbers on your arm in ink.

- Find the name and phone number of a highly rated local lawyer who specializes in civil rights or social justice cases. Write down their name and phone number on a piece of paper.

- Get and write down the phone number for the National Lawyers Guild Legal Support Hotline for your state (or the District of Columbia). You'll find this at nlg.org/massdefenseprogram. A few states have no hotline of their own; if you live in one of these, write down the number of the National NLG Federal Defense Hotline: 212-679-2811.

- If possible, get a good night's sleep the night before the demonstration.

- Eat some healthy food and drink plenty of water within an hour or two before you leave. It's harder to act from the best parts of yourself when you are tired, hungry, or very thirsty. If you're drowsy, drink some tea or coffee.

- Wear comfortable clothing that will keep you adequately warm or cool. If you anticipate temperature changes, dress in layers that can be easily removed.

- Wear comfortable shoes that you can run in, should you need to.

- If you usually wear contacts, leave them at home; wear glasses instead.

- If you are menstruating, wear a menstrual pad rather than a tampon, and bring a few extras. If you are detained, you may not have a chance to change tampons.

## What to Bring (in Your Pockets and/or a Small Backpack or Shoulder Bag)[89]

- your fully charged burner phone

- your driver's license or some other valid ID

- one major credit card, if you have one

- a small amount of cash—$10 to $20—in small bills

- several bottles of water, to avoid dehydration

- depending on your location and the time of year, sunscreen, a sun hat, insect repellent, hand warmers, and so on

- a small, basic first aid kit

- pens and paper

- tissues and/or wet wipes

- phone numbers for emergency contacts, a local lawyer, and your state's Legal Support Hotline (see above)

- any medications or other health-related items that you might need during the next twelve to twenty-four hours

- a flashlight, if the demonstration begins late in the day

- an umbrella or rain poncho, if rain appears likely

## What to *Not* Bring or Wear

- your wallet

- your regular phone

- jewelry, a necktie, or anything else that can be easily grabbed

---

89   I'm writing this chapter in the middle of the COVID-19 pandemic. If you're reading it during a serious infectious disease outbreak, of course wear a mask to the demonstration, and bring a few extra masks with you.

- anything expensive or valuable
- a weapon of any kind

## What to Do Shortly Before You Leave for the Demonstration

- Tell someone you trust who is *not* going to the demonstration where you are going and when you plan to return. (Let's call this person your *backup buddy*.) Promise your backup buddy that you will call them when you're safely back home, to let them know that you're okay. Agree on a time by which you will make this call. Give the person your burner phone number and the emergency numbers of people to contact if you do not call them back by the agreed-upon time.

- If you have long hair, tie it back so it cannot be easily grabbed.

- Do what you can to settle your body and nervous system, using some of the body activities in this book, especially the five anchors in Chapter 21.

## What to Do When You Arrive at the Demonstration Site

- With the other members of your posse, decide on a main meeting point and a meetup time. If anyone becomes separated from the group, this will be where and when all of you will reassemble.

- Set up a backup meeting point, in case the main one becomes inaccessible or dangerous.

- Agree on an exit strategy—how and when you will leave, should leaving become necessary.

- Locate, discuss, and agree on possible escape routes, should events turn perilous.

- Ground and orient yourself.

- Remind yourself to stay alert, use your discernment, settle your body as appropriate, and respond from the best parts of yourself.

## What to Do During the Demonstration

- Listen for and follow the directions of speakers, organizers, and marshals.

- If a problem arises, or you spot potential trouble, or you have a question, speak with a marshal.

- Stay alert. Ground and orient yourself often, so that you are always aware of what's going on 360 degrees around you.

- As necessary—if you are marching or if an existing escape route disappears—look for and note alternate routes.

- Use the five anchors and/or other body practices to stay as present, discerning, and settled as you can.

- If your body simply won't settle, remove yourself from what's happening for a few minutes. (Let your posse know what you're doing, why you're doing it, where you're going, and when you'll be back.) Find a relatively quiet and private spot; resettle your body; then return.

- If counter-demonstrators try to engage with you, ignore them as best you can. Simply walk past them—or walk away—without making eye contact.

- You are not—and should not be—a spokesperson. If someone in the media tries to interview you, point them to the demonstration's leaders and say, "Talk to them. They're the people with the clearest message."

- Obey the law. In the unlikely event that a speaker or leader urges you and other demonstrators to do something illegal, *pause*. Settle your body. Use your discernment to decide whether the situation is so unusual—and so dire—as to make lawbreaking the best course of action. If your body senses that it is not, leave the demonstration in a swift and orderly manner.

## What to Do If Trouble Breaks Out

- If the situation becomes potentially perilous, quickly gather your posse, check and evaluate your possible escape routes, swiftly agree on which route to take, and leave in as brisk and orderly a fashion as you can.

- If a swift escape is not possible, look around for the source or center of the danger and move away from it.

- If possible, look for a marshal, and, along with the rest of your posse, make your way over to them.

- If you are wearing sunglasses, remove them. When people cannot make eye contact with you, this may activate a *fight* response in their bodies, and they are more likely to try to hurt you.

- If the situation becomes violent or chaotic and you cannot move away, fall to the ground and don't move.

- If you are pushed or pulled, drop quickly into a sitting position. Stay there. Move as little as possible while remaining silent.

- Stay as calm and settled as you can.

- Do not expect police or the National Guard to keep you safe from right-wing activists, even if they provoke or attack you. In some locales, the police may side with them.

## What to Do If You Are Detained or Questioned by Authorities

- *Never* resist or run from police, the National Guard, or members of the military.

- If you are wearing sunglasses, remove them, for the reasons noted above.

- Keep your hands clearly visible at all times. You may wish to hold them above your head. This is especially important if you have a body of culture.

- If you are carrying an object of any kind, *very slowly* put it down, with your hands in full view at all times. *Do not put it in your pocket or backpack.*

- Be as relaxed and courteous as you can, so you will not be seen as a physical threat. This is triply important if you have a body of culture.

- Ask: *Am I being detained? Am I free to go?* (If the answer to the first is *no* and the answer to the second is *yes*, leave the demonstration as quickly and safely as you can.)

- You do not legally have to answer *any* question. You do not have to give your name or your reason for demonstrating. You have the legal right to remain completely silent.

- If you have been injured, clearly and firmly request medical assistance.

- Stay calm. Use the body practices in this book to settle your bodymind as best you can.

- If you are detained, threatened, or restrained by someone who is *not* a member of a police force, the National Guard, or the military, then it *may* be wise to resist, run, or fight back. Evaluate the situation, consult your body, and make the best decision you can.

## What to Do If You Are Arrested and Booked

- Know that the police may lie to you about anything. They may falsely tell you that the people you were with have been arrested. Or they may falsely claim that if you don't cooperate, you'll spend years in prison.

- Say very little. No matter what you are told or threatened with, repeat these words, over and over: "I invoke my right to remain silent. I want to speak with a lawyer. I want to make a phone call. I do not consent to a search."

- Contact a lawyer as soon as you can.

- Do not sign anything.

## What to Do After You Get Home

- Promptly contact your backup buddy and let them know that you are safely back home.

- Use the body practices of your choice to settle your body, review your experience (including the VIMBAS), and metabolize the energy. If you like, soul scribe.

- Talk about your experience with someone you trust.

By now, I hope it's become clear that preserving our country and beginning to build a living, embodied antiracist culture are not separate causes. Only when Americans collectively outgrow WBS will we create better connections with each other.

To that end, keep doing the body practices in this book—rep after rep, day after day. They will simultaneously help you heal, grow up, strengthen Somatic Abolitionism, encourage an emancipated democracy, and support the liberation of all Americans.

### BODY PRACTICE
### ORIENTING WITHIN CHAOS

This body practice reprises one of the practices from Chapter 10, Orienting for Safety. It leads you through the same steps but puts your body in a much more chaotic setting.

Go to a very busy public place that's filled with people on the move—a crowded subway platform during rush hour, a theater lobby during intermission, or a dancing throng at an outdoor concert.

Sit or stand in a spot where you are *not* out of the way, but part of the crowd. (However, you do not need to be at the exact center.)

Take a few long, slow breaths. Then, breathing normally, slowly turn your head and notice your surroundings. Look first to one side, then the other. Then swivel your shoulders and your head to each side, so that you can look behind you in each direction. Then look up, then down.

As you observe your surroundings, ask yourself these questions:

- Where are all the exits or paths leading away?

- What structures or objects will I need to move around in order to leave?
- Where are all the spots through which people can approach me?
- In the event of danger, what spots nearby may provide my body with protection?

Now turn your attention back to your body—but also remain aware of your location. Ask yourself these questions:

- In the event of any danger, what parts of my body will be most vulnerable?
- What can I do to quickly protect those parts of my body? (This might involve crouching, lying prone, or moving behind a structure or corner.)
- What parts of my body are reacting most strongly? Where do I experience constriction, or fear, or dread, or any other strong emotion?

If you like, soul scribe in response to this practice.

# 34

# WHITE BODIES AND HAND-WRINGING

*Take off your bedroom slippers. Put on your marching shoes. . . .*
*We are going to press on. We have work to do.*
Barack Obama

*Move past your white guilt. Guilt is an unproductive emotion.*
*Don't sit there mired in woe, just be better.*
Kesiena Boom

*Some people think social media is a substitute for action.*
*It's not. You have to get out and do something.*
Mary Frances Berry

*Get outside. Put your body in unfamiliar places with unfamiliar*
*people. Make new friends and march with them.*
Timothy Snyder

*The world is a dangerous place to live; not because*
*of the people who are evil, but because of the people*
*who don't do anything about it.*
Albert Einstein

In critical times, inaction is a form of complicity. In some situations, it's a form of surrender.

The Democratic Party has been guilty of such inaction time after time, year after year, for generations. (To be fair, it has also sometimes done the right thing at the right moment—or at the last possible moment, when forced into it.)

You already know that, if our country goes to war with itself—or if mob violence springs up in multiple locations—you will be forced to take a side. This will not be an intellectual exercise. You will need to act. You may also need to put your body in potential peril—perhaps multiple times.

As dangerous events unfold, pay close attention to your body. If you notice that a trauma response is being (or about to be) activated—if you find yourself about to *fight, flee, freeze, fawn,* or *annihilate*—then *pause*. Notice exactly what your body is experiencing, from head to toe. Stay with everything your body is experiencing. Then use the body practices in this book to help your body return to a more settled and tractable state.

If your body slips into a *freeze* response, be especially alert for an *avoidance loop*. This is a cycle of compulsive worrying, hand-wringing, and inaction—forms of dirty pain.

In an avoidance loop, someone stuck in a *freeze* response—like a deer caught in headlights—allows the chain of unfolding events to become more perilous. This increased peril re-activates the *freeze* response, generating more worrying, hand-wringing, and inaction. This cycle can continue indefinitely.

When faced with shocking and dangerous events, a body of any skin tone can temporarily move into an avoidance loop. But this is a particular danger for white bodies, because an avoidance loop is itself a common symptom of the complicit, collective variant and the progressive variant of WBS. As its name suggests, an avoidance loop is a way for a body to repeatedly avoid metabolizing its traumatic energy.

When a conflict is racialized, a white-body avoidance loop typically follows this pattern: the person (1) witnesses horrific injustice; (2) experiences shock, confusion, and other strong emotions; (3) fails to substantively act (though they may announce their allyship or solidarity with bodies of culture); (4)

experiences guilt, fatigue, and/or apathy; and (5) remains passive and inactive. Then, when the person witnesses a new injustice, the pattern repeats.

As we've seen, however, trauma is not destiny. Below are three practical, highly effective things you can do if you sense that your body is about to slip into a trauma response—or already has.

1.  Use the body practices in this book—especially the five anchors from Chapter 21—to help your body settle.

2.  Deliberately do *something* active and physical that might improve the situation and is unlikely to cause harm if the situation worsens. Go online, find a demonstration for a good cause, and join it. Locate an organization or initiative that strikes you as important, and volunteer for it. Buy and deliver needed food or supplies to people who are making a positive difference. No matter what else happens, you will have broken the loop by getting your body out into the world.

3.  Remind yourself, over and over, that inaction and passivity are detrimental to justice, equity, and humanness. Then remind yourself that your shift from inaction to action can help you heal. That shift may also help to save lives—and, perhaps, your country.

## BODY PRACTICE
# PUT YOUR BODY IN MULTIPLE IN-PERSON EVENTS

This body practice focuses on an often-overlooked benefit of reps: familiarity. Although I encourage everyone to do it, it is especially valuable for white bodies.

The more familiar you are with a situation or setting, the more nimbly you can act the next time you find yourself in it. You spend less time orienting yourself, so you can quickly begin to discern how to be most helpful and how to stay safe.

If our country faces widespread upheaval, you will probably need to join many public gatherings in support of integrity, justice, and human rights. But don't wait for that upheaval to put your body out in public. Start attending such gatherings now.

Show up in person for some of the following public events:

- demonstrations
- hearings on proposed legislation, rules, and/or policies
- forums sponsored by city, county, or state representatives
- trainings for demonstrators
- rallies for political candidates

You don't have to stay for the entire event. Do, however, stay long enough to absorb the dynamics, energies, and physical layout of each one.

# 35

# WHEN WHITE BODIES SAY, "TELL ME WHAT TO DO"

*If you have come here to help me, you are wasting your time. But if you have come because your liberation is bound up with mine, then let us work together.*

Lilla Watson

*Many of us want to do the right thing so badly, and yet sometimes it feels like we cannot predict the outcome of our well-intended efforts. So, some of us bottle up all of our good intentions and hold on to them, waiting for someone else to tell us exactly what to do, while others mistakenly end up burdening those already carrying more than their fair share in our rush to help. In these messy, uncomfortable struggles, however, we can awaken our capacity to do the deep work of transforming ourselves in order to change the world alongside others.*

Michelle Mijung Kim

*You become strong by doing the things you need to become strong for.*

Audre Lorde

Imagine that your six-year-old daughter says to you at supper, "Being an adult looks hard. Tell me what to do to become one."

Your answer won't be a checklist. Instead, you might say, "Well, butter bean, it's not just a list of things to do. It's a process. You live your life; you pay attention; you act from the best parts of yourself; and, day by day and year by year, you grow up."

"Wow," she says. "That sounds really hard. Can you do some of the growing up for me?"

"No, beanie," you'll say. "It doesn't work that way."

When I lead workshops, trainings, and classes in Somatic Abolitionism for groups of white-bodied people, I often encounter a similar dynamic. Even after some of these folks complete the training and read *My Grandmother's Hands*, they say to me, "Resmaa, I want to work closely with other white bodies to build a living, embodied antiracist culture. Now tell me what to do."

It doesn't work that way.[90]

First, a reminder: I am not anyone's guru, commanding officer, or surrogate dad. Second, culture doesn't get built by one particular person's decree. Third, I can't grow you up. That's your job. Fourth, the request is yet another instance of a white body saying to a body of culture, "I need you to protect me, save me, care for me, guide me, or do my work for me." The only compassionate answer to that litany of requests is no.

If you have a white body, you are not helpless. You are entirely capable of growing up and figuring out many things on your own.

If you're worried or afraid that those tasks are too daunting, remind yourself that this is a lie. That worry and fear are actually WBS talking.

Let's suppose that I often drive recklessly and inattentively. One day, as you cross the street, I sideswipe your elbow. At that point I don't get to say to you, "Sorry! Teach me how to drive." Instead, I need to do my own work to become a better driver—at my cost, not yours. I may also need to get you to a doctor.

Let me speak to one other aspect of *Tell me what to do*. When those words come out of a white body, often they are the beginning of this sentence: *Tell me what to do to support bodies of culture*. This is

---

90    There *are* situations in which *Tell me what to do* is the proper request: in demonstrations, marches, and other such group activities. Do follow the specific instructions of marshals at demonstrations and leaders in trainings, workshops, and classes. In these contexts, it's important to maintain group cohesion, so following instructions is essential. Don't go off and do your own thing, even if you have what you believe is a better idea.

yet another form of othering—and another subtle aspect of WBS. It presents the white body as the actor or subject and the body of culture as the object being acted upon. This very way of thinking is itself a problem. (Imagine how you might respond if I said to you, *People named Maria are great! Tell me what to do to support people named Maria.*)

If you have a white body, don't focus on helping or supporting bodies of culture. Instead, be concerned with growing up and with consistently acting from the best parts of yourself. As you do both of these, you will naturally help and support bodies of all skin hues.

Here's another reminder: if you have a white body and you're serious about helping our world grow out of white-body supremacy, you will need to commit yourself, and your efforts will cost you something. They will cost you time, effort, comfort, and repeated failure. They might also cost you some relationships, money, your current self-image, your social position, or even your job.

Don't try to figure out a way to avoid this cost. There isn't one.

*Pause.* Stay with this realization for a time, until you've metabolized it.

Often when white folks ask, "What can I do?," they really mean, "What can I do that won't cost me or hurt me or challenge me?" If that describes you, now you have to choose: either stop reading or commit to growing up.


How long does growing up require? You already know the answer: the rest of your life.

You also already know that Somatic Abolitionism isn't a blueprint or set of yoga poses to follow. That said, if you have a white body, there is one foundational practice that I now encourage for all white bodies who are serious about building a living, embodied antiracist culture. This practice will help you and two other white-bodied people begin to create a container that can hold the energies of race. You'll find it in the body practice that follows.

Beyond this initial practice, don't look to me for specific answers or for a playbook to follow.

Instead, on your own and with the other people you meet with, create your own answers, your own goals, and your own actions. Form alliances with other trustworthy people and groups. Try out some things, and evaluate the results. Keep doing what works, and learn from what doesn't.

Stay humble; don't expect that you will know all the answers or that you automatically deserve to lead. At the same time, offer whatever talents, support, and service you can. Notice what emerges; then decide and act, separately and together, over and over.

The best thing to do at any given time will depend on your situation, the people you know, your circle of influence, and the dynamics of the present moment. All of these will be emergent. Make the most of the skills, relationships, and opportunities you have. Watch for possibilities (and peril) as they unfold. As John Wesley counseled, do all the good you can, by all the means you can, in all the ways you can, in all the places you can, at all the times you can, to all the people you can.

Instead of following a playbook, you—along with many others—will write it and live into it.

## BODY PRACTICE
## **YOUR LIFELONG TRIAD**

*If you have a white body:*

Find two other white-bodied people you know and trust. Make this agreement with them:

*The three of us will get together weekly to work toward ushering in a living, embodied antiracist culture. Separately and together, we will practice, read, research, study, discuss, challenge each other, figure things out, and act from the best parts of ourselves.*

*This process will involve growth, discovery, and generative emergence. It is not a grim duty or an act of racial health maintenance. Together and separately, we will grow our discernment, expand our sense of resource, and explore joy.*

*We'll each do a lot of listening. But we won't just meet and converse. We'll also act—though we don't yet know what forms those actions will take.*

*We know that, along the way, we will face peril and possibility, make mistakes, learn from those mistakes, and keep going. Our path forward will be unknown, uncharted, and emergent. We will not follow a playbook; we will write our own.*

*This process will force each of us up against our edges and limitations. When this happens for one of us, we will support them as they examine those edges, move through any discomfort or pain, and metabolize the energy inside it.*

*We know that we must be humble. We will often need to follow in others' footsteps.*

*If one of us leaves the group for any reason, we will find another white-bodied person to join us, and we will continue.*

*We will do this for the rest of our lives. When all three of us are gone, the group will live on with different white bodies.*

Each time you meet in your three-person group, spend some of your time in what I call the resource triangle. This involves three positions: the sharer, the witness, and the observer.

The three of you will take each position in turn, so that each of you spends a few minutes in each position.

The sharer says whatever they wish to say. As they speak, they silently note what they experience in their own body—any movement, stuckness, contraction, expansion, freezing, releasing, trembling, quaking, and so on.

The witness listens closely to what the sharer says, without commenting, verbally judging, or interrupting. They also pay close attention to the sharer's body, voice, movements, energy, and vibe as they speak. After the sharer is done speaking, the witness tells the other two people what they witnessed about the sharer.

The observer also listens closely to what the sharer says, without commenting, verbally judging, or interrupting. Then they also listen closely to what the witness says. Throughout it all, they pay close attention to the movements, energy, and vibe of the group as whole, including themselves. After the witness is done speaking, the observer shares what they observed about this three-person communal body.

What will the three of you do during the rest of your time together? I don't know. That's up to you. But don't just chat. Do some of the other body practices together. Commit to taking specific positive action out in the world. Then hold each other accountable for taking that action.

What will each of you do to help usher in a living, embodied antiracist culture outside of these meetings? That's up to you, too.

Each of you has a circle of influence: people you know, relationships you can leverage, opportunities you can take or create or provide, and authority you can wield. Use them to build such a culture.

This might mean instituting (or lobbying for) changes in your workplace. It may mean having a discussion with an elected official. It might mean volunteering for an antiracist cause. It could mean bringing bags of food and bottles of water to a public demonstration. It might mean hiring someone, or firing someone, or changing jobs, or changing neighborhoods.

You doubtless have specific questions. Here is my answer to all of them: *This is a process. The three of you will have to live into it. No one can predict it. Just pay attention and act out of the best parts of yourselves.*

If enough white bodies commit to this foundational practice—and stay committed, year after year and generation after generation—perhaps in nine generations (or eight or ten) our descendants will be born into a living, embodied antiracist culture.

If you have a white body, this is your foundational body practice. It's the single most important thing for you to do. If you're not meeting regularly in triads with two other white bodies, you may (or may not) be of service to others, but you're not practicing Somatic Abolitionism.

Please do not look at this body practice as the ultimate resolution tool—or a rigid container that can hold and process every experience. It's simply one body practice among many. Like all human inventions, it's not perfect, and it shouldn't become static. Please leave room for emergence and change.

# 36

# PHYSICALLY PROTECTING YOURSELF AND YOUR FAMILY

*We've never advocated violence; violence is inflicted upon us.*
*But we do believe in self-defense for ourselves and for Black people.*
Huey Newton

*When it comes to self-defense, it is better to have the power*
*and not need it than to need it and not have it.*
Kevin B. Shearer

*Attackers don't care if you've found your spiritual center.*
*Honestly, neither do we.*
Poster advertising Krav Maga classes

It seems all but certain that the events of 2022 through 2025 will be hugely stressful for nearly all Americans and physically dangerous for many.

What will unfold in your own neighborhood, town, or community? Will there be violence or calm? Riots or peaceful demonstrations? Civil war or nonviolent confrontation? I can't know or even guess. Whether you live in Tampa, or Boston, or Pendleton, Oregon, or Pendleton, Indiana, your situation will be unique.

Here is what I *can* say:

First, stay alert about your local situation, which will likely change day by day and perhaps minute by minute. Pay close attention to local media reports. Connect with your neighbors, and arrange to stay in touch via texting or social media. Perhaps set up rotating neighborhood watches or patrols.

Second, it is always wiser to prepare than to scramble. I strongly recommend that you sign up for a self-defense class and/or a gun use and safety course as soon as you can. If you wait until violence unfolds, there may be hundreds (or thousands) of people in line ahead of you to get the same training.[91] More to the point, you may find yourself without the physical protection skills you need.

Here is a list of some of the ways in which you can physically defend yourself and your family, and how you can learn more about each one:

## Situational awareness training

- kravmaga.com/7-ways-to-improve-your-situational-awareness

- secondsight-ts.com/offerings-situational-awareness-for-safety

- en.wikipedia.org/wiki/OODA_loop

- searchcio.techtarget.com/definition/OODA-loop

## Basic self-defense moves

- realsimple.com/health/preventative-health/safety/4-essential-self-defense-moves-everyone-should-know

- lifehacker.com/basic-self-defense-moves-anyone-can-do-and-everyone-sh-5825528

- www.ucdc.edu/sites/default/files/uploads/documents/Other/Personal%20Safety.pdf

- howcast.com/guides/1064-basic-self-defense-moves

- verywellfit.com/best-online-self-defense-classes-5075581

---

91  I'm speaking here of in-person training, of course. Mini-courses in simple forms of self-defense are widely available online and will likely remain so.

## Self-defense classes
- www.kravmaga.com

## Choosing and using a personal alarm
- spy.com/articles/gadgets/electronics/best-personal-safety-alarms-95169

## Choosing and using a pepper spray
- www.safewise.com/blog/top-pepper-sprays
- www.pepper-spray-store.com/pages/choosing-pepper-spray
- reviews.chicagotribune.com/reviews/best-pepper-sprays

## Using dogs for protection
- offgridweb.com/preparation/dogs-for-defense-considerations-for-getting-a-protection-dog
- medium.com/@aliwoo7876/personal-protection-dogs-the-pros-the-cons-the-everything-in-between-aa86c4f77271

## Responsible gun use, ownership, and training[92]
- National African American Gun Association: naaga.co
- Gun Owners for Responsible Ownership: responsibleownership.org

One final thought: regardless of whether you face imminent danger, it is always worth learning how to keep yourself and your loved ones physically safe.

I need to say a few words about race and guns. (I could write a separate book about the subject, but fortunately I don't have to. Carol Anderson has written a brilliant and eye-opening volume

---

92    If you own a gun but have not yet been trained to use it safely and maintain it properly, sign up for such training ASAP. Also make sure that you are fully aware of the laws regarding gun use and ownership in your state and community—and that you abide by them.

on the subject, *The Second: Race and Guns in a Fatally Unequal America*, which I cannot recommend highly enough.)

For centuries, white bodies have used guns to control, maim, and murder bodies of culture, often with impunity. This is one of the central facts of American history. If you've ever wondered why so many white Americans lose their tempers—and their minds—at the mere mention of any restriction on the ownership of guns, the answer is WBS.

A single example from modern history will make this evident. For decades, white Americans railed vehemently against restrictions on gun use and ownership. Then, in 1966, the Black Panther Party (originally called the Black Panther Party for Self-Defense) was founded in Oakland, California. The Black Panthers promoted self-defense against police brutality. This included the legal ownership, carrying, and use of firearms. This scared the bejeezus out of many white bodies. So, in response, in 1967 the California legislature—with the support of Republican governor Ronald Reagan—passed the Mulford Act, which prohibited the open carry of loaded firearms.

But the restrictions did not end there. As Adam Winkler writes in his book *Gunfight: The Battle Over the Right to Bear Arms in America:*

> The law was part of a wave of laws that were passed in the late 1960s regulating guns, especially to target African-Americans, including the [federal] Gun Control Act of 1968, which adopted new laws prohibiting certain people from owning guns, provided for beefed up licensing and inspections of gun dealers and restricted the importing of cheap Saturday night specials [pocket pistols] that were popular in some urban communities.

Now buckle up and get ready: *In the 1960s, the NRA fought alongside government for stricter gun regulations.* If you don't believe me, Google it.[93]

For more recent evidence of this throughline, look at Officer Thomas Lane's bodycam video of the murder of George Floyd.

---

93   For a very brief (and very cogent) overview of the history of Black gun ownership in the United States, visit the website of the National African American Gun Association: naaga.co//black-tradition-of-arms.

(Google "Thomas Lane bodycam video.") Floyd had just purchased a pack of cigarettes at a mom-and-pop grocery store with a counterfeit $20 bill and was sitting behind the wheel of a van parked outside. As the store clerk who called the police explained, most people don't realize that they've passed a bogus bill, so if police officers can locate the person who used the bill, their usual response is to politely question that person about where they might have gotten it.

That is not what Thomas Lane did with George Floyd. Lane, who is white, knocked on the driver's side window with his flashlight, and Floyd opened the door. Almost immediately, Lane drew his gun and pointed it at Floyd. While Floyd said plaintively and repeatedly, "I didn't do nothing!," Lane kept his gun trained on Floyd and cursed at him.

As the prosecutor in Derek Chauvin's murder case noted, "The police officer could have written him a ticket, and let the courts sort it out." Instead, Thomas Lane saw a Black body sitting passively behind the steering wheel of a van and drew his gun.

Actually, it isn't necessary to go back in history to see how tightly white-body supremacy, gun "rights," and "freedom" are interwoven. First go on the website of the National Rifle Association (home.nra.org). When I visited this site in October 2021, here is what appeared on its home page:

- eight photos containing fourteen people, all of them white

- a box containing the message "Our rights are under attack like never before."

- a box containing the message "Dedicated to securing the future of freedom."

- the phrase "We're proud defenders of history's patriots."

Then visit the site of the National African American Gun Association (naaga.co). You'll find a serious, settled, and even-tempered site that focuses on the safe and responsible use of firearms.

Then ask yourself: *Which site appears to be run by sober and thoughtful adults?*

Let's examine the relationship of race and guns from one more angle. Compare these two stories of adolescent boys from the Midwest:

Boy #1, who did not have a driver's license, drove to a friend's home in another state, where he borrowed a semi-automatic rifle that he was legally too young to own or use. Then, in violation of a curfew that had been imposed, he prowled the streets late at night with the rifle, holding it in front of him, ready to shoot. A police officer threw him a bottle of water and said, "We appreciate you guys, we really do." About fifteen minutes later, the boy did shoot three people, killing two and seriously wounding a third.

Boy #1 was white. He was acquitted on all charges involving the shootings. His white judge, Bruce Schroeder, also dismissed two charges: possession of a dangerous weapon by a person under eighteen and failure to comply with an emergency order from state or local government. He was not charged with driving without a license.

Boy #2 was playing with a toy pistol in a public park, pointing it randomly at people. A witness called the local police department and reported what he saw, saying twice about the pistol, "It's probably fake," and adding, "He is probably a juvenile." Two police officers responded in a squad car. Before the car fully stopped, officer Timothy Loehmann, who was white, shot the boy through the car window, hitting him in the chest and killing him. Boy #2 was Black. Loehmann was not indicted.

You probably recognize boy #1 as Kyle Rittenhouse and boy #2 as Tamir Rice. Rittenhouse quickly became the Kim Kardashian of American gun fetishists—and a poster child for some white-body supremacy groups. Rice quickly became a corpse.

In these stories, you may also recognize three WBS-inspired throughlines:

1. White bodies are automatically assumed—by other white bodies—to be well-intentioned. Bodies of culture—especially Black and Indigenous bodies—are automatically assumed by white bodies to be up to no good.

2. For a white body with a weapon, the normal rules of law, safety, and engagement do not apply. (Recall the central ethic of plantation owners and conquistadors: *We're white*

*people with guns . . . do what we say or we'll kill you. We might kill you anyway.*)

3. Our courts are venerated as institutions of justice. But sometimes American courts kneel before the larger organizing structure of WBS.

The United States has a long, checkered, and complicated history with guns. Indeed, for many white American bodies, guns are the very symbol of safety and protection (and "freedom"). Historically, they are also a symbol of domination.

But protection is more than symbolic. Use your discernment to decide how to best protect yourself and your own family. Do what is wise, prudent, and legal, whether or not it involves firearms.

## BODY PRACTICE
## GROUNDING, ORIENTING, AND TELESCOPING

This body practice seems very simple, as if it primarily involves your eyes. As you will discover, though, it also involves and resonates through your whole body.

This practice may cause your body to do or experience some unexpected things. All kinds of VIMBAS might arise: urgency, or heat, or stuckness, or trembling, or a strong urge to move a particular set of muscles. It may make your body quake.

Most people do this practice by focusing and refocusing their gaze. But if you're visually impaired, you can do it with a visualization—either a memory or a set of images that you make up.

Keep pen and paper near you as you do this practice. Plan to soul scribe at three different points.

Stand or sit comfortably. Then focus your gaze on the most distant point you can see. If you're outdoors or looking out a window, this can be the horizon, or it can be a far-away person, tree, animal, or object, such as a water tower. If you're indoors and there is no window, focus on the spot in the room that's furthest from your eyes.

*Pause.* Take three slow, deep breaths.

Next, move your gaze to something else that's distant, but not as far away—say, a house, or a car, or a train, or the lamp across the room. *Pause* again. Take three more slow, deep breaths.

Shift your gaze once more, this time to something close to you. It might be a street lamp that you can almost touch, or the dog asleep on the rug by your feet, or the mailbox twenty feet away (but not any further away than that). Once more, *pause*. Slowly inhale and exhale three times.

Then shift your gaze to your own body or a specific part of it. *Pause*. Take three more deep, slow breaths.

Now, soul scribe about what your body is experiencing. Note any:

- vibrations
- images and thoughts
- meanings, judgments, stories, and explanations
- behaviors, movements, actions, impulses, and urges
- affect and emotions
- sensations

Next, reverse the process, so that your gaze telescopes out rather than in.

Begin by shifting your gaze back to the nearby street lamp, or dog, or mailbox. (If the dog has walked away, focus on the spot where the dog used to be.) *Pause*. Inhale and exhale slowly three times.

Then return your gaze to the person, object, or animal in the middle distance. *Pause* again. Take three more slow, long breaths.

Next, telescope out to the furthest point you can see. *Pause* once more. Inhale and exhale slowly three more times.

Soul scribe about your body's experience now. Note any:

- vibrations
- images and thoughts
- meanings, judgments, stories, and explanations
- behaviors, movements, actions, impulses, and urges
- affect and emotions
- sensations

Then pull in your gaze in one last time. Focus on the object in the middle distance; *pause;* take three deep, slow breaths.

Shift your gaze to whatever is close to you—the street lamp or dog or mailbox; *pause;* inhale and exhale slowly three more times.

Lastly, move your gaze back to your own body. *Pause.* Finish with three slow, deep, long breaths.

Now soul scribe one final time. Note any:

- vibrations
- images and thoughts
- meanings, judgments, stories, and explanations
- behaviors, movements, actions, impulses, and urges
- affect and emotions
- sensations

As you do this body practice, feel free to add any primal reps that your body might ask for, such as grunting, moaning, growling, humming, hovering, squeezing, wiggling, softening your face, and so on.

# 37

# EXPECT SITUATIONS, ALLIANCES, AND RELATIONSHIPS TO SHIFT

*If you're not careful, the newspapers will have you
hating the people who are being oppressed, and loving
the people who are doing the oppressing.*

Malcolm X

*The insurgent's goal is to make existing governments seem
powerless, feckless, and incapable of protecting the common
citizen—and then exploiting that vacuum to seize political power.*

Malcolm Nance

*When extremists decide to attack all our communities,
they must hope that there will be infighting. But we have
stood all for one and one for all. That is how we will win.*

Ben Jealous

*You do not have to be me in order
for us to fight alongside each other.*

Audre Lorde

*Alliance does not mean love,
any more than war means hate.*

Frances Parker Yockey

*Civil resistance works by separating the authoritarian ruler from pillars of support, including economic elites, security forces, and government workers. It attracts diverse groups in society, whose collective defiance and stubbornness eventually elicit power shifts. Mass, diverse participation empowers reformers and whistle-blowers and weakens the support base of hardliners.*

Maria J. Stephan and Timothy Snyder

*Pause.*

As we've seen, wannabe despots attempt to seize power through lies, confusion, fear, blood, mayhem, and chaos—and, wherever and whenever possible, turbocharging all of these.

First, despots create a clear, simple, easy-to-understand, and utterly false narrative—in this case, *Every Republican win was the result of a free, fair election. Every Republican loss was the result of widespread fraud committed by a conspiracy of traitors.* Then they and their surrogates repeat the lie relentlessly—everywhere, over all possible media, at all times, as loudly and forcefully as possible, until it becomes the single most common message that is broadcast, discussed, supported, denied, debunked, and argued over in the United States. This narrative will have clear but equally bogus villains—the five groups noted in Chapter 7.

A short-term goal of the people promoting this narrative will be to make *not* believing it so stressful, painful, exhausting, and potentially perilous that many bodies—especially many white bodies—will accept it, or at least go along with it, just to keep their jobs or get through the day.

Paired with this false narrative will be equally loud, profuse, and relentless attacks on *all* other ideas and narratives. Every other message will be branded a lie, fake news, Antifa propaganda, a threat from Black Lives Matter, or some form of critical race theory. The core message will be: *Everyone else is lying to you 24/7—not just about our elections but about everything. Every expert is lying. Every authority is lying. Every leader is lying. Every spokesperson is lying—except us. We are the only true, patriotic Americans, so we are the only people you can ever trust. Everything we say is the absolute truth; anything anyone else says is a traitorous lie.*

Some politicians, media figures, and other complicitors will add a variety of other hot-button (and WBS-related) sound bytes. These will involve "replacement theory," states' rights, "freedom fighters," "the American way of life," and whatever else infuriates and mobilizes large numbers of GOP loyalists.

Added to this will be accusations of ever-more-shocking (and ever-more-bogus) crimes that the fantasy villains from Chapter 7 will have ostensibly committed. These accusations will also be repeated endlessly in order to stoke rage and violence among Republican followers.

These accusations may strike you as absurd and laughable. But here is what you must understand: *The more true and obvious something is, the more virulently and vehemently it will be attacked, and the more absurd (or outright impossible) its replacement narrative will be. Some of these narratives will make folk heroes out of white lawbreakers (for example, Kyle Rittenhouse and Ashli Babbitt) and would-be autocrats (like Greg Abbott).*

I'm writing this chapter in October 2021. Several such widespread disinformation campaigns are already underway. Below are just five of the major ones. By the time you read this chapter, there will be dozens. All will be obviously and transparently false, and even self-contradictory, yet some may prove quite resilient and effective.

| Reality | False Replacement Narratives |
|---|---|
| Joe Biden is President of the United States. | Donald Trump is still President, because he did not lose or concede the election, and because he will soon be reinstated. |
| In the January 6, 2021 invasion of the US Capitol, five people died, and a hundred forty police officers were injured. | The January 6 Capitol invasion was simultaneously a peaceful protest in which no one was hurt; a normal visit by tourists; a traitorous attack by Antifa and Black Lives Matter; a false, staged event; the work of FBI operatives; and an act of great courage by patriotic Americans. The only death was the brutal murder of one of these patriots by agents of the Deep State. |

| Reality | False Replacement Narratives |
|---|---|
| Ashli Babbitt was a violent rioter who tried to force her way through a barricaded door into the House of Representatives chamber. She was shot and killed by police who were protecting the chamber. | Ashli Babbitt was an innocent, wonderful, patriotic woman who was also a brave freedom fighter and a martyr. She was deliberately and senselessly slaughtered by Democrats. |
| Many Americans of all skin tones recognize, object to, and are working to end the centuries-long dehumanization of bodies of culture. | Bodies of culture are collectively planning the mass genocide of patriotic white Americans (or white American Christians). |
| COVID-19 is a disease that has killed millions of people and infected hundreds of millions around the world. | COVID-19 is simultaneously a hoax; a deadly bioweapon loosed upon the world by China (and possibly Anthony Fauci); a creation of Big Pharma to help pharmaceutical companies make huge profits on vaccines; and a sleight of hand to enable the Deep State (or possibly Mark Zuckerberg or Bill Gates) to inject tiny tracking devices into our bodies. |

If, after reading the box above, you're confused and mentally exhausted, that is by design. The folks behind the civil war hope to steadily wear down and confuse enough Americans until they have no idea what is true, what is a lie, what or whom to believe, or what to do next.

*If you have a white body, you will be the primary target of these messages.* For this reason, the body practices in this book can be especially valuable for you.

Most bodies of culture are used to being lied to, gaslighted, and misdirected, so they have built some collective racial resilience and discernment around such disinformation. That said, the body practices in this book are no less important for bodies of culture, since they will almost certainly be some of the most common targets of mob violence.

In the next phase of the war, a wannabe despot—most likely Donald Trump—will try to knit together all this confusion with widespread fear. They will do this by inciting as much violence and chaos as they can, while also claiming, after each violent incident (as Trump did after January 6, 2021), that all they intended to do was inspire peaceful protest and a strong future voter turnout. They will also claim that America's enemies (Democrats, Black Lives Matter, Antifa, George Soros, et al.) are the real instigators of the violence.

These efforts will have two goals. The first is to create nationwide disorientation, confusion, and terror. The second is to get people to believe that all the institutions designed to protect them—police, the military, courts, legislatures, and so on—are helpless and useless against the people creating widespread havoc.

At this point, the wannabe despot will change their central message. It will now become:

*Look at where the Deep State, Antifa, Black Lives Matter, and the socialist, traitorous Democrats have gotten us—because, make no mistake, they are responsible for 100 percent of the carnage and terror that now surround us. This has been their plan all along, just like I told you. If we let them continue, our country will soon be destroyed—gone, poof, just like that, in a matter of weeks, maybe days. Your life will be ruined.*

*If you ever want to see the return of law, order, safety, and American values, I am the only person who can bring them back. No one else can be trusted. Support me, and I will save this country from all of its enemies. I'll lock up every single one of them. I promise you, not one will escape my righteous justice.*

*Patriots, are you with me? Are you going to help me take back America?*

In the midst of this chaos, here are some of the other things that may happen:

- Events may be cancelled, rescheduled, relocated, or shut down. Some may be abruptly ended in the middle, and attendees sent home.

- Some initial or potential rioters, surrounded by the chaos and bloodshed—or facing the prospect of arrest and imprisonment—may come to their senses and suddenly shift their support to legitimate institutions and unfettered democracy.

- In locales where rioters temporarily gain the upper hand, some people (especially those with white bodies) who have stalwartly resisted the attempted coup may suddenly decide that they are supporting a lost cause. They may stop resisting, or—imagining that it is their only hope—they may passively accept the coup. These folks may include some police officers, public officials, members of the military, judges, and other people whose jobs are to govern fairly, uphold justice, maintain public safety, and ensure that democracy supports and works for everyone.

- Some police forces, especially in small communities, may align with rioters. In other cities and towns, police officers and National Guard members may split into opposing groups, which may then turn on each other. The same may happen with city, county, and state boards and councils.

- Some chief executives of cities, counties, and states may declare themselves in favor of the attempted coup, especially if initial outbreaks of violence are not swiftly quelled.

- Some people you know—perhaps including some you are close to—may suddenly switch sides, particularly when the opposing side temporarily achieves a firm upper hand.

- Some people will flee their homes, or towns, or states, or the country, seeking safety. Others will leave their communities to join with people who are on the same side of the conflict.

- Some people will become spies and informants for the opposite side.

- Some people who switched sides once may switch again as the balance of power shifts in their locale.

As these events occur in real time—often swiftly and in quick succession—you will need to make one crucial judgment after another. Should you continue to trust someone whom you've trusted for years but whom you suspect may now be part of the coup attempt? Should you continue to stay in relationship with your father, or sister, or daughter who is now a supporter of the coup—or should you swallow hard and permanently cut your ties with them? Should you continue to trust your local police chief, or city council member, or mayor, or governor, or state representative, or member of Congress? Should you stay put, or hide, or defend yourself, or flee? Should you join the spontaneous pro-democracy demonstration that is forming in the nearby town square or parking lot?

You may often need to make swift decisions as events unfold. A quiet street corner may suddenly be taken over by a demonstration, or a mob, or a gunfight. One minute later, it may turn quiet again. The peaceful demonstration you march in may be attacked by violent thugs—or by a motorist who plows into it with their car.

There will be no blueprint or instruction manual to help you make these painful and difficult decisions. But you *will* have this invaluable resource: your bodymind.

Wealthy and powerful white bodies have a long history of splitting their opponents into factions and then turning those factions upon each other.

On this continent, the most successful such split they have engineered is, of course, between disempowered white bodies and (also disempowered) bodies of culture. But this is just one of many such divisions that the Republican Party will attempt to widen and weaponize as the years 2022 through 2025 unfold. Also expect the GOP to attempt to create as much friction as possible between[94]:

---

94    In each duality listed, one group will be encouraged to see itself as pure, superior, virtuous, wise,

- men and women
- people who embrace patriarchy and "traditional" gender roles and those who do not
- evangelical Christians and everyone else
- white evangelical Christians and everyone else
- evangelical Christians and all other Christians
- Trump loyalists and all other Americans
- Trump loyalists and all other Republicans and conservatives ("RINOs")
- white evangelical Trump-supporting Christians and everyone else
- Christians and non-Christians
- Christians and Jews
- Christians and Muslims
- non-Jews and Jews
- non-Muslims and Muslims
- heterosexual bodies and all other bodies
- cisgender bodies and all other bodies
- Black bodies and all other bodies of culture
- Asian bodies and all other bodies of culture
- Indigenous bodies and all other bodies of culture
- Latinx bodies and all other bodies of culture
- college graduates ("the elites") and people with fewer years of formal education
- residents of "red" states and cities ("patriots") and residents of "blue" states and cities ("elites," "socialists," "traitors," etc.)
- city dwellers and rural residents
- bodies born in America and all other bodies

and/or ordained by God, and the other group as inferior, sinful, foolish, despicable, and/or dangerous. This other group "deserves" contempt—and perhaps arrest, deportation, or destruction.

- white bodies born in America and all other bodies
- people who believe abortion is a sin and people who do not
- people who believe that nonhetero sex is a sin and people who do not
- QAnon believers and everyone else
- anti-vaxxers (and anti-maskers) and everyone else
- other conspiracy theorists and everyone else

This is only a partial list, of course. The GOP and most of its complicitors will attempt to drive as many wedges into as many people and groups as it can. In all cases, the strategy will be the same: attack, accuse, distort, divide, distract, lie, and infuriate every possible group. Sow chaos, distrust, and infighting. Meanwhile, encourage GOP followers to accept as gospel whatever Republican leaders tell them. Encourage everyone else to trust no one and believe no one. Get as many groups and people as possible to turn on one another and rip each other's hearts out.

The ultimate goal will be to fracture the country into a thousand angry splinter groups—until the largest of these groups is GOP loyalists who will do whatever they are told. Republican leaders will then instruct them to violently "take back" America.

Once the war begins, expect to be buffeted on all sides, 24/7, by these many strong winds. Use the body practices in this book, especially the five anchors, to *pause*; cultivate resource; settle your body; engage your discernment; and, over and over, act from the best parts of yourself.

If you have a white body, please take this especially to heart, because one of the most subtle and unexamined aspects of WBS is the white body's love of autonomy over solidarity.

Many people with white bodies will be tempted to quickly leave an alliance—or avoid joining one—if they object to one or two of its aspects, ideas, or key people. The GOP will push this autonomy button in as many white bodies as possible.[95]

---

95   In November 2021, an initiative appeared on the ballot in my hometown which would have replaced the Minneapolis Police Department with a Department of Public Safety. This initiative could have led to the creation of an expanded department that complemented and supported police officers

No alliance is perfect or seamless. In any effective alliance—as in any healthy family, romance, congregation, or workplace—there will always be disagreements, differences of opinion, and some people who don't get along especially well. There will also always be some questionable ideas, strategies, and/or messaging. Some people will be jerks some of the time. *All of this is normal.*

If you have a white body, please don't demand that any alliance be perfect or free of friction. Stay focused on the big picture, which is to support justice, equity, and the liberation of all Americans. Work with as many others as you can who also respect these vital causes—even when they do not otherwise think, believe, or live as you do.

Stay alert for an impulse to *flee* from other pro-democracy people and groups, and do not follow it capriciously. (*Do* follow it, of course, if you genuinely discern that a person or group is inhumane, immoral, or hopelessly dysfunctional.)

If you have a body of culture, you will face a different challenge—one that the GOP will also do its best to place before you, over and over.

You are used to taking and dodging metaphorical punches from white bodies. But a key part of the Republican strategy will be to stoke animosity from one group of bodies of culture toward another. If you have a Black body, you'll be encouraged to turn on bodies that are Indigenous, Asian, and/or Latinx. If you have an Asian body, you'll be encouraged to turn on Black, Latinx, and/or Indigenous bodies—and so on through every possible permutation.

We must not only resist this but do the opposite: encourage each other's growth and healing.

Don't forget that WBS lives in the bodies of nearly all Americans, regardless of their body pigmentation. We've also ingested a variety of other harmful ways of being—homophobia, sexism, anti-Semitism, and so on. The GOP will do everything

---

with other first responders, including social workers and mental health professionals. This initiative, known as Yes 4 Minneapolis, was closely watched by leaders and communities around the world. A variety of wealthy white bodies and their complicitors orchestrated a campaign that encouraged white voters to vote against the initiative because it was poorly written or too vague. This activation of white autonomy over solidarity helped to defeat the initiative.

it can to activate these in every one of our bodies—and then encourage us to wound each other.

As part of practicing Somatic Abolitionism—and moving toward justice and liberation—all of us need to examine how and where these harmful energies live in our bodies. Then we need to experience the clean pain of releasing them, metabolize that pain and energy, and grow and heal.

Many of us Americans are blessed with complex identities. For example, if you're a white Jewish lesbian, you simultaneously belong to a dominant group (white bodies) and two sometimes-dominated groups (Jews and lesbians).[96] Republican leaders will try to use this to their advantage in two ways.

First, expect Republicans and many of their complicitors to provoke whatever antipathy you might have for any other group. The GOP will try to incite you to fight with non-Jews, Muslims, straight people, gay men, and men in general.

Second, expect Republicans and their complicitors to encourage a similar fight *inside your own body*, with your Jewish, lesbian, and white energies all struggling against each other. The two body practices in Chapter 25, on untangling the energies of race, can help you separate, unhook, and work with these multiple energies.

## BODY PRACTICE
## PAUSE, NOTICE, DISCERN, AND ACT

All the body practices you've done, and all the reps you've put in, have helped you build your discernment. You've learned how to access and rely on all of your body's many intelligences, as well as the energies that flow through it. You have practiced cultivating many different types of resource. You have practiced the five anchors many times over. Your body is prepared.

Nevertheless, as events unfold, life will challenge you big time. Nothing can perfectly prepare you for widespread uncertainty, chaos or violence in the streets, or danger staring you in the face.

---

96   Academics and some activists call this *intersectionality*. I usually avoid the term because, to my bodymind, it is unnecessarily cerebral and academic sounding.

At each new decision point, slow yourself down. *Pause* and listen closely to what your body tells you. Stay in the moment. Ground and orient yourself. Settle your body as much as you can. Use your discernment rather than some predetermined strategy. And remind yourself that you have prepared your body for what it is experiencing right now.

## BODY PRACTICE
# STEPPING FORWARD, STEPPING BACK, PART 1

*If you have a body of culture:*

**Invited Rep**

Sit comfortably by yourself in a fairly quiet spot. Keep pen and paper nearby. Take a few slow, deep breaths.

Think back to an incident from your past when you were saying, doing, leading, organizing, or presenting something. Then, without asking—and without your explicit permission—one or more white bodies moved in, shunted you aside, and took over. In response, you reflexively stepped back, yielded control, and did not call out or challenge the move.

Mentally relive this incident. Pay close attention to what your body experienced, beginning with the moment when the white body (or bodies) first began to move in. Note any:

- vibrations
- images and thoughts
- meanings, judgments, stories, and explanations
- behaviors, movements, actions, impulses, and urges
- affect and emotions
- sensations

Soul scribe about your body's experience throughout this incident.

**Life Rep**

The next time you are leading something and one or more white bodies attempt a similar move, *pause.* Pay attention to what you experience in your body as the situation unfolds. If necessary, practice the five anchors from Chapter 21. Use your discernment to assess the situation and decide what to do. At all times, act out of the best parts of yourself.

Depending on the situation, you may choose to firmly and politely challenge the move. ("Hang on. My presentation isn't over yet. I'll be done in about five minutes. You're welcome to ask a question in the Q&A session immediately afterward.")

You may choose to challenge the move very assertively *without* politeness. ("This is a public forum. I have the floor right now. Be quiet until I'm done. When it's your turn to speak, I'll listen to you without interrupting.")

You may *choose* to yield to one or more white bodies. However, this will be a strategic decision based on your discernment of the situation, not a reflexive move.

You might also choose to yield *for now,* but to later challenge the move—for example, by speaking privately with the person or by speaking to their boss about what happened.

Afterward, if you like, soul scribe about your body's experience throughout the incident.

### *If you have a white body:*

**Invited Rep**
Sit comfortably by yourself in a fairly quiet spot. Keep pen and paper nearby. Take a few slow, deep breaths.

Think back to an incident when someone with a body of culture was in the middle of saying, doing, leading, organizing, or presenting something. Then, without asking, and without their explicit permission, you moved in, shunted them aside, and took over.

Maybe you had—or thought you had—a good reason for this. Maybe you were ordered to do it by your boss. Maybe you were the timekeeper at an event, and the person went well beyond their allotted time. Maybe the situation was becoming chaotic, and you chose to step in to restore order. Maybe something the body of culture said or did frightened you. For now, don't focus on your motives or reasoning. *This body practice is not about judging whether you were right or wrong to step in.*

Mentally relive the entire incident. Pay close attention to how the other person responded to your intervention. Also notice what your body experienced in each moment, beginning with when you first felt a need to move in and take over. Note any:

- vibrations
- images and thoughts

- meanings, judgments, stories, and explanations
- behaviors, movements, actions, impulses, and urges
- affect and emotions
- sensations

Soul scribe about your body's experience throughout this incident.

**Life Rep**
The next time you experience an urge to attempt a similar move with a body of culture, *pause*. Pay attention to what you experience in your body as the situation unfolds. If necessary, practice the five anchors from Chapter 21. Use your discernment to assess the situation. Ask yourself these questions:

- Is it necessary for me to follow this urge?
- Will inserting myself into the situation genuinely improve it? If I do, what is the likely outcome?
- If I do intervene, what is the person likely to say or do in response? How are they likely to experience my intervention? Afterward, how will they likely assess my actions?
- Who stands to benefit from my potential intervention? Who stands to lose?
- Would I feel this same urge—or would I be equally likely to act on it—if the person were white?
- What options do I have besides directly and assertively intervening right now? Might one of these other choices be wiser?

Once you've answered these questions, act from the best parts of yourself.

Afterward, if you like, soul scribe about your body's experience throughout the incident.


BODY PRACTICE
## STEPPING FORWARD, STEPPING BACK, PART 2

*If you have a body of culture:*

**Invited Rep**
Sit comfortably by yourself in a fairly quiet spot. Keep pen and paper nearby. Take a few slow, deep breaths.

Think back to an incident from your past when you were part of a group and another body of culture was leading, organizing, or presenting something. Suddenly, one or more white bodies moved in, shunted the person aside, and took over.

Mentally relive this incident. Pay close attention to what your body experienced, beginning with the moment when the white body (or bodies) first began to move in. Note any:

- vibrations
- images and thoughts
- meanings, judgments, stories, and explanations
- behaviors, movements, actions, impulses, and urges
- affect and emotions
- sensations

Then answer these questions:

- Did you experience an urge to directly call out or challenge the move?
- Did you interrogate that urge? If so, what did you discover or conclude?
- Did you follow the urge? If you didn't, why not? If you did, how did events unfold afterward?
- Afterward, did you reach out to the other body of culture about the incident? If you did, why, and how did your communication with them unfold? If you didn't, why not?

Soul scribe about your body's experience throughout this incident.

### Life Rep
The next time you are part of a group that another body of culture is leading, and you witness one or more white bodies attempting to move in and take over, *pause.* Pay close attention to the situation as it emerges. Closely observe all of the bodies involved.

Also carefully note what you experience in your body as the situation unfolds. If necessary, practice the five anchors from Chapter 21.

Ask yourself these questions:

- Should I speak up and challenge the move right now, in front of everyone?
- If I do, what effects is it likely to have on my fellow body of culture? On the situation in general?

- Should I wait a bit and see how the situation further unfolds?
- If my fellow body of culture has not yet challenged the move, should I give them more time to make (or not make) their own challenge?
- Is my wisest and most compassionate move to not do anything?

As events unfold, you may need to move through these questions more than once.

Afterward, if you like, soul scribe about your body's experience throughout the incident.

### If you have a white body:

**Invited Rep**

Sit comfortably by yourself in a fairly quiet spot. Keep pen and paper nearby. Take a few slow, deep breaths.

Think back to an incident when you were present as someone with a body of culture said, did, led, organized, or presented something. Then, as you watched, one or more white bodies moved in, shunted them aside, and took over.

Mentally relive this incident. Pay close attention to what your body experienced, beginning with the moment when the white body (or bodies) first began to move in. Note any:

- vibrations
- images and thoughts
- meanings, judgments, stories, and explanations
- behaviors, movements, actions, impulses, and urges
- affect and emotions
- sensations

Then answer these questions:

- Did you experience an urge to directly call out or challenge the move?
- Did you interrogate that urge? If so, what did you discover or conclude?
- Did you follow the urge? If so, how did events unfold afterward? If not, why not, and how did events unfold?

- Afterward, did you reach out to the body of culture about the incident? If so, why, and how did your communication with them unfold? If not, why not?

Soul scribe about your body's experience throughout this incident.

## Life Rep

The next time you are part of a group being led by a body of culture, and you witness one or more white bodies stepping in to take over, *pause.* Pay attention to what you experience in your body as the situation unfolds. If necessary, practice the five anchors from Chapter 21.

Ask yourself these questions:

- Should I speak up and challenge the move right now, in front of everyone?
- If I do, what effects is it likely to have on the body of culture? On the situation in general?
- Does it appear that the body of culture will want or appreciate my intervention?
- Should I wait a bit, see how the situation further unfolds, and give the body of culture more time to respond?
- Would I feel this same urge—or would I be equally likely to act on it—if the person being interrupted were white?
- What options do I have besides directly and assertively intervening right now? Might one of these other choices be wiser?
- Is my wisest and most compassionate move to not do anything?

Once you've answered these questions, act from the best parts of yourself.

Afterward, if you like, soul scribe about your body's experience throughout the incident.

# 38

# RELIGIOUS GROUPS WILL SUPPORT AND ATTACK YOU

*The next two weeks are probably the most important two weeks in
the history of America. I pray the army of the Lord is ready. . . .
I rebuke the news in the name of Jesus. We ask that this false
garbage come to an end. . . . It's the lies, communism, socialism.*

Rev. Tim Remington, pastor of the Altar Church, in his sermon four
days after the January 6, 2021 invasion of the US Capitol

*Today, for an alarming number of white conservative Christians,
the mark of Christian faithfulness is not a love that inspires them
to lay down their lives for their friends, but a defensiveness that
lures them to take the lives of their fellow citizens.*

Jennifer Rubin

*When the forces of extremism become so overwhelming that they
depress the hope of the people, the prophetic voice and mission
is to connect words and actions in ways that build restorative
hope, so a Movement for restorative justice can arise.*

Rev. Dr. William J. Barber II

Throughout the history of religion in America, two long-standing—and irreconcilable—narratives stand out:

- Religious leaders, groups, and movements have firmly supported human rights, liberation, dignity, and equality.

- Religious leaders, groups, and movements have firmly *opposed* human rights, liberation, dignity, and equality.

There's no dodging this contradiction. Like white-body supremacy, it is baked into every American institution that is intertwined with religion. It is in the water we drink and the air we breathe. And it shows up whenever a new moral dilemma arises—fundamentally unchanged but dressed in new clothes.

This contradiction goes back at least to the Puritans. The Puritans were an extremist Protestant sect that came to this continent with the rallying cry of "Freedom of religion!" Then, soon after they arrived and put down roots, many of them began trying to convert as many Indigenous people to their version of Christianity as they could.[97]

The imminent civil war will surely follow this same pattern. On one side will be folks—mostly white Protestants—who will be convinced that a violent coup is righteous, holy, and ordained by God. They will be quite sure that murdering other Americans en masse, violently overthrowing our elected government, and replacing it with a Protestant (or white Protestant) theocracy is the height of virtue. These people will demonize you—perhaps literally, by claiming you are in league with the Devil.

This interweaving of conquest and religiosity in the Americas goes back well before the Puritans, to the Spanish missionaries and conquistadors of the sixteenth and seventeenth centuries. As you'll recall, they came to the Americas with a single clear message: *We're white people with guns, cannons, lots of other weapons, and the full support of our God. We're taking everything and taking over. Do what we say, or we'll kill you. We might kill you anyway.*

---

97   Many of today's current social, political, and cultural fights can be traced back to the Puritans. To give just one example, Puritans were deeply and bitterly divided over vaccination (which, back then, was in a primitive stage). Cotton Mather, who was pro-vaccination, had his house stink-bombed by an angry anti-vaxxer.

The toxic combination of conquest, religiosity, and white-body supremacy actually goes back even earlier, to Pope Nicolas V. In 1452 and 1455, Nicolas issued a series of papal declarations that granted Portugal the "right" to "capture, vanquish, and subdue" all sub-Saharan Africans and "reduce their persons to perpetual slavery."[98] (Today, some white Christian Republicans continue to make the same argument. It goes like this: *From the time Europeans first set foot on this continent, God decreed that it rightfully belongs to white Christians and only white Christians. Everyone else deserves to die, be deported, or be subjugated.*)

On the other side will be folks of all skin tones—people from many religions, including many Protestant denominations—who will organize, demonstrate, and perhaps die to support justice, dignity, equity, emancipated democracy, and liberation for all people. As the war unfolds, you may want (or need) to build (or strengthen) relationships with one or more of these groups. If civil war breaks out and violence becomes widespread, these groups' buildings may also provide you with urgently needed safety and sanctuary.

You will of course need to use your discernment to decide whether any particular religious group or organization is trustworthy.

If you currently belong to a congregation or religious group— especially one with lots of white bodies—now is a good time to take the moral temperature of its members and leaders. As the war unfolds, every congregation, group, and leader—like every individual American—will be forced to take a side. If you are less than certain that your own group will stand firmly for democracy, justice, and liberation in the face of widespread mayhem, you may be wise to dissociate yourself now.

One possible scenario for some congregations is a schism. If that takes place in a group with which you are involved, keep in

---

98    Church leaders argued that enslavement would serve as a Christianizing influence among these Africans. It will perhaps not surprise you that, during the nineteenth century, Catholic priests and nuns regularly bought and sold enslaved people. For example, Georgetown Visitation Preparatory School in Washington, DC, founded by nuns who championed free education for the poor, owned over one hundred enslaved men, women, and children and sold dozens of them to help finance the construction of a new chapel. Georgetown University profited from the sale of over two hundred enslaved human beings. These institutions were not outliers. As journalist Rachel Swarns has noted, "The Catholic Church established its foothold in the South and relied on plantations and slave labor to help finance the livelihoods of its priests and nuns, and to support its schools and religious projects."

mind that the folks on the other side of the schism may consider you the worst of all possible enemies—and one of their most urgent targets.

BODY PRACTICE
## BUTTERFLY ON YOUR CHEST

The practice below, called the Butterfly Hug, was developed by therapist Lucina Artigas, who originally created it for use with survivors of catastrophes.[99] It can help anyone to settle their body, especially when they face stress or conflict.

Cross your arms over your chest in the following way:

- Place the tip of your middle finger of each hand just below your collarbone, on the opposite side of your body.
- The middle finger of your left hand should be roughly below your right eye. The middle finger of your right hand should be roughly below your left eye. Your hands should automatically cross at the wrists.
- Let your fingertips rest comfortably on your upper chest.
- Keep your fingers as close to vertical as you can, without creating discomfort. They should point more toward your neck than your arms.
- If you like, interlock your thumbs.

This creates a pair of metaphorical butterfly wings on your chest.

Breathe slowly and deeply. Close your eyes.

Begin alternately flapping the butterfly wings on your upper chest. Lift one set of fingers; then tap them just below your collarbone. Then let these fingers rest where they are; lift the other set, and tap them just below your collarbone on the other side.

Continue with this alternating movement for five minutes, or for as long as your body tells you to.

---

99    Artigas developed this practice in 1997 during her work with survivors of Hurricane Pauline, one of the deadliest Pacific hurricanes to make landfall in Mexico. Artigas's original practice involves a more detailed script and protocol. In a therapeutic setting, it is typically used in concert with Eye Movement Desensitization and Reprocessing (EMDR) to help people metabolize the energies of trauma. The version provided here is much simpler and has a more modest purpose: to help human bodies settle in the face of stress or conflict. The Butterfly Hug creates what therapists call *bilateral stimulation*: a positive tactile and energetic experience on both sides of the upper chest. You can find the full Butterfly Hug protocol at emdrfoundation.org/toolkit/butterfly-hug.pdf.

You'll find a photo of someone doing the Butterfly Hug at emdrfoundation. org/toolkit/butterfly-hug.pdf (scroll down to the bottom of the web page).

As you do this practice, pay close attention to your body. Note any:

- vibrations
- images and thoughts
- meanings, judgments, stories, and explanations
- behaviors, movements, actions, impulses, and urges
- affect and emotions
- sensations

If you like, soul scribe afterward about your experience.

# 39

# LISTEN TO BLACK WOMEN

*You may not always have a comfortable life and you will not always be able to solve all of the world's problems at once, but don't ever underestimate the importance you can have, because history has shown us that courage can be contagious and hope can take on a life of its own.*

Michelle Obama

*You got to give up the shit that weighs you down.*

Toni Morrison

*Do not allow setbacks to set you back.*

Stacey Abrams

*To a certain degree, our entire future may depend on learning to listen, listen without assumptions or defenses.*

adrienne maree brown

*Listen to Black women. . . . If America has a future, Black women need to have a prominent place in leading.*

Van Lathan

*Black women have been saving this republic since its founding.
That was especially so during the Trump era when their turnout
helped elect Democrats in unlikely places such as Alabama
and Georgia. Their votes put Joe Biden in the White House.*

Jonathan Capehart

*Pause.*

My distant ancestors, like yours, were Black Africans. Mine were still Black Africans five generations ago. If yours left that continent millennia ago, then over many generations their skin may have grown lighter, or darker, or lighter for a time and then darker once again.

Regardless of those changes, though, the mitochondria we all share are 1,500 centuries old. That is vastly older than white-body supremacy, which has been around for much less than a millennium. While all of our bodies are vulnerable to WBS, our shared ability to heal goes back many thousands of generations.

As you have moved through this book and followed its process of growth, healing, and restoration—day by day and rep by rep—you have been calling on this elemental, embodied healing response.

We all share the same mitochondrial Great Mother. Scientists believe that she lived about two hundred thousand years ago in what is now the Kalahari Desert in southern Africa but back then was a land of lakes, forests, and grasslands.

Every living human on Earth is descended from the Great Mother. In our cells, each of us has some of the same mitochondria that she did. All of us diversified from her.

But the Great Mother is actually a fairly recent player in your (and everyone's) origin story. Yes, we can all trace ourselves back to that Black African woman who lived more than five thousand generations ago. But we can trace the elements and energies of our bodies far further into the past, into the primordial blackness of creation. Nearly all the elements in our human bodies were formed in stars billions of years ago.

This creative blackness is not a one-time phenomenon that occurred in a far distant past. It is always with us. It will still be here long after the human race dies out, millions of years from now.

The universe constantly changes and emerges from this blackness. In each moment, it expresses the same energies of creation that birthed our solar system, life on Earth, our mitochondrial Great Mother, you, and me. It is the blackness of the womb, of earth, and of space. It is the source of all potential and possibility—and it is where all movement, and all life, ultimately returns and rests.

The Great Mother is the earliest of many, many Black women who have much to teach us. By *us*, I mean all of us—people of all skin tones, ages, genders, and backgrounds. And when I say *Black women*, I include Black women who are trans, queer, and femme.

Unfortunately, too many of us—again, people of all skin tones, ages, genders, and backgrounds—have paid insufficient attention to what wise Black women can teach us. That has been our enormous loss. It hasn't done wise Black women any good, either.

As part of your commitment to Somatic Abolitionism—and as part of your resistance to the attempted destruction of American democracy—I urge you to listen to the words of some or all of the women listed below. Read their books, blogs, articles, essays, and social media posts. Watch their videos or performances. Listen to their audio interviews.

By *listen to*, I mean *bring your whole bodymind to their words and voices*. Let your body be a natural receiver and amplifier for their words. Listen not just for information but for energies and guidance that can transform you and the world.

When you turn your attention to each of these women, let her words—and their resonances—ripple through you. Listen without judging, without critiquing, without internally debating, and without preparing a response. When you hear contradictions, allow yourself to be in those contradictions without having to do something about them. Do the same with things that you find confusing—or just plain wrong.

Listening doesn't mean agreeing. If something that one of these women says strikes you as wrong, or crazy, or inflammatory, or shocking, just note your reaction and keep listening.

You can learn a great deal from someone even when you disagree with them—sometimes *especially* when you disagree. When you've finished listening, let yourself wrestle with what you just heard. If you disagree with something, just stay with that disagreement for a time, without trying to resolve it or make the other person wrong.

Disagreeing with someone—like conflict in general—is a normal part of life. You don't have to take sides. If you agree with some things a Black woman (or any other human being) says, and disagree with some other things, that's normal. I'm not asking you to become anyone's fan or sycophant.

The point is to listen with your whole body.

By *listen to*, I also mean *start listening to*—that is, *start taking Black women seriously*. Sadly, many of us—once again, people of all skin tones, ages, genders, and backgrounds—haven't recognized Black women as a widespread source of wisdom.

The following list of wise Black women could easily have been far longer. But here are some voices (in reverse alphabetical order) to get you started:

- **Rev. angel Kyodo williams**

  angelkyodowilliams.com

  en.wikipedia.org/wiki/Angel_Kyodo_Williams

  facebook.com/zenchangeangel

- **Maxine Waters**

  waters.house.gov

  en.wikipedia.org/wiki/Maxine_Waters

  facebook.com/MaxineWaters/

- **Sonya Renee Taylor**

  sonyareneetaylor.com

  en.wikipedia.org/wiki/Sonya_Renee_Taylor

  facebook.com/profile.php?id=100052496942731

- **Amanda Seales**
  en.wikipedia.org/wiki/Amanda_Seales
  facebook.com/AmandaSealesTV

- **Layla F. Saad**
  http://laylafsaad.com
  en.wikipedia.org/wiki/Layla_Saad

- **Angela Rye**
  angelarye.com
  en.wikipedia.org/wiki/Angela_Rye
  facebook.com/TheAngelaRye

- **April Ryan**
  aprildryan.com
  en.wikipedia.org/wiki/April_Ryan
  facebook.com/AprilDRyanWhiteHouse

- **Nova Reid**
  novareid.com
  facebook.com/novareidofficial

- **Ladonna Sanders Redmond**
  ladonnasandersredmond.com
  columinate.coop/consultants/ladonna-sanders-redmond/
  facebook.com/ladonnaredmondconsulting/

- **Ijeoma Oluo**
  ijeomaoluo.com
  en.wikipedia.org/wiki/Ijeoma_Oluo

- **Tamika Mallory**
  untilfreedom.com/our-team/
  en.wikipedia.org/wiki/Tamika_Mallory
  facebook.com/TDMallory

- **Audre Lorde**
  alp.org/about/audre
  en.wikipedia.org/wiki/Audre_Lorde

- **Catrice M. Jackson**
  catriceology.com
  shetalkswetalk.com
  facebook.com/CatriceJacksonSpeaks

- **bell hooks**
  bellhooksinstitute.com
  globalsocialtheory.org/thinkers/hooks-bell/
  en.wikipedia.org/wiki/Bell_hooks
  facebook.com/bellhooksfansJemele Hill
  en.wikipedia.org/wiki/Jemele_Hill
  facebook.com/jemelehillworks

- **Nikole Hannah-Jones**
  nikolehannahjones.com
  en.wikipedia.org/wiki/Nikole_Hannah-Jones

- **Zahara Green**
  womensmediacenter.com/shesource/expert/zahara-green
  transcendingbarriersatl.org/our-team-1
  facebook.com/zahara.green.7

- **Alicia Garza**
  aliciagarza.com
  en.wikipedia.org/wiki/Alicia_Garza
  facebook.com/ChasingGarza/

- **Angela Davis**
  humanities.ucsc.edu/academics/faculty/index.php?uid=aydavis
  en.wikipedia.org/wiki/Angela_Davis
  facebook.com/AngelaDavis26

- **Tiffany D. Cross**

  tiffanydcross.com
  en.wikipedia.org/wiki/Tiffany_Cross
  facebook.com/TiffanyDCrossSayItLouder

- **Laverne Cox**

  lavernecox.com
  en.wikipedia.org/wiki/Laverne_Cox
  facebook.com/lavernecoxforreal

- **Rachel Cargle**

  rachel-cargle.com
  en.wikipedia.org/wiki/Rachel_Cargle
  facebook.com/rachelecargle

- **adrienne maree brown**

  adriennemareebrown.net
  en.wikipedia.org/wiki/Adrienne_Maree_Brown
  facebook.com/emergentstrategyideationinstitute

- **Yaba Blay**

  yabablay.com
  en.wikipedia.org/wiki/Yaba_Blay

- Black mothers who have lost children at the hands of police, including Valerie Castile, Katie Wright, Samaria Rice, Lezley McSpadden-Head (Michael Brown's mother), and so many others.

## BODY PRACTICE
## EMBODIED GRATITUDE

Think of a Black woman who has had a significant positive impact on your life. She might be a relative, friend, partner, teacher, neighbor, boss, coworker, elder, actor, musician, singer, writer, artist, spiritual leader, employer, activist, inventor, chef, business owner, employee, customer, client, trainer, advisor, mentor, therapist, or healthcare professional.

Find an image of this person—on the internet, on your phone, in an old photo album, or anywhere else you can. Sit alone in a quiet, comfortable place with this image in front of you. If you can't find an image of her anywhere, then close your eyes and envision her.

Take a few deep, slow breaths. Then simply say aloud, "Thank you."

Repeat the deep breaths and the words *thank you* two more times.

As you do this practice, pay close attention to your body. Note any:

- vibrations
- images and thoughts
- meanings, judgments, stories, and explanations
- behaviors, movements, actions, impulses, and urges
- affect and emotions
- sensations

If you like, soul scribe about your body's experience with this practice.

# 40

# THE LEGACY OF
# WHITE-ON-WHITE OPPRESSION

*Through new laws passed by the Virginia assembly [between
1667 and 1705], plantation owners consciously encouraged
racial hatred between blacks and poor whites. . . . In this way,
the legal construction of racism helped diffuse the threat of
insurrection. Poor white people would now see themselves as
allied with those far wealthier than themselves, and would
define themselves by race rather than by class.*

Vanessa Williamson

*There is a simple truth to American history for the majority
of people who have ever been American: the worse the black
experience, the worse everyone else's experience, including whites.*

Quinn Norton

As we saw in Chapter 16, when the modern concept of race was
invented, its central strategy was to get poor, exploited, working-
class whites to identify with wealthy white landowners, rather
than with poor, exploited, working-class Blacks. Once this
imaginary solidarity was accomplished, wealthy white bodies
used it constantly to their advantage. After nearly three hundred
fifty years, this strategy—the most successful and enduring scam
in American history—continues to prove as resilient as ever.

Here is how it works, explained from the viewpoint of a powerful white body:

- Teach less powerful white bodies that whiteness is what separates the worthy from the unworthy, the deserving from the undeserving, the virtuous from the nonvirtuous, winners from losers, and humans from subhumans.

- Relentlessly stress the ostensible bond between wealthy, powerful white bodies and white bodies with less money and power.

- Just as relentlessly, emphasize the supposedly unbridgeable gap between whites with little power and bodies of culture.

- Under this banner of faux solidarity, swindle, cheat, exploit, and oppress less-powerful white bodies.[100]

- Swindle, cheat, exploit, and oppress bodies of culture as well, but also demean, incarcerate, brutalize, and murder them in large numbers.

- Tell the oppressed white bodies that they too will someday be wealthy and powerful, just like you, because of their whiteness.

- Show off your own wealth and power, so that oppressed white bodies will both envy you and identify with you.

- If you like, run for public office. Tell oppressed white bodies that their country and way of life are being attacked, mostly by bodies of culture; that you and only you stand with them; and that you and only you can save them from the dire, ongoing threat that bodies of culture pose. Repeatedly encourage them to not only vote for you but donate to your campaign. Put as much of their donations into your own pocket as you can.

- Whenever oppressed white bodies begin to recognize their own disempowerment and become angry, tell them over and over that bodies of culture are the cause of their plight. Whip them into a state of fury against bodies of culture;

---

100  In 1960, then-Vice President Lyndon Johnson, a Democrat, said this: "If you can convince the lowest white man he's better than the best colored man, he won't notice you're picking his pocket. Hell, give him somebody to look down on, and he'll empty his pockets for you."

tell them that they are righteous, caring patriots; and encourage them to set things right by attacking bodies of culture—their fellow Americans.

This worked like a charm in Virginia in the late seventeenth century. It worked beautifully throughout the United States in the three centuries that followed. Today it is as successful as ever. It remains one of the primary strategies of the GOP and Donald Trump. It also continues to be enabled by the fecklessness and complicity of the Democratic Party.

The coming conflict may take the form of a racialized civil war, and it may be driven largely by self-interest, anger, and hatred. But there is another, less visible side to the conflict: just as in the 1600s, wealthy and powerful white men (and a few wealthy and powerful white women) are duping and taking advantage of many millions of oppressed white bodies.

One way to measure the success of this swindle is to examine fundraising for dubious political causes. As one example, we know that 2020 Trump voters were overwhelmingly white, and that in the twelve months *after* he lost the 2020 election, he raised over $250 million, ostensibly to "stop the steal," "reinstate" him as president, and "save America." Very little of this $250 million went to any of these efforts.

Another way to measure the success of this scam is to count the number of white bodies that rise up to violently "take back" the country.

For more than a millennium—originally in Europe, and now in the United States and many other countries—rich and powerful white bodies have oppressed poor, less-empowered white bodies. As a result, long ago, trauma became stuck in many millions of European bodies. Because this trauma went largely unexamined and unhealed, it got passed down through generation after generation of these bodies.

Eventually, many of these poor, oppressed white bodies made their way to what is now the United States, primarily from

Holland, Britain, Spain, Portugal, and France.[101] When these folks arrived, multiple generations of unhealed trauma was in their blood, bones, soul nerves, soul muscles, and genes.

Some of these bodies swiftly begun to blow that trauma through one another—as, for example, the Puritans did by routinely torturing and murdering each other. Others took on the role of oppressors, blowing their trauma through Indigenous bodies, then Black bodies, then bodies of culture in general. Most of these people failed to examine—or, in many cases, even acknowledge—the long legacy of brutality and exploitation that their ancestors suffered.

Sadly, until these folks' modern-day descendants metabolize the trauma energy that has been passed on from one generation of white bodies to another, that unhealed trauma will burst forth as white rage. They will then direct this rage largely at bodies of culture—as they have done for the past three hundred fifty years.

## BODY PRACTICE
## YIELD THE CARETAKING

*If you have a body of culture:*

WBS tells its white-bodied sufferers: *It is the role of bodies of culture to serve you, protect you, and defer to you.* The bodies of culture variant of WBS sends its sufferers a parallel message: *It's your role to serve, protect, and defer to white bodies.*

Both of these messages are lies, of course. But WBS embeds them deep inside our bodies.

The body practice below is a life rep that you will have the opportunity to repeat many times.

The next time a white body asks (or demands or expects) you to serve, protect, or defer to them, *pause.* Notice what arises in your body. In particular, notice any urge to reflexively respond to that request. *Do not follow that urge.* Instead, ask yourself:

- How and where do I experience that urge in my body? What constriction, discomfort, and/or sensations are emerging?

---

101   Denmark, Norway, Russia, and Sweden also established colonies in North America.

- What is the likely outcome for the white body if I do as I'm asked?
- What is the likely outcome *for me* if I do as I'm asked?
- What is the likely outcome *for me* if I say no or don't do their bidding and politely but firmly explain why?[102]

Then use your discernment to choose your best course of action. As always, act from the best parts of yourself.

Here are some common opportunities for practicing this life rep:

- You are a sales associate, and a white-bodied customer asks you to do something that's clearly not part of your job, such as carry their purchases to their car a block away.

- You have a service job. One of your white-bodied clients asks you to do something unusual that is not technically outside of your job description, but will take a great deal of your time and cut into your ability to assist other clients.

- You are on a team with several white bodies. One of the white-bodied people tries to maneuver you into essentially acting as their assistant.

- In public, a white body encounters a problem that they can handle on their own. But instead of taking care of themselves, they call for help, either explicitly or implicitly (for example, they shout, "Oh, dear God!").

- Your boss takes you aside and asks you to treat a particular white-bodied colleague, customer, client, or visitor with unusual deference, because the person is "prickly" or "high-strung" or "a piece of work."

An important note: you may discern that your wisest course of action is to carry out the white body's request or demand. That's fine. This rep is not about reflexively saying no. It's about learning to notice your body's urges and not reflexively following them.

If you like, after the incident, soul scribe about what your body experienced.

---

102  As appropriate, you might also suggest an alternative, such as, *See that red-headed man over there? He can find someone to help you.* Or, *This is something you can easily learn to do yourself with a little practice; when I come back this afternoon, I'll show you how.*

BODY PRACTICE
## CHECK YOUR ADVANTAGE

*If you have a white body:*

WBS tells its white-bodied sufferers: *It is the role of bodies of culture to serve you, protect you, and defer to you.* The bodies of culture variant of WBS sends its sufferers a parallel message: *It's your role to serve, protect, and defer to white bodies.*

Both of these messages are lies, of course. But WBS embeds them deep inside our bodies.

The body practice below is a life rep that you may have the opportunity to repeat multiple times.

If you find yourself starting to ask, expect, or demand that a body of culture serve, protect, or defer to you, immediately *pause.*

If you haven't yet made the request, hold up your hand and say, "Hang on a second, please. Let me start over."

If you already made the request, shake your head and say, "Wait. Sorry, scratch that. Let me start over. Give me a moment, please."

Take that moment to reconsider your request. Answer these questions:

- Given your relationship to the other person, is the request legitimate for you to make of them, regardless of their race?
- Would you have made the same request of this person—and made it in the same way—if they had a white body?

As you answer these questions, notice what you experience in your body.

Based on your discernment and your answers to these questions, resume your conversation. If appropriate, modify or withdraw your request. If you realize that your original request was fine, simply restate it. As always, act from the best parts of yourself.

If you like, after the incident, soul scribe what your body experienced.

## BODY PRACTICE
## **YIELD YOUR ADVANTAGE**

*If you have a white body:*

Below is a life rep that may present itself to you when you are in a public space with one or more bodies of culture, and no clear leadership roles have been established.

If, as events unfold, you experience an urge to step forward and claim a leadership role, *pause.*

Take a few deep, slow breaths. As you do, answer these questions:

- Where in your body do you experience this urge to claim leadership?
- Why do you believe you're qualified for this leadership?
- Do you sense that you're entitled to simply step forward and assume this role? If so, how do you sense this in your body?
- Might anyone else around you also be as qualified or perhaps more qualified?
- Is it clear to everyone involved that you are the only person who is genuinely qualified to take the lead?

After you've answered these questions, *pause* again.

If the answer to the final question above is genuinely yes (for example, if something is on fire and you are the only firefighter in the room), then step forward.

Otherwise, *don't.* Let someone else take the lead.

If you sense that one of the bodies of culture is qualified to lead in this situation, you may also—based on your discernment—gently encourage them to step forward.

As this person begins leading the group, pay close attention to what your body experiences.

If you like, after the incident, soul scribe about this body practice.

## 41

# WHEN WHITE BODIES DEPUTIZE OTHER WHITE BODIES

*Black people are always on trial. We are always being policed: in how we fight, how we mourn, and how we die. We are always being asked to produce evidence for why we should be allowed to live, and we can be beaten or killed at a moment's notice should we fail to give the right answer.*

Elie Mystal

*Bear witness. If you are a white person and you see a person of color being stopped by police, if you see a person of color being harassed in a store: bear witness and offer to help, when it is safe to do so. Sometimes just the watchful presence of another white person will make others stop and consider their actions more carefully.*

Ijeoma Oluo

*The only thing more contagious than a good attitude is a bad one.*

David Goggins

It happens in stores, workplaces, gyms, restaurants, hotels, places of worship, sports arenas, and many other locations. It's an experience that's familiar to almost every American body of culture.

It begins when a body of culture and a white body get into a conflict, or when a white body simply starts to experience some discomfort in the presence of a body of culture. The white body summons another white body to their side and asks them to use their experience, knowledge, skills, or authority to help resolve the issue.

Often this situation is exactly what it looks like, with no racialized undertones.

Sometimes, though, a different dynamic is at work. The first white body is deputizing the second: bringing in reinforcements in order to outnumber the body of culture and create a show of unified white-bodied strength. The underlying message from the first white body to the second is: *This body of culture may be getting out of line. Help me police them.*

When this occurs, the encounter quickly transforms. Even if it began as a legitimate conflict that could have been resolved on its own terms, it is now a power struggle and a show of white-bodied power and unity. The white bodies' message to the body of culture is *There are two of us and one of you. There can quickly be more of us, if necessary. You're outnumbered. Surrender.*

In many cases, all of this takes place outside of white bodies' cognitive awareness. But the body of culture often sees clearly what's going on.

Sometimes the dynamic is less clear. The body of culture then has to discern whether the underlying conflict is still the issue or whether the situation has morphed into a power struggle and a show of white-bodied authority. This may not become clear until the situation unfolds further. Unfortunately, the further it unfolds, the more dangerous it may become. Just ask George Floyd's relatives.

One little-discussed aspect of WBS is the policing energy that is present in many white bodies. When these bodies encounter a body of culture, they automatically assume it's their duty to monitor that body for a potentially threatening move—and, if necessary, to step in and control that body. (These white bodies may be cognitively unaware that this is what they're doing.) The deputization of one white body by another often draws on a shared, implicit acceptance of this role.

This monitoring function is sometimes called the white gaze, which I wrote about in Chapter 22. If you have a body of culture, you encounter it all the time. I regularly see it in the bodies of white police officers, security guards, teachers, bus drivers, store managers, sales associates, and other white bodies in positions of authority. Sometimes, though much less often, I also experience it with bodies of culture in these roles.

In any given encounter, the body behind the white gaze may be relaxed or tense, friendly or distant, happy or grim. But the energetic message they send is always: *Stay in line.* Or *Fall in line.*

If a civil war emerges, the attempted deputization of white bodies by other white bodies may become an everyday occurrence.

If you have a body of culture, such encounters will require you to quickly discern whether someone with a white body is on your side. This may require all the presence and discernment you can muster.

If you have a white body, you will need to be just as watchful and discerning. What will you do when you realize—or suspect—that another white body is attempting to deputize you? If you reflexively step to their side, you will implicitly declare your loyalty to WBS—and your opposition to bodies of culture.

You have another, better option. You can slow yourself down, pause, use your discernment, and fully evaluate the situation. If you realize or suspect that you have been called on largely because of your whiteness, you have several aikido-like moves to choose from.

For example, instead of answering the other white body's call, you can turn to the body of culture, smile, and say, "Is there something I can help you with?"

If you're the white body's superior, you can say to them, "Thank you; I can take it from here." Then you can turn and offer your assistance to the body of culture.

Or you can briefly smile at the body of culture and then stand next to them, so they can sense that your energy and support are with them, not with the other white body.

All the reps you've done, and all the discernment you've built, will help you decide when to step forward, when to step back or stand aside, what to say, and how to navigate the resonance and dissonance fields of the situation.

Whatever happens, you can use the five anchors. Whatever emerges, act from the best parts of yourself.

If you have a white body, you may have lived most or all of your life without seriously interrogating the ramifications of your whiteness. As I hope you now see, if and when a civil war emerges, you will no longer have that luxury.

BODY PRACTICE
## APPREHENDING THREE BODIES

Recall a recent incident in which you witnessed a Black body being apprehended, detained, or arrested by police.[103] Briefly relive that incident from beginning to end. As you do, pay close attention to your body. Note any:

- vibrations
- images and thoughts
- meanings, judgments, stories, and explanations
- behaviors, movements, actions, impulses, and urges
- affect and emotions
- sensations

*Pause.* Take a few slow, deep breaths.

*Now recall* a recent incident in which you witnessed a white body being apprehended, detained, or arrested by police. Briefly relive that event from beginning to end. As you do, pay close attention to your body. Note any:

---

103   If you yourself have been apprehended, detained, or arrested by police, you are welcome to use that incident for the type of body you have.

- vibrations
- images and thoughts
- meanings, judgments, stories, and explanations
- behaviors, movements, actions, impulses, and urges
- affect and emotions
- sensations

*Pause* again. Take a few more deep, slow, breaths.

*This time, think of* a recent incident in which you witnessed a body of culture who was not Black as they were apprehended, detained, or arrested by police. Briefly relive that incident from beginning to end. As before, pay close attention to your body. Note any:

- vibrations
- images and thoughts
- meanings, judgments, stories, and explanations
- behaviors, movements, actions, impulses, and urges
- affect and emotions
- sensations

*Pause* once more for a few breaths. Then ask yourself these questions:

- What elements did all three incidents have in common?
- What elements, if any, did the incidents involving the two bodies of culture share?
- What was unique to the apprehension, detention, or arrest of the white body?
- What was unique to the event involving the Black body?
- What was unique to the incident involving the body of culture who wasn't Black?

If you like, soul scribe about your experience of this practice.

**42**

# WHEN WHITE BODIES TURN ON EACH OTHER

*People turned against each other
cannot turn against those responsible.*

DaShanne Stokes

*Gangster capitalism has taught us that
the best food available is each other.*

Van Lathan

*If you look at the people in your circle and you don't get
inspired, you don't have a circle, you have a cage.*

Nipsey Hussle

*He [The Dalai Lama] made it his mission to say,
"We can't afford to squabble over minor differences;
we have to concentrate on what we have in
common, our common mission."*

Pico Iyer

*It is time for us to turn to each other,
not on each other.*

Jesse Jackson

In all the work I and my colleagues have done with racialized trauma, the most difficult and explosive situations are usually those in which everyone in the room is white.

When I work with large groups on the healing of racialized trauma, I temporarily separate the white bodies from the bodies of culture, then assemble each group in a separate room. I lead the roomful of bodies of culture, and one of my white colleagues works with the white bodies.

Typically, the bodies of culture swiftly create a relaxed vibe and an open atmosphere where people are able to speak pretty freely. We're usually able to do a lot of work in a short space of time.

Also typically, within an hour—sometimes much more quickly—some of the white bodies lose their cool, flip into *fight* responses, and turn on each other.

This is not because most of them are bad people or secret white nationalists. It's because, as we've seen, their bodies have little agility or acuity around race. They can't handle the charge, or speed, or texture, or weight of race—because, throughout their lives, they haven't had to.

As a result, when their racialized trauma is activated, they can't simply stay with its clean pain—even when they're surrounded by other white bodies. They try to blow that pain through those bodies. There are often fireworks. Sometimes people storm out, or ditch the whole training, or declare me and/or the white facilitator to be their enemies, or start their own splinter groups.

If you have a body of culture, you already know that when a white body starts to experience discomfort, especially around matters of race, they may suddenly flip into *fight* or *annihilate* mode, and try to blow their dirty pain through you (or some other body of culture nearby).

However, you also need to be ready for when two white bodies turn on each other. You will need to be present and discerning. Depending on what emerges, you may need to quickly leave. You may need to create a distraction. You may need to enlist the help of someone in authority. And you already know that if you say or do the wrong thing, both white bodies might suddenly stop bickering and, together, turn on you.

If you have a white body, when a racialized situation emerges and you sense that your racialized trauma is being activated, *pause*. Pay close attention to your body. Experience the clean pain without trying to do anything about it.

If you sense that you might soon lash out at someone, physically remove yourself from the situation. Settle and resource your body as best you can. Above all, don't try to blow your pain through another human being.

This is why getting your reps in, especially with the five anchors, is so essential.

### BODY PRACTICE
## TWO BODIES COMING TOGETHER

Do this body practice with one other person. *If you have a body of culture,* do it with another body of culture; *if you have a white body,* do it with another white body. Otherwise, your counterpart can be any adult who is happy to do the practice with you. (If the two of you are doing this practice during a pandemic, wear masks and take all other appropriate safety precautions.)

Find a quiet spot where the two of you can have five uninterrupted minutes together. This can be either indoors or outdoors, so long as it has an open area of about fifteen feet. Bring a pen and paper with you, but set them aside until the end of the practice.

Begin by standing about fifteen feet apart, facing each other, with the open area in between you.

Once you begin this practice, both of you will stay silent. Look at one another, but not directly in each other's eyes. Keep your gaze soft rather than piercing.

To begin the practice, simply say aloud, "Let's begin."

Together, take two slow, long breaths. Then, very slowly, begin walking toward each other. As you do, pay close attention to your body.

When you can sense your counterpart's body—when you don't just see it, but begin to experience its energy field—stop walking. Hold up your open palm in a *stop* gesture, so that the other person stops as well. (If the other person senses your energy field first, then they will stop and hold up their own palm. When they do this, stop walking.)

Notice what has changed in your body as a result of being near the other body. What in your own body has constricted or relaxed, opened or closed? What signals is your body receiving or sending? What comfort or discomfort do you experience, and where do you experience it? What other vibrations, images, thoughts, urges, impulses, emotions, or physical sensations do you experience? Has your breathing changed, and, if so, how?

After a few breaths, lower your palm (or your counterpart should lower theirs). Now, both of you take two more slow steps forward—then stop.

Once again, pay close attention to your body. What has changed in it now that your bodies are closer together? What different vibrations, images, thoughts, urges, impulses, emotions, or physical sensations do you experience? What do you sense or notice about the other body that you didn't notice before?

After a few more breaths, one of you (it doesn't matter which one) raises both palms. This is the signal for both of you to take five slow, small, *careful* steps backward—and then to stop again.

As you move back—and once you've stopped—notice what changes you experience in your body, and how it responds to the greater distance between the two of you.

Then soul scribe about this body practice.

If both of you wish, you can also discuss what each of your bodies experienced during it.

# 43

# POLICING WHITE RAGE: A LIFE REP FOR WHITE BODIES

*White rage recurs in American history. . . .*
*For every action of African American*
*advancement, there's a reaction, a backlash.*
Carol Anderson

*Researchers have repeatedly documented*
*that racial resentment is the single most*
*important factor motivating Republicans*
*and Republican-leaning voters.*
Dana Milbank

The most reliable way to motivate many white Republicans is to activate their racialized trauma by stoking their rage over race. GOP leaders and media figures know this very well. So if they are able to incite a civil war, white rage will be tightly wrapped inside it.

Rage is not the same as anger. As Dr. Ken Hardy taught me, rage is anger that has aged.

A great deal of white rage follows a predictable trajectory. First a white body becomes uncomfortable around the topic of race, or an event that has become racialized, or even the simple presence of a body of culture. Sometimes just the words *white rage* (or *white fragility*, or *critical race theory*, or *racism*, or *white-body supremacy*) may engender this discomfort.

Because that white body is unwilling or unable to handle the discomfort—and the charge it experiences around race—those sensations may activate a *fight* or *annihilate* response in the form of rage.

The white body may then express this rage through words, violence, or both. Its central message to nearby bodies of culture is typically, *I'm furious. Therefore you're in trouble. I'm going to make you pay.*

Carol Anderson has written a greatly insightful history of white rage in America over the past one hundred fifty plus years. Her book *White Rage: The Unspoken Truth of Our Racial Divide* provides a throughline for this widespread, unhealed trauma response.

On his website, eand.co, Umair Haque has written three deeply observant essays about white rage: "This Is Why Minorities and White People Can't Get Along in America," "White Rage Is Destroying America," and "Why the American Right Is Having a Meltdown About Race."[104] I strongly urge you to read all three, in the order in which I've listed them. If you have a body of culture, they will validate what you have long known. If you have a white body, they will help you experience in your own body what so many bodies of culture experience in theirs.

Here are a few brief excerpts from these essays[105]:

- We minorities are terrified of triggering white rage. Because when it erupts, it is totally disproportionate, relentless, abusive, and hateful. All the boundaries that even the good white liberal imagines they never cross are suddenly OK to cross. White rage is a law unto itself.

- A white person can erupt in rage at you, over anything, anytime, but you can never respond in an angry way to a white person. . . . The minority can never, ever respond angrily, or even be offended. We have to respond to the

---

104   Here are the web links, in order: eand.co/we-need-to-talk-about-white-rage-28cbf5ec3d1b; eand. co/white-rage-is-destroying-america-4cb285d73959;     eand.co/why-the-american-right-is-having-a-meltdown-about-race-e519b529e0c7. On his site, Haque has also often noted that we live in an age of trauma.

105   I've removed Haque's boldface type, which he uses to call out key points. The bold face makes sense in the context of the full online essays but would be visually confusing here.

often murderous rage that's directed at us *politely*. We have to keep our cool. . . . Because if we react angrily, if we are offended, if we get a little hot under the collar—all of which are normal human reactions to being attacked, remember—then White Rage goes from being an explosion to being a chain reaction. All those white people who step in, after a time, to cool down the angry white person, will turn on *us*.

- White Rage is about *power*. A certain kind of power. Not empowerment and not liberation. It is the power to put you back in your place. It is about the power to violently force you back into submission. With a threat of annihilation.

- White rage is about power, and that is why *only another white person can tell a white person to calm down* when White Rage has been triggered. You can't do it, as the minority—you will only ever make things much, much worse. If you make that mistake, the White Rage will only explode further and hotter.

As Haque wisely observes, bodies of culture often have no good choices in the face of white rage. They can walk away and risk being harmed or attacked from behind. They can outwardly keep their cool and suffer through the rage—and still risk being harmed. Or they can push back or express their own legitimate anger and put themselves in still greater potential danger.

The person or people expressing the rage also have no good choices. Remember, they're stuck in a traumatic *fight* or *annihilate* response. They are partly or entirely out of control.

In these situations, the people with the most power to defuse the situation, or mitigate the harm, are other, more settled white bodies who observe the rage.

If you have a white body, I strongly urge you to practice the body activity below. Use it whenever you become a witness to white rage. Also use it when you sense that another white body may soon erupt in a rage attack. Your efforts, and your settled body, could prevent a great deal of harm—or even save lives.

## BODY PRACTICE
# POLICING WHITE RAGE

### *If you have a white body:*

This is a vitally important life rep that you will probably have the chance to practice often, especially if we slide into civil war or widespread chaos and violence.

### Part 1

The next time you witness another white body—or multiple white bodies—on the verge of flying into a rage in the presence of one or more bodies of culture, do the following:

First, *pause.* If there is time, take two or three deep breaths.

Then, using your discernment, assess the situation as best you can. Ask yourself these questions:

- Does a white body look like it might become physically violent toward a body of culture?

- Does the body of culture seem afraid? Do *they* look like they may become physically violent?

- What do I experience in own my body right now—especially any urge to *flee, freeze,* or *fight*?

- What should I do next? Call the police? Start recording the incident on my phone? Simply stand by, watch, wait, and see what unfolds? Leave now, because the situation has already become violent? Or step in to try to de-escalate it?

If you decide to try to de-escalate the situation, what strategy seems most likely to work? Here are some possibilities:

- Move in closer, so it is clear to everyone that you are bearing witness to the unfolding events.

- Move in closer, nod and smile at the body of culture, and stand beside them, so it is clear to everyone that you are aligned with them.

- Move in closer, smile and nod at the body of culture, and ask them, "Can I help with anything here?"

- Move in closer, then smile and nod—first at the body of culture, then at one or more of the white bodies—and ask everyone, "Anything I can help with here?"

- Move in closer, and ask everyone a distracting question, such as "My dog ran off. Has any of you seen an unleashed Doberman?" or "Do any of you know how to get to Hennepin Avenue?"

Whatever you decide, act from the best parts of yourself.

Keep in mind that, at any moment, one or more of the bodies involved could slip into *fight* or *annihilate* mode—and perhaps focus their rage on you.

Afterward, if you like, soul scribe about the incident. Focus on what your body experienced as events unfolded.

## Part 2
The practice above involved an encounter with one or more white bodies who were on the verge of rage. But there will also be times when one or more white bodies have *already* flipped into rage. Such a situation will be much more potentially perilous. Do the following:

First, *pause.* If there is time, take two or three deep breaths.

Then, using your discernment, assess the situation as best you can. Ask yourself these questions:

- Does a white body look like it might become physically violent toward a body of culture?
- Does the body of culture seem afraid? Do *they* look like they may become physically violent?
- What do I experience in own my body right now—especially any urge to *flee, freeze,* or *fight*?
- What should I do next?
    - Call the police?
    - Start recording the incident on my phone?
    - Simply stand by, watch, wait, and see what unfolds?
    - Leave now, because the situation has already become violent, and then call the police?
    - Step in and try to separate people, or stand in between them?
    - Try to contain an aggressive white body?
    - Try to contain an aggressive body while shouting to other bystanders, "I need help here! I don't know this guy! Help me contain him so no one gets hurt!"?

- Try to de-escalate the situation? (If so, consider the potential risks of doing this.)

If you decide to attempt de-escalation, what strategy seems most likely to work? Here are some possibilities for situations that have not yet turned violent:

- Move in closer, so it is clear to everyone that you are bearing witness to the unfolding events.

- Move in closer, nod and smile at the body of culture, and stand beside them, so it is clear to everyone that you are aligned with them.

- Move in closer, smile and nod at the body of culture, and ask them, "Can I help with anything here?"

- Move in closer, then smile and nod—first at the body of culture, then at one or more of the white bodies—and ask everyone, "Anything I can help with here?"

- Move in closer and ask everyone a distracting question, such as "My dog ran off. Has any of you seen an unleashed Doberman?" or "Do any of you know how to get to Hennepin Avenue?"

Whatever you decide, act from the best parts of yourself. Keep in mind that, at any moment, one or more of the bodies involved could slip into a *fight* or *annihilate* response and attack you.

Afterward, if you like, soul scribe about the incident. Focus on what your body experienced as events unfolded.

After you have experienced both types of life reps—that is, both Part 1 and Part 2—compare the two events. Take note of your body's experiences, the decisions you made and how you made them, the ways in which you responded, and the outcomes of the two situations.

# 44

# LIVING WITH UNCERTAINTY, AMBIGUITY, AND LOST BATTLES

*Civil resistance is strategic. Movements . . .
must endure inevitable setbacks—like arrests, counter-
mobilizations by regime supporters, and legislative
defeats—while maintaining momentum.*

Martha J. Stephan and Timothy Snyder

*Sometimes the fight against evil feels heavy and hopeless. But
it's not hopeless. Plot, plan, strategize, organize and mobilize.
You start by yourself. You plot our what you want to see in the
world, you maybe do a little planning by yourself. But then you
begin to strategize with others around you—in your building,
on your street, in your office. And then you organize with
others. And then, finally, you mobilize together. In that struggle,
we discover solidarity with other human beings—and that is
something that no evil can take away from us.*

Michael Render, aka Killer Mike

*Freeing ourselves from the need to understand everything
can bring about a tremendous amount of peace.*

Sonya Renee Taylor

*Sometimes, you have to take steps back
to take one step forward.*
Nipsey Hussle

*Don't cry to give up, cry to keep going.*
ET, the Hip Hop Preacher (aka Eric Thomas)

*Should I just stop trying and give up? But then,
that's exactly what they're waiting for me to do.*
Tupac Shakur

*You cannot achieve success without failure.*
P. Diddy

If civil war erupts, everything about your life may swiftly become much more difficult and perilous. Even everyday decisions— *Do I go out to buy groceries? Do I smile and wave at my neighbor, who has stopped making eye contact with me?* —may require careful thought and the weighing of potential risks. You may also have to regularly make deeply important decisions:

- Do I go to work and meet my deadline, or go on strike and join the marchers in the street?

- Do I let my child go to school?

- Do I need to sign up for self-defense training? Do I need to sign up my kids as well?

- Do I need to learn to shoot a handgun? Do I need to keep one by my bedside? Do I need to put one in the glove compartment of my car? Do I need to carry one as I go about my day?

- Who are all these people I don't recognize driving through my neighborhood? What, if anything, should I do in response?

All of this may create a level of stress that is new to you, especially if you have a white body. While you didn't cause this stress, you will need to accept its clean pain and metabolize its energies.

If we face widespread violence, there are two other types of clean pain that you (and all of us) will need to accept and metabolize: uncertainty and loss. Often, your next day, hour, or breath may be utterly unpredictable. Just as often, you may need to let go of a relationship, plan, or hope that has long been important to you.

As in any war, the news will not always be positive. There may be disappointments, discouragements, setbacks, and lost battles. But one defeat or missed opportunity does not mean a lost war.

The January 6, 2021 riot was brought under control within hours. Multiple, widespread, or ongoing riots will not be so easily quelled. Your life may become a roller-coaster ride of alternating successes and failures, relief and disappointment, safety and peril.

The rioters, coup supporters, and their leaders will attempt to capitalize on this. One of their primary weapons may be relentlessness. Through sheer persistence, they may try to create widespread exhaustion, then resignation and apathy, then acquiescence. Their plan is to force you (and everyone else) into a difficult choice: either stop everything else in your life and put all your time, energy, and attention into resisting them, or let them sweep in and take control.

If these genuinely become your only options, you already know what choice you must make: the strong but clean pain of steadfast resistance.

All of this is why it is crucial to regularly:

- Cultivate and access resource.

- Do the body practices in this book. *Get your reps in.*

- Reach out to other people you trust and who care for you.

- In situation after situation, act from the best parts of yourself.

BODY PRACTICE
# DISAPPOINTMENT, GRIEF, IMPATIENCE, AND UNCERTAINTY

Find a quiet spot where you can be alone for about fifteen minutes. Keep paper and a pen near you.

Scan through your memories of incidents in which you experienced profound disappointment. Then make a list of five or six of these incidents.

For now, you don't need to describe or recall any event in detail. Just write a few words that enable you to easily recall it—for instance, *eleventh birthday,* or *boating accident,* or *Thurgood the cat.*

Of these disappointing incidents, pick one that ultimately led to a positive—perhaps profoundly positive—outcome.[106] For example, it might have:

- taught you something important that later enabled you to succeed
- changed you in a positive way
- woke you up to something important you hadn't seen before
- helped you to avoid disaster later
- turned out to be temporary; your dashed hope or expectation was eventually fulfilled

Now relive the disappointing event from beginning to end. As you do, pay attention to your body, and note any:

- vibrations
- images and thoughts
- meanings, judgments, stories, and explanations
- behaviors, movements, actions, impulses, and urges
- affect and emotions
- sensations

Now return to the here and now. For a few breaths, contemplate the positive outcome that eventually unfolded out of the disappointing incident.

---

106 If your initial list doesn't include an incident that later led to something positive, scan your memory further for another handful of initially disappointing incidents.

*Now* notice what you experience in your body. Is it relief? Gratitude? Astonishment? Wonder? A sense of justice?

Soul scribe about what your body is experiencing now. As always, note any:

- vibrations
- images and thoughts
- meanings, judgments, stories, and explanations
- behaviors, movements, actions, impulses, and urges
- affect and emotions
- sensations

The next time you do this body practice, focus on an incident that involved profound *grief* rather than disappointment—but eventually led to a positive outcome. For the rep after that, focus on an incident involving profound *impatience;* for the rep after that, focus on one involving profound *uncertainty.*

When you reach rep number 5, go back to *disappointment,* but choose a different incident that unfolded into something positive.

# 45

# CREATING A LIVING, EMBODIED ANTIRACIST CULTURE

*What we practice at the small scale sets the patterns for the whole system. . . . Every member of the community holds pieces of the solution, even if we are all engaged in different layers of the work.*

adrienne maree brown

*Instead of trying to build a brick wall, lay a brick every day. Eventually, you'll look up and you'll have a brick wall.*

Nipsey Hussle

*We will not go back to normal. . . . We should not long to return, my friends. We are being given the opportunity to stitch a new garment. One that fits all of humanity and nature.*

Sonya Renee Taylor

*We are fighting for a different world, and we are building new muscles to do so.*

Alicia Garza

*We're all midwives trying to give birth to a new American. In the past, every time we came to the moment in which the new American could be born, white supremacy was the umbilical cord wrapped around the baby's neck, and we let it snuff the life out of it. Let's be better midwives, as we try to be better people.*

Eddie S. Glaude Jr.

Somatic Abolitionism does not just require that we all be fair and compassionate to each other, though this is very much worth doing. It demands that we create a living, embodied antiracist culture. This will involve the ongoing efforts of many people, acting separately and together, over multiple generations.

Creating culture is not a volunteer opportunity that you sign up for, or a playbook that you follow. It's a reality that you, and I, and many others will create together as our lives unfold.[107]

In *My Grandmother's Hands*, I wrote this about creating culture: "Change culture and you change lives. You can also change the course of history. . . . More than anything, culture creates a sense of belonging—and belonging makes our bodies feel safe. This is why culture matters to us so deeply." If you want a good example of how to create culture, watch what the GOP is doing—and has been doing for years. It uses slogans, chants, colors (red and white), rallies, music, talking points, and products (T-shirts that say "DEPLORABLE," "Don't Fauci My Florida" drink koozies, hoodies that say, "My Mask Is As Useless as Jill Biden's Doctorate," etc.) to bond people around a common identity and a common purpose.

The Republican Party and their active complicitors also understand that, in addition, they need to provide a compelling vision and an equally compelling underlying myth. The GOP has been so effective in spreading these that when you read the myth below, it will seem quite familiar:

*The America you know and love is falling apart. Everything that once made it great is being systematically taken away from you by a wide-ranging group of anti-American bad actors.*

*They don't deserve this country. But you do.*

*You're a genuine, true, patriotic American. You know this in your body—probably because you're white, or Christian, or a white male Christian, or a particular type of Christian.*

*America once belonged to you and others like you. It was created by God for people like you. That's partly what made it great. Now it is all being stolen by people who are not like you, and who want to destroy*

---

107   As I wrote to white readers in *My Grandmother's Hands*: "Not only is it not my business to lead you out of white-body supremacy, but I would do you a profound disservice by trying to do so. You need to develop, lift up, and follow your own leaders in the work of dissolving white-body supremacy. If you don't—if you choose to follow a Black Pied Piper—you will collectively reaffirm the myth of white fragility and helplessness in racialized contexts. You will also have no one to pass the baton to when your Black savior retires, dies, or moves on (or turns out to be flawed, like all human beings)."

*everything you deserve and hold dear.*[108] *They have already pulled off the biggest election fraud and cultural heist in history, and they are planning more of the same.*

*You can have it all back—but only if you are willing to take it back, by any means necessary.*

*Our candidates will fight alongside you. But first you must give us your money, elect us, hate the people and ideas we tell you to hate, believe everything we tell you, disbelieve everyone else, and do whatever we say.*

*If you do these things, the America that once was great—and that once belonged to you and people like you—will be great once more and will be returned to your control.*

The Republican Party and their complicitors have one huge advantage: they do not have to tell the truth about *anything*. Indeed, the GOP base consistently rejects truth and clamors for comforting, angry lies.

For us to create a living, embodied antiracist culture, however, we must rely on truth—so we shouldn't dabble in falsehoods braided into myth. But we can create a compelling vision of the future—one based on reality, and on human beings' inborn ability to grow up.

This reliance on truth and reality—and a willingness to build structures and create relational glue based on truth—provides us with a huge advantage: everything we say can be verified through people's own eyes, bodies, and experience.

I don't know what this vision will ultimately look like. But here is what it needs to be:

- profoundly positive—much more than the simple eradication of white-body supremacy

- embodied

- both individual and communal

- tied to creation and to the creative energy that flows through all of us (and all of the universe)

- an expression of our humanity that is timeless—a returning to and remembering of what we have always been

---

108 This is the same essential message that almost every wannabe dictator throughout history has used to galvanize and mobilize their followers. The GOP has simply customized it for twenty-first-century America.

- vivid and compelling enough to engender a sense of belonging

- expansive enough to include all aspects of human experience

- fluid and flexible enough to be manifested through science, art, music, education, law, activism, literature, communal policing, and most other important human endeavors

The process of creating this vision cannot be purely cognitive. It will need to arise from the interaction of multiple bodies—and from the energies of creation.

I can't foresee the trajectory by which this vision will become reality, because—as you already know—I am not your leader or prophet or guiding light. Nor is such a person even necessary. Me Too, Black Lives Matter, and Twelve Step programs—to name just three—have emerged and grown without a single grand guru, visionary, or charismatic figure leading the way.

Notice that this vision includes far more than mere accountability.

The guilty verdicts in the murder of George Floyd by Derek Chauvin and the murder of Ahmaud Arbery by Travis McMichael, Gregory McMichael, and William Bryan, Jr. are welcome examples of accountability. But it's important not to conflate accountability with the emergence of a safer, more just, and more vibrant world.

It's equally important not to use others' accountability as a way to dodge your own. (Many white bodies, especially those with the complicit, collective variant of WBS, may be tempted by this thought: *Because some white murderers of bodies of culture have gone to prison, I don't need to examine or change anything about myself. I don't need to confront or change anything about the world. And I don't need to work to create a living, embodied antiracist culture.*) Resist that temptation, because you (and I and all our fellow human beings) need to do all of them.

As we move forward with Somatic Abolitionism, we need to continue to cultivate and access the energies of creation. Separately and together, we need to get our reps in with a variety of body practices. Some of these practices will be from this book; others may come from my other books and blog entries; still others will emerge from other bodies. You may discover a few new ones yourself.

If, at any time in this process, you lose your way, simply return to these six pillars of Somatic Abolitionism:

- the definitions of white-body supremacy and Somatic Abolitionism (on page ix)

- your awareness of the manifestations and energies of WBS, as described in Chapter 16

- the practice of *pausing*

- your body's six intelligences, or VIMBAS: vibrations; images and thoughts; meanings; behaviors, impulses, and urges; affect and emotions; and sensations (see Chapter 6)

- the five anchors (see Chapter 21)

- your body as a toy box (see Chapters 6 and 29)

As you, I, and others stay steeped in these—and as we get our reps in, individually and collectively—we can create an environment in which a living, embodied antiracist culture can emerge.

## BODY PRACTICE
## CLAIMING AND LETTING GO

*If you have a body of culture:*

Go to a quiet spot where you can sit comfortably alone, without distraction, for fifteen minutes. Bring pen and paper with you.

Take a few slow, deep breaths. Spend the next minute or two doing whatever simple reps help you settle your body.

Then, at the top of a page, write in all capital letters: WHAT I WILL CLAIM.

Next, ask yourself: *What power, authority, or agency am I willing to claim that I haven't yet claimed in order to help heal racialized trauma?*

Sit with this question for a few breaths. Then write down a list of whatever specifics come to mind.

An item can be general (*full ownership of my own body*) or very specific (*I will not let Harriet pressure me into going with her to her batshit hair stylist again*). It can be global, local, or personal.

Make a list of at least five such items. But don't automatically stop at five. Keep adding to the list until the full fifteen minutes have passed.

Now read your list aloud, slowly. Listen closely to the sound of your own voice and to each specific item you intend to claim. As you do, envision yourself actually claiming each item by taking a specific action.

Then turn your attention to your body. Notice any:

- vibrations
- images and thoughts
- meanings, judgments, stories, and explanations
- behaviors, movements, actions, impulses, and urges
- affect and emotions
- sensations

If you like, soul scribe about what your body experiences.

Although soul scribing is optional for this body practice, the following activity is not:

Over the next month or two, *follow your own plans*. Item by item, act to claim everything on your list and make it a part of your life.

Repeat this body practice until you have claimed every item on your list. Then, for your next rep, create another list, and begin anew.

### If you have a white body:

Go to a quiet spot where you can sit comfortably alone, without distraction, for fifteen minutes. Bring pen and paper with you.

Take a few slow, deep breaths. Spend the next minute or two doing whatever simple reps help you settle your body.

Then, at the top of a page, write in all capital letters: WHAT I WILL LET GO OF.

Next, ask yourself: *What advantage, power, or authority am I willing to give up that I haven't yet released, in order to help heal racialized trauma?*

Sit with this question for a few breaths. Then write down a list of whatever specifics come to mind.

An item can be general (*when people come to me for advice as an ostensibly wise elder, I'll refer them to younger, darker, equally wise folks*) or very specific (*serving on my condo association's board*). It can be global, local, or personal.

Make a list of at least five such items. But don't automatically stop at five. Keep adding to the list until the full fifteen minutes have passed.

Now read your list aloud, slowly. Listen closely to the sound of your own voice and to each specific item you intend to let go of. As you do, envision yourself living without that advantage or form of authority. Then envision yourself taking a specific action that releases that advantage or authority.

Then turn your attention to your body. Notice any:

- vibrations
- images and thoughts
- meanings, judgments, stories, and explanations
- behaviors, movements, actions, impulses, and urges
- affect and emotions
- sensations

If you like, soul scribe about what your body experiences.

Although soul scribing is optional for this body practice, the following activity is not:

Over the next month or two, *follow your own plans*. Item by item, act to release everything on your list, and accept the changes that this will create in your life.

Repeat this body practice until you have let go of every item on your list. Then, for your next rep, create another list, and begin anew.

# 46

# EMERGENCE

*When a seed sprouts, it's a violent process. The skin breaks and splits in two. Something dies and something is born.*

Michele Cassou

*The force of life is first and foremost expression, intention, and intelligence.*

Liz Koch

*When you put love out in the world it travels, and it can touch people and reach people in ways that we never even expected.*

Laverne Cox

*I'm not saying I'm gonna change the world, but I guarantee that I will spark the brain that will change the world.*

Tupac Shakur

*When we liberate ourselves from the expectation that we must have all things figured out, we enter a sanctuary of empathy.*

Sonya Renee Taylor

*We must recognize and nurture the creative parts of each other without always understanding what will be created.*

Audre Lorde

*It's not magic, but it feels like magic.*

Doyne Farmer

Physicist David Pines defines emergence this way:

> When electrons or atoms or individuals or societies interact with one another or their environment, the collective behavior of the whole is different from that of its parts. We call this resulting behavior emergent. . . . Examples of emergent behavior are everywhere around us, from birds flocking, fireflies synchronizing, ants colonizing, fish schooling, individuals self-organizing into neighborhoods in cities—all with no leaders or central control—to the Big Bang, the formation of galaxies and stars and planets, the evolution of life on earth from its origins until now. . . . Indeed, we live in an emergent universe in which it is difficult, if not impossible, to identify any existing interesting scientific problem or study any social or economic behavior that is not emergent.

Emergence is inherent in every atom, every particle, every wave, and every bit of matter and vibration of energy in the universe. It is an interplay of flows and forces that manifests itself anew in each moment, in an unfolding process that never ends.

We come from creation. We are representations of creation itself. And creation is ongoing. Each new moment is a manifestation of the universe emerging before us and through us.

As we saw in the previous chapter, human beings will need to build a living, embodied antiracist culture, as well as a vision to help drive its creation. But this process will be emergent—not scripted or centrally planned. It will include us but not be wholly determined by us. Sometimes it will move in ways and directions that surprise us.

Over months, years, decades, and generations, in ways that you and I cannot foresee, Somatic Abolitionism will unfold, transform, and emerge.

Perhaps you've heard of the biology term *imaginal cells* or *sleeping cells.* These are the cells that transmute a caterpillar into a butterfly—and, more generally, many types of insects from one stage of growth to another. (These cells bear some similarities to the *stem cells* in human embryos, which have the potential to divide into any type of cell in the human body.)

As a caterpillar ages, it spins (or molts into) a chrysalis. Once it is surrounded by the chrysalis, it dissolves into a soupy mush. Out of this soupy mush grows a butterfly that contains the same DNA as the caterpillar.

That caterpillar contained imaginal cells when it hatched from an egg, but those cells do not become profoundly activated until the caterpillar dissolves. Here is how Marc Winn describes the process that follows: "The imaginal cells . . . multiply, and they connect with one another, forming clusters. They start to resonate with the same frequency and communicate in the same language, passing information backwards and forwards until there is a tipping point—when they stop acting as individual, separate cells and instead, become a multiple-celled organism: a butterfly."

Every new moment of our lives is like an imaginal cell—a fresh encounter with the cosmos containing immense potential. Each of us can also be an imaginal cell within the human collective.

How might tomorrow's Somatic Abolitionism evolve and emerge? Here is Marc Winn again: "When systems are breaking down, you can either collapse and die or rise to the challenge of creating something better—and achieve the next stage of evolution. . . . As ideas spread and like minds connect, the possibilities grow exponentially to transform systems, policies, and processes to meet the greatest challenges."

Who knows what Somatic Abolitionism will look like three years from now, or ten, or fifty? It may look as different from what I describe in this book as a butterfly differs from a caterpillar. But as long as it keeps the same DNA, it will continue to support the growth and healing of human beings.

## BODY PRACTICE
## THE WAY FORWARD

You and I do not know how the future will unfold. But we can commit, individually and collectively, to helping liberation, justice, belonging, and community emerge.

All of these are much more than mere ideas. They grow and thrive inside human bodies.

Find a quiet place where you can be alone for a few minutes. Place a pen and paper nearby. Take a few long, slow breaths. Settle your body.

Speak the words below aloud. As you say them, listen closely to your own voice. Pay attention as it resonates through your body.

"I am not done. This is not over.

"I will defend myself, the people I love, my community, and my dream of a just, emancipated American democracy.

"I will work to create a living, embodied antiracist culture.

"I will often pause—to settle my body, to discern, to process pain, and to metabolize trauma—but I will not quit these efforts. I will also discern the difference between pausing and quitting.

"I will not sink back into the status quo of WBS."

If you have a white body, also add this: "I will not rest on my white-body advantage, but will let go of it."

Pay close attention to your body as you say these words. Note any:

- vibrations
- images and thoughts
- meanings, judgments, stories, and explanations
- behaviors, movements, actions, impulses, and urges
- affect and emotions
- sensations

Lastly, soul scribe about your body's experience with this practice.

# 47

# THE END OF THE WAR

*What I see everywhere in the world are ordinary people willing to confront despair, power, and incalculable odds in order to restore some semblance of grace, justice, and beauty to this world.*
Paul Hawken

*Transformation is not magic.*
*It's hard work. But it's also doable work.*
Sonya Renee Taylor

*All great achievements require time.*
Maya Angelou

*Now go show the world what people who matter can do.*
Wab Kinew

Just as no one can know how the war will play out, no one can know how it will end. It may cease as quickly as the US Capitol riot, with local police and National Guard units moving quickly to arrest rioters and restore order. Or perhaps the war will last days, or weeks, or years. Some locations may face multiple riots, while others may remain calm and trouble-free. Some states (and/or parts of states) may attempt to secede from the union, and it is anyone's guess whether any such attempt will succeed.

In any case, when peace does return, it will not involve a million-body healing circle where everyone sings "We Shall Overcome." Peace will be neither pretty nor comfortable. It will simply be the absence of physical fighting.

Ending or preventing an imminent civil war will surely not mean the end of racialized conflict. Indeed, for the past four hundred years, there has *never* been a time without racialized conflict on this continent. At best, the conflict will continue unabated, but without widespread violence.

Folks with vehement and devout WBS in their bodies may put down their guns and return home for now. But, like the Taliban and ISIS when they were pushed out of a locale, they may plan to return for renewed warfare when the circumstances are right. Like many white Americans after the end of the Civil War, they may play the long game, just as they have for centuries. They may support white-body supremacy in every way and situation they can, hoping to eventually win the day—whether that day comes three years later, or thirty, or three hundred.

It's possible that, chastened, the Republican Party may return to its former ideology of small government, low taxes, and limited regulation[109]—but I seriously doubt it. Too many GOP voters would gladly accept widespread government intervention, high taxes, and strong regulation if they were coupled with autocracy and white-body and/or Christian supremacy. And many Republican voters have already decided that violence is the proper way to settle political differences.

Indeed, based on what I see in late 2021, most Republican voters would accept *anything*—including their own impoverishment and the deaths of their children—if Donald Trump favored it or if it could help return him to power.

Similarly, the Democratic Party may morph into a strong and unified voice for equality, dignity, liberation, safety, and an unfettered democracy for all Americans—but I doubt that, too. Too many white-bodied Democrats have acted fecklessly for

109 In practice, of course, the GOP never followed this ostensible ideology very closely. A more accurate description of its actual ideology would be *Low taxes and limited regulation for rich and powerful people, no taxes and limited regulation for Christian churches.* According to GOP ideology, other folks—such as Muslims, people seeking abortions, and bodies of culture in general—need to be carefully controlled and regulated, and sometimes highly taxed, by robust government authorities, including police, courts, the National Guard, and election commissions.

years, decades, and generations, squabbling and compromising on contentious issues in ways that hurt many Americans, especially bodies of culture.

Many political and racial conflicts will remain unresolved. Anger and resentment will continue to simmer in many bodies. But white Americans will not be at their fellow citizens' throats. That is what peace may look like.

Nevertheless, this peace will open up new possibilities—and of course new peril—for our nation. Perhaps, once the war is over (or prevented), our country will at last be ready to embrace Somatic Abolitionism and make it an ongoing part of American life.

I invite you to join with me and many other Americans in this healing and growing up.

By now you've seen that Somatic Abolitionism, and the body practices in this book, aren't intended just for our current era of peril and possibility. Somatic Abolitionism is a lifelong and multigenerational effort, and it is as necessary to Americans' health and sanity in peacetime as it is during war.

In fact, once peace is restored, it will become more essential. In the past, during times of peace, many white bodies reflexively stopped confronting white-body supremacy in themselves, in other bodies, and in our culture. They imagined that regular confrontation was no longer necessary to ensure their own safety and comfort. Of course, this very urge to withdraw is itself a pernicious aspect of WBS.

Should many white-bodied Americans yet again attempt to do this, then you, I, and many other Americans of all skin tones will need to call out this reflexive behavior and hold our fellow citizens' feet to the fire.

Eventually, when enough people do the right thing over and over, and when they share something valuable with each other enough times, it becomes culture.

When that culture gets passed down from generation to generation—and when we teach our children, grandchildren, and great-grandchildren to consistently act from the best parts of themselves—then someday our Somatic Abolitionist vision will become reality.

## BODY PRACTICE
# AT YOUR BEST

Recall a time in your life when you were particularly strong, resilient, or resourceful—or all three.

This might be a general time in your life, such as your junior year of high school or your first month at your current job. It could also be a specific process, such as learning to play the trumpet, or a particular event, such as the day you and your college basketball team won the conference championship.

Find a comfortable, quiet place where you can be alone. Think back to this incident or time, and relive it in detail. Notice all the times when you were doing or being your best. During each of these times, pay attention to what you experience in your body. Note any:

- vibrations
- images and thoughts
- meanings, judgments, stories, and explanations
- behaviors, movements, actions, impulses, and urges
- affect and emotions
- sensations

If you like, soul scribe about your experience.

Now, remind yourself that strength, resilience, and/or resourcefulness remain in your body *right now.*

How do I know this? For the same reason that you do: you just accessed them moments ago, as you relived key moments from your life.

Today, or at any time in the future, you can access and experience them again.

# 48

# THE NEW RECONSTRUCTION

*There was white resistance to emancipation after the
Civil War, after Reconstruction, after Jim Crow, after
desegregation, and after the Civil Rights movement. In each
case calls to restructure society to support racial equality
were lampooned as misguided or a bridge too far.*

Citizen Stewart

*Only when justice isn't a surprise to anyone,
can the whole nation move ahead.*

Petula Dvorak

*If you're walking down the right path and you're willing
to keep walking, eventually you'll make progress.*

Barack Obama

*The aim of this work is truth—seeing it, owning it,
and figuring out what to do with it. This is lifelong work.
Avoid the shortcuts, and be wary of the easy answers.*

Layla F. Saad

*It is our right and responsibility to create a new world.*

adrienne maree brown

The period following the end of the first American Civil War, from roughly 1865 through 1877, is known as Reconstruction. Its first few years were among the most vibrant and hopeful in American history. In 1866, Congress passed the Civil Rights Act and four Reconstruction Acts. This guaranteed Black American men—at least on paper—the right to vote. Beginning in 1870, voters in eight states elected over a dozen African American men—some of whom had formerly been enslaved—to the US Senate and House of Representatives. For a very brief period, the healing of America's widespread racialized trauma seemed genuinely possible.

Starting in 1868, however, white-bodied Americans, especially in the South, began fiercely pushing back. Southern elections were marred with increasing violence. The Ku Klux Klan took vigilante action against both free African Americans and the white Americans who stood in solidarity with them.

Back then, it was the Democratic Party that stood for vehement and devout white-body supremacy. Democrats in both the South and the North did everything they could to suppress Black voting and regain power.[110] In the 1870s, paramilitary groups such as the Red Shirts and the White League worked openly to intimidate Black voters and turn Republicans (who were then generally supporters of racial equality) out of office.

All of this surely sounds familiar. So will this: in 1876, there was an intensely disputed presidential election that threatened to tear the country apart. A bipartisan election commission was established to find a solution. Eventually, in January 1877, a deal was reached between the Republicans and Democrats, in a party-line vote of 8 to 7. Democrats agreed to acknowledge the political rights of African Americans and conceded the election to the Republican candidate, Rutherford Hayes. In exchange, Republicans agreed to withdraw federal troops from the South.

---

110 Although the modern Democratic Party has a much better record than it did in the nineteenth century, its leaders' stances on civil rights during the last fifty years have often been underwhelming. President Joe Biden was a crusader for mass incarceration (mostly of African Americans) in the 1980s and 1990s; in the mid-1970s, he was an equally ardent opponent of busing white children to majority-Black schools and Black children to majority-white schools. During that same period, one of the best-known Democratic senators was Sam Ervin from North Carolina. In 1974, even as he worked to bring down President Richard Nixon in the Watergate hearings, Ervin was a staunch proponent of racial segregation and Jim Crow laws. More recently, some Democratic politicians have been, at best, lukewarm advocates of civil rights policies and legislation. By now, none of this should surprise you.

What happened next will also strike a familiar chord. After the compromise, some angry Democrats complained that their candidate, Samuel Tilden, had been cheated. There was talk of creating armed militias that would attack Washington. Then-President Ulysses Grant, reading the tea leaves, tightened military security in Washington, and nobody marched on the city.

However, as soon as the federal troops were gone, Southern Democrats reneged on all their promises. All the Southern state legislatures passed Jim Crow laws that made it impossible for most African Americans to vote. This enabled white Democrats— many of them former Confederate officials and slave owners— to quickly return to power. With the backing of the US Supreme Court, they effectively repealed the Fourteenth and Fifteenth Amendments and the Civil Rights Act of 1875 in their states and imposed devout and vehement white-body supremacy on their citizens for the next ninety years.

By 1877, all the former Confederate states had rejoined the Union, drafted new constitutions, acknowledged (on paper) the Thirteenth, Fourteenth, and Fifteenth Amendments, and pledged their renewed loyalty to the US government. But in those states, the widespread oppression and murder of African American bodies had resumed. Although enslavement was no longer legal, the devout and vehement variants of WBS were once again the law of the land throughout the South.

After the coming civil war ends—or is prevented—America will be at a similar crossroads. We will have an opportunity to grow up as a nation and as individuals, to heal our racialized trauma, and to create a widespread antiracist culture.

If we do, however, there will surely be fierce pushback from advocates of white-body supremacy, not just in the South but throughout the country.

Most of this will of course be from the GOP and their active complicitors. But don't be surprised if (or, more likely, when) some of the pushback comes from "centrist" Democrats. They may claim that they seek compromise, or bipartisanship, or unity. They may insist that their resistance supports economic stability, public safety, or the maintaining of property values. These are all tried-and-true, generations-old excuses for backing away from liberation and justice, and for throwing bodies of culture under a bus. Tragically, while actual buses have evolved dramatically over these many decades, the motivations, declarations, excuses, actions, and inaction of many Democrats have barely budged.

When all of this occurs, will we stand up to opponents of liberation and justice, time after time, day after day, year after year? More to the point, will most white-bodied Americans stand up to them consistently over time? That is the challenge that history will likely soon pose to every American with a white body.

I need to remind you that, whatever happens, turning the United States into an antiracist nation will take time. It has been in thrall to white-body supremacy for over a dozen generations. It will take many years to untangle, outgrow, and heal all that trauma.

When the second American civil war ends (or is avoided), we will have taken only a few steps forward on that multigenerational journey. We will need to keep walking.

In Chapter 24, I suggested that it will take roughly nine generations for Americans to grow a living, embodied antiracist culture and for the great majority of Americans of all skin hues to fully live into that culture. But that's an estimate, not a proclamation. No one can say how long it will take—or if it will ever be possible.

In any case, creating a timeline isn't the point. Regardless of how long America's healing may take, our job is to put our shoulders to the wheel right now, and again in the next moment, and the next. If we don't, we may deprive many future generations of the sweetness of liberation.

## BODY PRACTICE
## INVITING THE ENERGIES OF RACE

This practice builds on the body practices from Chapter 26, Untangling the Energies of Race, Parts 1 and 2. It can help you further metabolize any racialized trauma still stuck in your body. It can also help you resolve any embodied conflicts about race that remain.

Find a quiet place where you can sit comfortably and alone at a desk, table, or other flat surface.

Rest your elbows on the desk or table so that each elbow is directly in front of a shoulder. Keeping your elbows on that flat surface, point both your forearms and hands straight up.

For a few breaths, notice the energy that's present in your hands. *Pause.* Take a few more breaths.

Bring your attention to one of your hands. (It doesn't matter which one.) This hand holds the energies of white-body supremacy—the energies of colonization, perpetration, and discrimination. *Pause* again, and take several more breaths.

Then move your attention to the other hand. This hand holds the energies of healing, growth, and the metabolization of trauma. *Pause* once more for a few breaths.

Now, slowly, bring your hands together. Lightly interlock your fingers. Pause once again.

Focus your attention on your clasped hands. For ten breaths, just stay with their energies. Don't try to visualize or imagine anything. Don't try to move anything—or hold it still. Just pay attention.

What moves? What emerges? What grows? What do your hands do or want to do? What does the rest of your body do or want to do? Note any:

- vibrations
- images and thoughts
- meanings, judgments, stories, and explanations
- behaviors, movements, actions, impulses, and urges
- affect and emotions
- sensations

Now say aloud: "I am healing from white-body supremacy. I will continue to heal."

Slowly unclasp your hands.

If you like, soul scribe about your experience with this body practice.

# 49

# Y2K, COVID-19, AND SOMATIC ABOLITIONISM

*Do not expect neat, tidy resolutions, or assume that we will instantly fix the world's ills. . . . We can, however, get closer to those goals if we are willing to be uncomfortable.*

Sonya Renee Taylor

*You really can change the world if you care enough.*

Marian Wright Edelman

*The time for sitting back and taking Democracy for granted is over. The time for doing nothing has passed. The time for you to step up is now. Whether we keep our Democracy or lose it is completely up to you and no one else. Get smart, get tough, get going, and keep going.*

Greg Jenkins

If you're older than thirty, you probably recall the crisis that we now call Y2K.

Human beings had no trouble making the shift from the year 1999 to 2000. But, as techies warned us in the late 1990s, most computer programs would have a lot of trouble making that transition, because they had been designed to calculate each year based on three digits, not four. Just as old-style car odometers would turn from 99,999 miles to 0 miles, many types of software would suddenly shift from 1999 (or, from the software's viewpoint, 999) to the year 0.

As the turn of the millennium approached, no one knew for certain what would happen inside most software when January 1, 2000 arrived. But tech people around the world were very worried that all kinds of systems, large and small, could go haywire. Some thought that power grids, or satellite communications, or the thermostats in hundreds of millions of homes, might all stop working at once.

A small minority of people shrugged off the issue. "We'll be fine," they said. "You techies are a bunch of doomsayers. Calm down."

But most governments, public utilities, corporations, and other large organizations took the warnings very seriously. They invested many billions of dollars—and tens of millions of person-hours—in updating millions of pieces of software. This became one of the most concerted and unified efforts that humankind has ever undertaken in peacetime.

These efforts paid off in a big way when January 1, 2000 arrived. Around the world, 98 percent of computer programs made the transition smoothly. There were some minor hiccups, but nothing serious or deadly.

Some of the forward-thinking techies had the bright idea to do an experiment. As a test, they let some of the original, un-updated software continue to operate some small, nonessential systems. Many of those systems failed when 1999 became 2000. The tech folks discovered that they had accurately predicted the potential for disaster and properly communicated the urgency of the problem.

Nevertheless, as the world celebrated the turn of the millennium, some of the people who had said, "Calm down," shook their fingers at all the people who had worked so hard to prevent the crisis. "See?" they said. "We told you there was nothing to worry about."

Our world faced a similar situation with the spread of COVID-19. Some governments—for example, those of New

Zealand, Rwanda, Denmark, and Australia—quickly saw the potential for widespread disaster and took swift and coordinated steps to prevent it. As a result, by the end of 2021, fewer than 7,500 people died of COVID in all four countries combined—out of a total population of nearly 50 million. That's about 1.5 deaths per 10,000 people.

In other countries, leaders ignored or denied the crisis. They called COVID imaginary, or nothing to worry about, or "a little flu." In just two of those countries, the United States and Brazil, which have a combined population of 539 million, by the end of 2021 over 1.4 million people died of COVID-19. That's about 25 deaths per 10,000 people—a death rate about seventeen times that of the countries noted above. In the US, far more people died from COVID than from the Spanish flu during the epidemic of 1918–20.

In early 2021, when the Republican Party become fully authoritarian and anti-democratic, I and others clearly saw not only the dangers that the transfigured party posed but the playbook from which it had begun to operate. I quickly also saw the need to set aside the book I had been working on—a sequel to *My Grandmother's Hands*—and create this book first.

Some folks may look at this book, shake their heads, and say, "We'll be fine. Resmaa, you're a doomsayer. Calm down." My answer to that is, "Let's see what happens" (or, perhaps, "Look what's happened since 2022 began"). And if the person making that comment is a white Christian, I'll add, "It's much easier for someone who doesn't have white skin—or someone who is Muslim or Jewish—to recognize what's going on than it is for a white Christian."

My hope is that this book will ultimately reach far beyond the current crisis, help people to recognize and heal from their racialized trauma, stand up to forces of totalitarianism around the world, and claim or reclaim their rightful places as participants in emancipated democracies.

Perhaps, together, we will succeed in preventing the civil war of 2023 (or 2022, 2024, or 2025).

If we do, and if the person who called me a doomsayer says, "See, Resmaa? I told you there was nothing to worry about; the civil war you wrote about never happened," then my answer to them will be, "You're welcome."

BODY PRACTICE
## WHAT COMES NEXT

Find a quiet space where you can sit by yourself in front of a desk, table, or other flat surface for at least twenty minutes. In front of you, place your notebook, journal, or whatever you have used for soul scribing since you began this book. Keep a pen nearby.

Open your journal or notebook to the beginning. Over the next few minutes, page through it slowly, reading the words that you soul scribed over the past months. As you do, pay attention to your body. Note any:

- vibrations
- images and thoughts
- meanings, judgments, stories, and explanations
- behaviors, movements, actions, impulses, and urges
- affect and emotions
- sensations

Now turn your attention to what has happened in the world, and in your life, since you began reading *The Quaking of America*. Spend a few minutes reflecting on the many perils, possibilities, and changes that have unfolded.

Next, shift your attention slightly, from how the world has changed to what it most needs *right now* to heal from war, upheaval, or widespread discord—and from white-body supremacy. Reflect on this topic for as long as you like.

Pick up your pen. In your notebook or journal, at the top of a blank page, in all capital letters, write: WHAT THE WORLD MOST NEEDS RIGHT NOW TO HELP IT HEAL. Then write a list of at least five items. Take whatever time you need to create this list.

Next, at the top of the following page in your journal or notebook, write in all capital letters: WHAT THE WORLD MOST NEEDS *FROM ME* RIGHT NOW TO HELP IT HEAL. Reflect on this topic, and then write another list containing at least five items. Again, take as much time as you need.

Turn to the next page in your notebook or journal. At the top, in all capitals, write: WHAT I WILL DO NEXT TO HEAL MYSELF AND THE WORLD. Reflect on this topic; then write a list of five or more things that you commit to doing in the days and weeks ahead.

Put down your pen. *Pause.* Take a few deep, slow breaths.

Reread the three lists you've just written. As you do, pay close attention to your body. Notice any:

- vibrations
- images and thoughts
- meanings, judgments, stories, and explanations
- behaviors, movements, actions, impulses, and urges
- affect and emotions
- sensations

Now, say aloud, "I know what to do next."

If you like, soul scribe about your experience with this body practice.

## 50

# VITAL RESOURCES AND NEXT STEPS

*We're not only disasters; we're also miracles.*

Eddie S. Glaude Jr.

*Let them remember that there is a meaning beyond absurdity.
Let them be sure that every little deed counts, that every word
has power, and that we can—every one—do our share to
redeem the world in spite of all absurdities and all frustrations
and all disappointments. And above all, remember that the
meaning of life is to build a life as if it were a work of art.*

Abraham Joshua Heschel

*It always seems impossible until it's done.*

Nelson Mandela

*Hope is invented every day.*

James Baldwin

To learn more about Somatic Abolitionism, visit my website,
resmaa.com, or my Somatic Abolitionism blog for Psychology
Today, psychologytoday.com/us/blog/somatic-abolitionism.

To enroll in my free five-session video course on racialized trauma through the Cultural Somatics Institute, go to culturalsomaticsuniversity.thinkific.com/courses/cultural-somatics-free-5-session-ecourse.

To access a full array of my free articles, podcast and television interviews, videos of my live presentations, and other helpful resources, visit resmaa.com/links. You can also use this QR code:

You'll find hundreds of free videos, articles, and other posts on my Instagram page, instagram.com/resmaamenakem/?hl=en.

You can listen to my podcast, *Guerilla Muse* (also known as *Gorilla Muse;* both are correct), available wherever you get your podcasts.

## Here are some of the most important books[111] on racialized trauma and/or communal healing around race:

- *The Second: Race and Guns in a Fatally Unequal America* by Carol Anderson (Bloomsbury, 2021)

- *White Rage: The Unspoken Truth of Our Racial Divide* by Carol Anderson (Bloomsbury, 2016)

- *We've Got Answers: Honest Conversations on Race in America* by Charlamagne Tha God (Brilliance Audio, 2021)

- *Nice Racism: How Progressive White People Perpetuate Racial Harm* by Robin DiAngelo (Beacon Press, 2021)

- *White Fragility: Why It's So Hard for White People to Talk About Racism* by Robin DiAngelo (Beacon Press, 2018)

---

111    As of this writing, Charlamagne Tha God's *We've Got Answers* is available only in audio.

- *Healing: The Act of Radical Self-Care* by Joi Lewis
  (Wise Ink, 2019)

- *My Grandmother's Hands* by Resmaa Menakem
  (Central Recovery Press, 2017)

- *Be a Revolution* by Ijeoma Oluo (HarperOne, 2022)

- *State of Emergency: How We Win in the Country We Built*
  by Tamika D. Mallory (Atria/Black Privilege, 2021)

- *The Reckoning: Our Nation's Trauma and Finding a Way
  to Heal* by Mary L. Trump (St. Martin's Press, 2021)

The Libraries for Liberation website offers an excellent list of suggested books that center the experiences of bodies of culture: librariesforliberation.com/which-books.

**These brief, highly readable books shed light on the current attempts to destroy American democracy:**
- *Why We Elect Narcissists and Sociopaths—and How
  We Can Stop!* by Bill Eddy (Berrett-Koehler, 2019)

- *On Tyranny: Twenty Lessons from the Twentieth Century*
  by Timothy Snyder (Tim Duggan Books, 2017)

- *How Fascism Works: The Politics of Us and Them* by Jason
  Stanley (Random House, 2018)

**These organizations provide a wealth of invaluable information on organizing, demonstrating, and stopping or preventing attempted coups and insurrections:**
- Indivisible, indivisible.org. Offers many useful webinars, trainings, organizing tools, books, articles, and other forms of practical information on demonstrating, organizing, and supporting American democracy.

- Choose Democracy, choosedemocracy.us. Offers many helpful articles, books, and videos, including:

  – *4 Ways to Defeat a Coup* (video)

  – "How to Stop an Election-Related Power Grab"
     (training slides)

- – "10 Things You Need to Know to Stop a Coup" by Daniel Hunter (article)
- – "How to Face Right-Wing Violence While Defending an Election" (interview with George Lakey)
- – *The Anti-Coup* by Gene Sharp (book, available as a free PDF)
- – Civil Resistance Against Coups: A Comparative and Historical Perspective by Stephen Zunes (book, available as a free PDF)
- – "Resisting Stolen Elections: Lessons from the Philippines, Serbia, Ukraine, and Gambia" by Stephen Zunes (article)

• Black Lives Matter, blacklivesmatter.com. Under this site's Resources tab, you'll find useful toolkits on healing action, healing justice, conflict resolution, and other topics.

• Albert Einstein Institution, aeinstein.org. This organization's credo is "Advancing freedom with nonviolent action." Its site offers a wide array of helpful free resources, including books, films, interviews, talks, and a news feed. I especially recommend its list of 198 methods of nonviolent action: aeinstein.org/wp-content/uploads/2014/12/198-Methods.pdf.

• Amnesty International offers many free, helpful toolkits and guides at amnestyusa.org/tools-and-reports/toolkits-guides, as well as a succinct and valuable one-page guide, "Safety During Protest," at amnestyusa.org/pdfs/SafeyDuringProtest_F.pdf.

• The ACLU (American Civil Liberties Union) sponsors this excellent "Know Your Rights" page for protest participants and organizers: aclu.org/know-your-rights/protesters-rights.

• New York University's Center on Race, Inequality, and the Law offers a variety of protest tips and resources: law.nyu.edu/centers/race-inequality-law/protest-tips.

- WikiHow has a good set of pages called "How to Protest" (wikihow.com/Protest) and another called "How to Protest Safely" (wikihow.com/Protest-Safely).

- Natural Resources Defense Council (NRDC) provides a brief, helpful guide called "How to Protest Safely": nrdc. org/stories/how-protest-safely.

**Below are some other essential resources on movement building and responding effectively to attempted coups and insurrections:**

- *The Purpose of Power: How We Come Together When We Fall Apart* by Alicia Garza (One World, 2021)

- *We Are Indivisible: A Blueprint for Democracy After Trump* by Leah Greenberg and Ezra Levin (One Signal/Atria, 2019)

- *How We Win: A Guide to Nonviolent Direct Action Campaigning* by George Lakey (Melville House, 2018)

- *Indivisible: A Practical Guide for Fixing Our Democracy*, indivisible.org/democracy-guide

- "How Nonviolent Activists Helped Oppose the Coup" by Stephen Zunes, Yes! Magazine, January 20, 2021, yesmagazine.org/democracy/2021/01/20/trump-coup-nonviolent-activists

- The Hollaback! website, ihollaback.org, offers a wealth of information, tools, and strategies for supporting the safety of your block and neighborhood, for responding effectively when you witness the public harassment of a person or group, for organizing a protest or march, and for de-escalating conflict. The lists of what to do and not do in Chapter 33 are adapted from Hollaback!

The three guides below were originally written for the 2020 election. However, each one provides information, resources, and links that will be useful in the 2022 and 2024 elections. Updated versions may be published shortly before either or both of these elections.

- *Daniel's Guide to Taking Action,* sourceful.us/doc/550/daniels-guide-to-taking-action-in-the-2020-electio
- *Hold the Line: A Guide to Defending Democracy* by Hardy Merriman, Ankur Asthana, Marium Navid, and Kifah Shah, digitalcommons.unl.edu/cgi/viewcontent.cgi?article=1000&context=oersocialsci. A related podcast interview with Merriman is at mettacenter.org/ppr/hold-the-line-a-guide-to-defending-democracy.
- *Stopping the Coup: A Disruption Guide to 2020,* sourceful.us/doc/601/stopping-the-coup-the-2020-guide

## To better understand the relationship of emergence, activism, and the human body, read these enlightening books by adrienne maree brown:

- *Emergent Strategy: Shaping Change, Changing Worlds* (AK Press, 2017)
- *Holding Change: The Way of Emergent Strategy Facilitation and Mediation* (AK Press, 2021)
- *Pleasure Activism: The Politics of Feeling Good* (AK Press, 2019)
- *We Will Not Cancel Us: Breaking the Cycle of Harm* (AK Press, 2020)

## Below are some helpful resources for healing racialized trauma:

- Resources in the Wake of Community Trauma and Beyond (from the State of Minnesota's Department of Health): health.state.mn.us/communities/mentalhealth/trauma.html
- Racism and Mental Health (from St. Olaf College): wp.stolaf.edu/wellness/racism-and-mental-health
- Healing from Racial Trauma (from Augsburg University): augsburg.edu/cwc/self-help/recovering-from-racial-trauma

- How to Cope with Traumatic Events (from the Jed Foundation): jedfoundation.org/resource/how-to-cope-with-traumatic-events

- Coping with Grief After Community Violence (from the US Substance Abuse and Mental Health Services Administration): store.samhsa.gov/product/Coping-With-Grief-After-Community-Violence/SMA14-4888

- Toolkits and Resources from Black Emotional and Mental Health (BEAM): beam.community/tool-kits-education

- Center for Healing Racial Trauma: centerforhealingracialtrauma.com/resources

- Mental Wealth Alliance: mentalwealthalliance.org. MWA promotes Charlamagne Tha God's vision to address the mental health gap facing Black communities. MWA raises awareness, reduces stigma, and expands access through training, teaching, and treating.

- The Safe Place (a Black-centered app) is available from Google Play and the Apple app store.

- Liberate (liberatemeditation.com) is a daily meditation app by and for Black bodies. It's available from Google Play and the Apple app store.

- The twenty-eight-lesson e-course on racialized trauma that I created for the Cultural Somatics Institute is available at courses.culturalsomaticsinstitute.com/courses/racialized-trauma-home-study-course. (A much briefer, five-session e-course is also available, at no charge, at courses.culturalsomaticsinstitute.com/courses/cultural-somatics-free-5-session-ecourse.)

## Some mental health and crisis support phone lines:

- SAMHSA (Substance Abuse and Mental Health Services Administration) Disaster Distress Helpline: call 800-985-5990 or text "TalkWithUs" to 66746, for 24/7 confidential, free crisis counseling.

- National Suicide Prevention Lifeline: 800-273-TALK (8255). Open 24/7. Free, confidential counseling is available in English and Spanish.

- NAMI (National Alliance on Mental Illness) Helpline: 800-950-6264, Monday–Friday, 10 a.m.–8 p.m., Eastern Time; or text "NAMI" to 741741, 24/7. Counseling is free and confidential.

## Some legal support phone lines:

- National Lawyers Guild Legal Support Hotline for your state (or DC): find your state at nlg.org/massdefenseprogram. If your state has no hotline of its own, call the National NLG Federal Defense Hotline, 212-679-2811.

## Organizations that (unlike the NRA) support responsible gun ownership, use, and training:

- National African American Gun Association: naaga.co

- Gun Owners for Responsible Ownership: responsibleownership.org

## Deeply worthwhile—and deeply relevant—film, TV, and video productions:

- *Exterminate All the Brutes* is a four-part HBO docuseries directed by Raoul Peck. It revisits and reframes two of the most notable—and brutal—aspects of American history: the genocide of Indigenous bodies and the enslavement of Black ones. The series also examines the implications of these events for human beings today.

- *High on the Hog* is a four-part Netflix series hosted by Stephen Satterfield. It relates a history of the United States through the lens of foods created, cooked, and eaten by Black bodies.

- *How to Become a Tyrant* is a six-part Netflix series that examines the playbook by which murderous dictators rise to power and maintain it. Narrated by Peter Dinklage, the series focuses on Idi Amin, Muammar Gaddafi, Adolf

Hitler, Saddam Hussein, Josef Stalin, and Kim Jong-un and his father and grandfather.

- *Lovecraft Country* is an HBO series set in the 1950s that combines horror, drama, history, and an inspired (and terrifying) bizarreness. The formal setup involves Atticus Freeman and his friend Letitia, both of whom are African American, driving across the Jim Crow South in search of Atticus's missing father. However, this does not begin to convey the experience of watching this series. Let me simply say that Atticus and Letitia often encounter monsters, only some of which are human.

- *Enslaved* is a six-episode Epix docuseries narrated by Samuel L. Jackson, which explores 400 years of human trafficking from Africa to the Americas.

**To receive training in psychological first aid, start with one of these websites:**

- National Child Traumatic Stress Network (NCTSN) Learning Center: learn.nctsn.org/course/index.php?categoryid=11
- American Psychological Association: apa.org/practice/programs/dmhi/psychological-first-aid/training
- American Red Cross: redcross.org/take-a-class/classes/psychological-first-aid%3A-supporting-yourself-and-others-during-covid-19/a6R3o0000014ZIg.html

**You'll find information about training in Critical Incident Stress Management (CISM) at these websites:**

- simplilearn.com/cyber-security/cism-certification-training
- trainingcamp.com/training/cism-certification-bootcamp

**Materials I've created for folks who want to mindfully interrogate their racialized trauma and dive deeply into Somatic Abolitionism:**

- *Somatic Abolitionist 12-Month Practicebook.* This is a detailed, hands-on workbook that guides the reader on a year-long journey of inquiry. There are three versions of the *Practicebook*: one for bodies of culture, one specifically for Black bodies, and one for white bodies. Each *Practicebook*: is intended for groups of three or more people, who work together as a cohort for a full year. *Practicebooks* are thus sold in packages of three. You can order these at resmaa.com/merch.

- The CORE Assessment measures the qualities of an individual's racialized energies: confidence, outgoing, reliable, and easygoing. Each person's energy profile includes an analysis of their virtues, opportunities, limitations, and threat tendencies—both individually and communally. The CORE Assessment does not measure someone's racism or bias, and it is not a personality test. You can learn more about the CORE Assessment at https://www.culturalsomaticsinstitute.com/core-assessment.

You can use the Wyser app on your smartphone to access a wide range of additional web content related to each chapter of *The Quaking of America*. *See page* 369 for details and a QR code.

## BODY PRACTICE
## **YOUR DAILY REBIRTH**

Each day when you wake up, you emerge into a new world—one that is different from the world the day before, the hour before, and the moment before.

You are different, too. Like the rest of the world, you are always changing, always emerging.

Each new day—and each new moment—is your rebirth and the rebirth of the cosmos.

Here's a set of simple primal reps that I do each morning. Try them out daily for a week or two. Thereafter, continue to practice them each day—or adapt or replace them in whatever ways your body wants you to.

Begin by stretching in any way or direction your body desires. Hold the stretch for three breaths.

Then, for a single breath, do a different primal rep. Grunt, or moan, or wiggle, or pump, or growl, or push and pull, or hum, or yawn, or etc.

Repeat this process ten times.

You can do the same stretch over and over, or you can change it to a different one whenever your body wants to. Ditto for the primal rep in between stretches.

As you do this very simple practice, you are grounding and orienting; you are settling your body; you are broadcasting and receiving signals and energy flows; and you are reminding your body that it belongs in the precise space it occupies, at this exact moment in time.

From now on, when you first get out of bed each day, spend five to ten minutes reconnecting with the primal energies of the elements, the planet, and the cosmos in this way.

Then go forth and live into the new and ever-emergent world.

# AFTERWORD: US

*This is no ordinary moment in the course of our democracy. It is a moment of great peril and risk.... Defenders of democracy in America still have a slim window of opportunity to act. But time is ticking away, and midnight is approaching.*

Letter signed on November 29, 2021 by 196 scholars of democracy

*The death of democracy has reached America's door . . . and the ones who are supposed to be protecting us are a bunch of frail-ass, shook-ass, punk-ass cowardly donkeys.*

Charlamagne Tha God

*Democrats: get your butts in gear and get passionate about saving this damn country. You're not doing it.*

Don Lemon

*This is nation-ending stuff we're dealing with here and folks better wake up soon. I'll do my part. Think about what yours is.*

US Senator Chris Murphy

*Republicans are making their intentions clear. The crisis is already here, and we have to treat it with the urgency it deserves.*

Paul Waldman

*Today's GOP is how democracies die.*

Dean Obeidallah

*Our great nation now teeters on the brink of a widening abyss.
Without immediate action, we are at genuine risk of civil conflict
and losing our precious democracy.*

Former President Jimmy Carter

*The strength of democracy is that it empowers the people. The
fragility of democracy is this: if we are not vigilant, if we don't
defend it, democracy will not stand. It will falter. And it will fail.*

Vice President Kamala Harris

*We are living at an inflection point in history. . . . We're engaged
anew in a struggle between democracy and autocracy.*

President Joe Biden

*Pause.*

At first glance, the Republican agenda in 2022 and beyond appears to be to destroy the United States as a democracy. That is an incomplete view.

The current GOP plan is to destroy the United States not only as a democracy but as a nation and as a civilization.[112]

Five centuries ago, when Spanish and Portuguese armies arrived in the Indigenous ancestral homelands that we now call the Americas, this was their message: *We're powerful white bodies with guns, cannons, swords, crossbows, and halberds. We're destroying your civilizations and taking everything. Obey us or we'll kill you. Sometimes we'll kill you anyway.*

A century later, human traffickers kidnapped millions of Africans and sent them across the ocean to a strange and dangerous land. This was the kidnappers' message to the human beings they captured and trafficked: *We're powerful white bodies with lots of guns. We're taking your bodies and destroying your cultures. Obey us or we'll kill you. Sometimes we'll kill you anyway.*

---

112   This statement is not hyperbole. It is my most realistic and accurate description of unfolding events in early 2022. That said, as part of its strategy, the GOP will insist—loudly, constantly, everywhere—that the actual villains are the Biden administration, the Democratic Party, Black Lives Matter, George Soros, the Deep State, refugees, immigrants, bodies of culture, and perhaps this book. Republican strategists hope that some folks will believe these weaponized lies and that others will imagine that the parallel accusations cancel themselves out, creating a rhetorical standoff.

For over two centuries in North America, plantation owners and other enslavers required many generations of Black bodies to toil for no pay as forced laborers. This was their message: *We're powerful white bodies with lots of guns. Your bodies belong to us. We have destroyed your cultures. Obey us or we'll kill you. Sometimes we'll kill you anyway.*

For many decades, as white Americans pushed beyond the original thirteen colonies into the interior of the continent, they killed many millions of Indigenous people, captured and relocated millions more, and stole their land. This was their message: *We're powerful white bodies with lots of guns. We're taking everything and destroying most of your cultures. Obey us or we'll kill you. Sometimes we'll kill you anyway.*[113]

Fast forward to the third decade of the twenty-first century. The gang violence at the US Capitol on January 6, 2021, which shocked the world, is only one small, early part of a much larger, pro-mayhem and pro-chaos GOP agenda.

Look at what's unfolding around our country. Thousands of Americans have threatened violence and murder against healthcare professionals, teachers, election monitors, school board members, government officials, judges, political candidates, and elected representatives. Meanwhile, right-wing media propagate one Big Lie after another, 24/7. And, in plain sight, GOP operatives across the country make plans to subvert and overthrow future elections.

Yet this is only the surface layer. Also notice the ever-growing emphasis on guns and violence as the solutions to all disputes. The demonization of everyone who has not pledged complete subservience to Donald Trump. The creation of endless imaginary threats, from the faux spreading of COVID by refugees, to the nonexistent indoctrination of children in critical race theory, to the ostensible imminent disappearance or destruction of suburbs,

---

113   Compare this with the following list: *truthfulness, love, bravery, wisdom, honor, respect, humility, generosity, compassion.* As I wrote this Afterword in October 2021, a new installation by Dakota artist Angela Two Stars opened at the Walker Art Center, about two miles from my Minneapolis home. The installation, which is at once a large work of visual art and an amphitheater-like space with a fountain in the center, highlights these and seven other Dakota values, which are presented in large lettering, in the Dakota language, on dozens of concrete benches. The list I've provided is Two Stars' rough translation of the Dakota words, which are (in the same order as the English words above): *wówićake, wótheĥiŋda, wóohitika, wóksape, wóyuonihaŋ, woohoda, wicowaĥba, wóoĥ'aŋwaśte,* and *wówauŋśida.* A more nuanced translation of each Dakota word would of course be far more detailed. For more about this installation and the words that anchor it, visit www.walker.org/two-stars.

windows, and cows.[114] The ongoing murder of bodies of culture by police—and police forces and unions that strenuously resist holding the murderers to account. The relentless stoking of white fury. The Confederate flags. The contempt for laws. The contempt for science. The contempt for honest elections. The contempt for public discussion and debate. The contempt for respectfulness and civility. The contempt for intelligence. The contempt for compromise. The contempt for women. The contempt for the elderly. The contempt for children. The contempt for everyone who is not an American-born white Christian male. The contempt for the very people the GOP hopes to provoke to mob violence. The contempt for reason. The contempt for thought. The contempt for community. The contempt for economic stability. The contempt for kindness. The contempt for generosity. The contempt for honesty. The contempt for responsibility. The contempt for integrity. The contempt for ethics and morality. The contempt for safety. The contempt for human health. The deep and abiding contempt for truth. The total contempt for democracy. And the deepest contempt of all for justice and liberation.[115]

The GOP's current core message is clear, simple, and time-tested: *We're white bodies with lots of guns. We plan to take everything, destroy culture, implode democracy, and replace it with rule by raw power. Obey us. Patriots, join us—and Make America Great Again.*

As configured in 2022, and very likely beyond, this is what the Republican Party stands for. Stop imagining anything different. Continue to prepare for what is to come: mayhem.

*Pause.*

Mayhem and chaos are central parts of the GOP's plan.

What will this mayhem and chaos look like where you live? Will the local police protect you and your family from it? Will the National Guard? Will the military? Will you and your neighbors work together to protect one another? You may want to work on this. Are you and your family prepared to defend and protect each other? You may want to work on this, too.

Will the Democratic Party protect you from this mayhem and chaos? You already know the answer. They did not protect

---

114    You read this right. At various times, Trump claimed that if Joe Biden were elected president, he would somehow take away or destroy suburbs, windows, and cows.

115    Compare this list, too, with the list of Dakota values in the footnote on page 364 – 365.

America from the rise of Trump. They did not protect America from the Big Lie. They have not protected untold numbers of bodies of culture from being murdered by police.

For decades, Democrats have dithered; wrung their hands; fought each other; called for bipartisanship; tried to reach across the aisle; held hearings; issued subpoenas, which were often ignored; and made strong statements to the press. All the while, they have often eaten their own young and repeatedly thrown bodies of culture to the lions, attempting to appease the GOP. The GOP and their followers have responded with scorn, baseless attacks, and death threats.

Meanwhile, in full view of the entire world, the Republican Party has constructed a huge media ecosystem of lies and subterfuge—and used it to stoke fury, WBS, and bloodlust in tens of millions of armed citizens.

Go online right now. Look at what the Democratic Party is doing today. Does it look like a full-court press for justice, liberation, and an emancipated democracy? Or are the Democrats, wittingly or unwittingly, just another group of GOP complicitors?

I'm writing this toward the end of 2021. The Dems have an opportunity to pass voting rights bills with real backbones and at last create an unfettered democracy for all citizens. They have an opportunity to pass a "Build Back Better" bill that deeply invests in a safer, healthier, cleaner, more secure, and more prosperous future for all. They have an opportunity to pass legislation that substantively addresses the ever-worsening climate crisis.

The Dems also have the opportunity to finally grow up, wield their power, choose clean pain over dirty pain, and do what is just and liberatory for all Americans—precisely *because* it is just and liberatory.

In December 2021, there are signs that they will do all of these things. There are equally strong signs that they will do few or none.

It's true that, in late 2021, the Dems are in multiple double binds. But the only way through any double bind is to grow. This means doing something that frightens you but that you know is right. Or doing something you hadn't previously considered or believed was possible. Or doing something you imagined you weren't capable of doing. Or doing something you thought—or pretended—you weren't *permitted* to do. It often means living into Nelson Mandela's words: "It always seems impossible until it's done."

To you, the year 2021—and the Dems' actions in it—are history. Perhaps, as I hope, the Democrats summoned the grit and courage and unity and wisdom that they so often lacked in the past. Perhaps they did the right things *because* they were the right things. Perhaps they finally earned the loyalty (and votes) of the many millions of bodies of culture whose support they routinely needed—and counted on—but for whom they so rarely delivered. Perhaps *they* were the wise people who helped us to avert a civil war.

Or, perhaps, as they did so many times before, the Dems let most or all of it slip through their fingers. Perhaps they threw tens of millions of American bodies, especially Black women's bodies, to the wolves yet again. Perhaps they chose to be idle and complicit in helping our planet burn ever hotter. Perhaps historians will say of the Democratic Party, *They could have pulled our country back from the edge of an abyss, but instead they helped push it over that edge.*

If that is what the Democrats choose, then civil war may be a mere harbinger of worse things to come.

The game is up. The reckoning is here. The conflicts that have been building for centuries are now in our streets and in our faces. The contradictions baked into American culture can no longer be swept aside or denied. How will we resolve them?

The Republican Party hopes to resolve them with lies, autocracy, violence, and brutality.

The Democratic Party hopes to address them with legislation, policies, programs, and litigation. These can be helpful, but they are not remotely enough.

You, I, and all of us who want an emancipated democracy *must* vote—in every general election and in every primary. But that, too, is not remotely enough.

We will only resolve our centuries-old conflicts and contradictions through justice and liberation.

Now it is up to us.

# DEEPENING YOUR EXPERIENCE OF THIS BOOK

I invite you to use the Wyser app to get more out of this book. Wyser provides a chapter-by-chapter set of links that will take you to videos, websites, articles, essays, podcasts, and other relevant information and perspectives.

To download and use Wyser on your smartphone, scan the QR code below.

# ACKNOWLEDGMENTS

As you answer the question *How will I help to create a living, embodied, antiracist culture?*, perhaps the creation of this book will serve as a model.

*The Quaking of America* began as nothing more than an idea—a seed that needed to be planted and a sense that the world would soon need what would grow from that seed.

At first, these were all I had to work with: an idea and a sense of necessity. Yet, out of these, a vision emerged—and then, step by step, day by day, and breath by breath, this book.

I could not have created *The Quaking of America* on my own. It involved the work of a great many other human beings. Let me shout out some of the most important ones.

My longtime collaborator and literary agent, Scott Edelstein, worked closely with me throughout the project. This is my third book with Scott, and I expect us to collaborate on at least one or two more. I'm deeply grateful for his work as my co-author. I also appreciate how, as my agent, he has always had my back, while putting my interests front and center.

The key people at Central Recovery Press—my editors Valerie Killeen and Lucy Vilankulu, copy editor Beth Wright, the sales and marketing wizard Patrick Hughes (who now practices his wizardry elsewhere), special markets manager John Davis, and publisher Jeff Speich—provided many forms of steadfast support. My profound thanks to all six. With my enthusiastic blessing, CRP has established a line of Somatic Abolitionism books and will publish at least one new title each year.

Scott, Valerie, Patrick, and I originally envisioned this book as a sequel to *My Grandmother's Hands*. But in February 2021, Scott said, "Resmaa, I think the sequel is going to have to wait. Just look at what's happened to our country in the past two months. Americans are going to need a very different book than the one we've been writing." I knew immediately that he was right.

When we told Valerie and Patrick, "We're going to deliver a very different book; here's what it will look like," and outlined *The Quaking of America* for them, we did not know how they and their colleagues would respond. It was yet another situation of peril and possibility. Fortunately, everyone at CRP quickly understood the need for this book. They pivoted without objection—as did the people at their distributor, Consortium—and we all quickly realigned.

My thanks to my primary publicist, Sam Mattingly, and her close collaborator, Josh Baran, who have been ingenious, persistent, and brilliantly effective. They're also good people.

A talented team of professionals handles hundreds (sometimes thousands) of tasks a day on my behalf, including my correspondence; my Somatic Abolitionism blog for PsychologyToday.com; my social media presence (involving a multitude of platforms); my videos; my online classes, workshops, and trainings; my in-person events; my workbooks; the CORE assessment, which measures racialized energy; my day-to-day-schedule; my *Open Hands* newsletter; and a great deal more. Multiple thank-yous to (in reverse alphabetical order) Zanib, Scott, Patti, Lucy, Lechon, Karine, Jason, Erin, Dee, David, and Carlin.

My thanks to my transcriber Cara Weberg, who by now has typed hundreds of thousands—possibly close to a million—of my words.

I want to express my appreciation to Rachel Martin of Cultural Coherence, who has often been my collaborator in working with groups—and who was the first (to my knowledge) to observe that, in America, issues of race are spring-loaded.

Thanks to my longtime friend Ariella Tilsen for several important concepts in this book, for her many helpful suggestions for making it as strong as possible, and for helping in a multitude of other ways.

Over a hundred other professionals deserve my thanks for their guidance, insights, influence, support, and ideas. I can't list them all, but I've called out some of these folks elsewhere in this book, and I'll mention a few others here:

Dr. David Schnarch, who died in 2020, was my longtime mentor, an ongoing inspiration, and a good friend. I will always miss him. Dr. Bravada Garrett-Akinsanya has also been a longtime mentor and friend. Mahmoud El-Kati has been another influential mentor—to me and a great many others—for decades.

Dr. Ken Hardy has helped me to more deeply understand the importance of connection and friendship. He has also given me some important insights into anger and rage.

Larry Tucker of Kente Circle has given me ongoing support and friendship. Thank you, Larry. I send mine in return.

I'm grateful to Angela Rye and Charlamagne Tha God, who have been open, caring, loving, and hugely supportive.

My thanks to Damario Solomon-Simmons and the Justice for Greenwood Coalition, Sonya Renee Taylor, Layla F. Saad, Nova Reid, Dr. Aruna Khilanani, and adrienne maree brown for their deeply important work. Further thanks to the many Black women who are pushing, pulling, spurring, and sometimes dragging the human species forward and upward. I call out about thirty of these in Chapter 39, but there are many, many more.

The most important and influential Black woman I know is my wife, Maria, who literally saved my life when I returned from Afghanistan. I had spent the previous two years in a war zone, managing the wellness and counseling services for civilian contractors on fifty-three US military bases. Maria held me accountable—and simply held me—when I brought the Afghan war back with me inside my body. I'm endlessly grateful that she did not give up on me. She also has one of the best laughs on the planet.

My thanks to Repa Mekha for being a big cuz, a mentor, a protector, and a beautiful man.

Thank you to my longtime friends Steve, Chaka, Rodney, Keith, Greg, Fred, and Dicky. I'm glad to still have all of you in my life. Even though your bellies have gotten bigger, y'all still my dawgs.

I'm grateful to the two best brothers anyone could have, Chris and Cameron. They see the world differently than I do at times, but they have always been there when I needed them—and I have always been there for them.

Thanks to my babies (who are now both full-grown adults), Brittney and Tezara, for helping me understand that it is not my job to try to control the outcomes of their lives. They have been two of my biggest teachers.

I send my great gratitude to my mom, Amanda, for loving me and showing me how to love without getting or expecting something in return. I offer equal gratitude to my dad, Walter, who demonstrated that, even if life hands you a pail of shit, you can still turn that shit into things of value. I'm very proud of both my parents.

I thank the Akhepran community for nurturing my African spirit.

To all American bodies of culture—particularly Black and Indigenous ones: I appreciate everything you and your ancestors have done, separately and together, to resist conquest, colonialism, land theft, exploitation, genocide, and enslavement. I see the work that you continue to do to heal your ancestors and your descendants and to bring about justice and liberation. I'm honored and humbled that you are doing this work alongside me. Thank you.

Lastly, my thanks to everyone who reads this book and takes it to heart. Together, we can get through the current crisis of democracy with our bodies, souls, and safety intact.

Then, working separately and together, we can build a living, embodied antiracist culture for our descendants.

# ABOUT THE AUTHOR

Resmaa Menakem is a healer, a longtime therapist, and a licensed clinical social worker who specializes in the healing of trauma. He is also the founder of the Cultural Somatics Institute, a cultural trauma navigator, and a communal provocateur and coach.

Resmaa is best known as the author of the *New York Times* bestseller *My Grandmother's Hands: Racialized Trauma and the Pathway to Mending Our Hearts and Bodies*, and as the originator and key advocate of Somatic Abolitionism, an embodied antiracist practice of living and culture building. He is also the author of *Psychology Today's* Somatic Abolitionism blog, psychologytoday.com/us/blog/somatic-abolitionism.

For ten years, Resmaa cohosted a radio show with former US Congressman Keith Ellison on KMOJ-FM in Minneapolis. He also hosted his own show, *Resmaa in the Morning*, on KMOJ. Resmaa has appeared on both *The Oprah Winfrey Show* and *Dr. Phil* as an expert on family dynamics, couples in conflict, and domestic violence. He has also been a guest on Charlamagne Tha God's Comedy Central TV program, *Tha God's Honest Truth,* and on iHeart radio's *The Breakfast Club with Charlamagne Tha God and Angela Yee.* He currently hosts the *Guerilla Muse* podcast, available wherever you get your podcasts.

Resmaa has served as the director of counseling services for Tubman Family Alliance, a domestic violence treatment center in Minneapolis; the behavioral health director for African American Family Services in Minneapolis; a domestic violence counselor for Wilder Foundation; a divorce and family mediator; a social worker for Minneapolis Public Schools; a youth counselor; a community organizer; and a marketing strategist.

From 2011 to 2013, Resmaa was a community care counselor for civilian contractors in Afghanistan, managing the wellness and counseling services on fifty-three US military bases. As a certified military family life consultant, he also worked with members of the military and their families on issues related to family living, deployment, and returning home.

Resmaa helps people rise through suffering's edge. His work focuses on making the invisible visible. You can learn more about Resmaa and his work at his website, www.resmaa.com; on his Instagram feed, instagram.com/resmaamenakem/?hl=en; or by scanning this QR code: